SYSTEMIC FAILURES OF INDIAN POLITY

SYSTEMIC FAILURES OF INDIAN POLITY

In Defence, Diplomatic and Internal-Insurgency Fields

Mahinder N. Gulati

GYAN

Systemic Failures of Indian Polity

ISBN : 978-81-212-1137-6

Published in 2012 in India by
Gyan Publishing House
23, Main Ansari Road, Daryaganj,
New Delhi - 110002
Phones : 23282060, 23261060
Fax : (011) 23285914
E-mail: books@gyanbooks.com
website: gyanbooks.com

Laser Type Setting : Rajender Vashist, Delhi
Printed at : Chawla Offset Printers, Delhi

CONTENTS

SECTION -II

SECTION-III

LIST OF MAPS AND SKETCHES

PREFACE

I started working on this manuscript, off and on, about seven years back while in the US. The libraries in the Universities of Berkley and Stanford are extremely well organized, well stocked and easy to access. So are the community libraries of Fremont where we lived as well as in neighboring Milpitas. These facilities were a great boon for doing research on the subject of my choice.

The title of the book might give an impression of being negative in content. No, it is not really so. Since there are innumerable works by renowned scholars on the 1857-Mutiny, Freedom Struggle, Mahatma Gandhi, Pandit Jawaharlal Nehru, Indira Gandhi, *et al*, it was therefore pointless to add on these aspects of our famous personalities whose achievements and performance needed no further elaboration. However, what I found sadly lacking in the literature were the various failings of our top polity from time to time. After all, no human being is perfect. All make mistakes, big and small. So did our polity, the senior echelons of our political leadership, sometimes in concert with their military counterparts; hence the choice of content of my proposed work.

Having completed the first draft of the manuscript I approached Mr. Gadkari, President of BJP, to write the Foreword. Since he is a VVIP intensely involved in political activities, obviously, he did not find the time to do so although I got an impression from his Principal Secretary that he was inclined to do so. So I said to myself in the usual Army lingo: To hell with the Foreword; I shall do so myself as part of the Preface!

Concurrently, I submitted the manuscript to Gyan Publishing House, New Delhi. The CEO-MD was quite enthusiastic about the title of the proposed book and expressed his readiness to publish the same, advising certain improvements at the same time:

In order to make the work more comprehensive and improve the Book to a reference book standard in libraries, he advised that I should add about 100 odd pages covering other events of recent history; e.g. Hyderabad Police Action, Indian Military Action in Portuguese Territories in India, Sri Lanka Operations, etc; Secondly: he asked me to substantiate some of the statements-observations I had made in the texts to lend credence to the same.

As for the first suggestion, I have complied with it as best as I could. However, I found that description of battles, operations, etc., tended to make the work sound more like a treatise in military history, rather than a political commentary. Since the book is aimed at general lay public, it has to be reader-friendly. Therefore, for his second suggestion I could do so only partly for reasons set forth in succeeding paragraphs.

I started my professional career at the young age of twenty and published my first article at age 22 titled: "Forty Days Among the Lushais" (now Mizos). Since Army rules prohibited publishing any material in civil newspapers-magazines without prior clearance from the Army Intelligence Department—and that involved getting embroiled in endless correspondence and red-tape—I decided to write under a pseudonym. A number of articles were published in some newspapers, anthropological magazine, journals etc. besides some on operational-war experiences where personal experiences and observations formed the basis of my writings. For instance:

- When Pakistan Prime Minister Liaquat Ali Khan showed a close fist as a gesture of threat, a number of military units were posted on Indo-Pak border in 1952-53. I was commanding a platoon group deployed in Khasi and Jaintia Hills district of Assam on Dawki border;
- In Sino-Indian War of 1962, I was serving in 4 Infantry Division that bore the brunt of Chinese offensive and was located in Tac HQ of the Division close behind the forward, defences in Thagla Ridge-Namkach Chu Valley;
- In Indo-Pak War 1965 I served in an independent armoured Brigade both in the Lahore and Khemkaran Sectors where my unit, like other fighting arms, was allotted a sub-sector to hold as a defensive position;
- In the Bangladesh War 1971, I was on the operational planning staff of Eastern Command where I had the privilege

of attending numerous planning sessions one of which was a top secret operational conference chaired by Field Marshal Manekshaw, MC, besides Mr. D.P. Dhar, Adviser to Prime Minister Indira Gandhi. D-Day was given out by the Field Marshal to this select group of Planning Staff to enable us to work out the 'Time and Space' factor and allied 'nuts and bolts' of the operations;

- Thereafter I was based in Dhaka and was entrusted the responsibility of organization and deployment of resources for rehabilitation of infrastructural facilities like roads, bridges, powerlines, etc of the war ravaged country.

I have narrated the above not to beat my own drum, but merely to emphasize that during the aforesaid varied experiences one gathers large number of impressions, observations and personal thoughts which have a cumulative impact on one's mind. When the same are later recorded on paper, it becomes virtually impossible to substantiate the same with academically convincing evidence; hence my inability to fully comply with the second advice of CEO-MD, while in some cases it may not be even desirable to do so. Dealing with high personalities is a delicate matter after all ... I trust he would forgive me for this deficiency, more so because now at age 80+ memories of many of those long past events are becoming rather hazy.

Since Nehru-Menon combine suffered paranoia of military coups in the region during late 1940's till about mid 1960's, perks and pay in the Army were a pittance, not at all enough to make both ends meet. I therefore sought premature retirement and served as consultant on construction projects, as a Projects Manager in a foreign Government, in a private company in another country and then yet in another war-torn country and so on, to earn some petro-dollars.

August 2011 **MNG**

GRATITUDE

At the very outset I am grateful to my friend Brigadier P.S. Kulkarni, VSM, for suggesting modification of the rather longish title that I had selected for this book. The present one sounds much better, and conveys better the gist of the content.

Geographical descriptions and military campaigns cannot be understood adequately unless suitable maps-illustrations are provided along with the text. And I am no artist to have been able to do justice to this aspect. Mrs. Jagriti Chopra, Ph.D. came to my rescue. She has a Doctorate in Arts (Ph.D.) and is a reputed teacher on the subject, besides English language. I am profoundly grateful to her for sparing her valuable time for the commendable job that she has done. While on this, I might as well add that in order to make it reader-friendly, I have taken recourse to large number of maps-sketches to explain the military aspects of wars-battles.

This work would not have seen light of the day but for the encouragement and sound advice rendered by Gyan Publishing House, New Delhi. I am thankful to him for having published this humble effort. My gratitude is also due to his editorial staff for painstakingly correcting my numerous errors in composition and formatting, and for taking all the trouble to print the maps-sketches. Thank you all indeed.

MNG

SECTION-I
FREEDOM STRUGGLE

1

HISTORICAL BACKGROUND

"What is now in the past was once in the future" –
Prof. F.W. Maitland, Cambridge University Historian

An odd foreigner, Chinese-Persian-European, did visit India in early part of the Christian era; but these visits merely brought to light the existence of a big country in the Arabian-Indian ocean complex. And that's about all. The ransacking and destruction of Shiva Temple at Somnath by Mahmud of Ghazni in 1025 was in the nature of a mere raid, a looting expedition to collect rich booty and go back home with all the riches and women to enjoy the fruits. It made practically no impact on the rest of the Indian subcontinent. And that holds good for the first European sea-voyage to Indian shores in 1498 by Vasco da Gama, sailing around Africa, a voyage of discovery, not even exploration, and the world class sailors were soon back home without leaving behind any worthwhile landmark. It was only in 1505 that the Portuguese started governing their possessions when they appointed Francisco da Almeida as their first Viceroy stationed at Kochi, later shifted to Goa in 1510. The Portuguese were expelled from Hoogly in 1631 retaining their enclaves on the West coast at Daman, Diu, Dadra and Nagar Haveli as of 1947.

The first Englishmen who sailed to India were William Davis and R. Bechar who arrived at Hoogly Port on February 25, 1551 by a ship flying the Union Jack. In 1600 Queen Elizabeth signed the Charter granting monopoly over trading rights to "Governor and Company of Merchants of London" for trading into East Indies. The Charters of 1676 and 1683 conferred on the East India Company the powers to create a sort of trading-empire in India. The first clash between the intruders and the Nawab's army took place at Hoogly Bazaar in which three British soldiers were killed. Nonetheless, Calcutta remained the base for East India Company to expand its operations towards the rest of the country.

The French East India Company was founded in 1604 in France. Two French ships sailed for India in 1615 and established the French East India Company in 1642. Its possessions included Pondicherry, Karakul, and Yangon on Coromandel Coast besides Mahe on the Malabar Coast. These covered an area of 203 sq miles of which Pondicherry alone was 113 sq miles. The French were forced to withdraw from Calcutta area and they established their colony at Chandernagar in Bengal.

The foregoing stray incursions-incidents merely pointed to the existence of a vast geographical area lying open for exploitation. But that by itself did not open the flood gates for the Mughal invasion and subsequent large-scale occupation of India by foreign forces, besides kick-starting the process of integrating bits and pieces of India into a unified country. That happened only after Akbar undertook a powerful military expedition in 1565 to extend Mughal power to Deccan.

The Mughal Empire in India continued to expand. By the end of the 17th century it reached its zenith. What goes up must come down, more so if it is based on untruth and cruelties. So did the Indian Mughal Empire. The death of Emperor Aurangzeb in 1707 marked the beginning of the end of the Empire. It disintegrated as fast as it had built up on the ashes of atrocities committed in the process of conversion of Hindus to Islam. This was the opportunity the East India Company was seeking over the past many years. It lost no time and embarked on a career of territorial conquests by hook or crook, by force of arms or clever diplomacy amongst the ever so mutually suspicious and jealous princes of various Indian states. The Company made a grand start of empire building in 1757, when it defeated Nawab Sirajuddaulah in the Battle of Plassey. Within a short span of one hundred years the Company established its undisputed control over the bulk of Indian subcontinent.

At this point in time it may be recalled that before Akbar, the Mauryan Emperor Ashoka who converted to Buddhism in 265 BC, had unified bulk of the subcontinent, but mostly North India, besides adding the peripheral territories under his Empire. And Kushana

Emperor Kanishka (AD 78-102) followed by Chandragupta I (AD 320) kept up the good work in North India till AD 480 after which Sri Harsha re-established the North Indian Empire c.640.

However, it was the Arabs who took the first step to occupy part of India by conquering Sind (and Samarkand) in AD 712. They adopted the Indian numeral system around AD 760 and developed algebra and trigonometry. Muslim rule took roots in India during 8th to 14th century. The Arab conquest of large chunk of Indian Territory was followed by a large massive invasion of India by Muhammad Ghauri in 1175 leading to founding of Sultanate of Delhi in 1206. Mongol conquest of Asia provided the necessary spark for establishment of the Sultanate.

Invaders in the Garb of Traders

Practically speaking, the English came to India in the 17th century as mere traders. It was not long before they discovered that the country they came to trade with was not a single unified country *per se*; it was in bits and pieces controlled by rulers of various hues – the landlords, rajas (rulers) and bigger rajas, the maharajas, each a master of whatever his ancestors had managed to grab, more as their personal fiefdom rather than as a 'state' in political or constitutional sense. In fact, the very concept of a constitution to govern in a lawful manner did not exist. Nonetheless, most rulers acted within bounds of a self-imposed moral code, albeit it may have been modified from time to time to meet constraints of a difficult situation. Thus, each ruler was his own master. However, religion and tradition provided a unifying influence. In such a fragile political set-up the British discovered a long-term application of trade and territorial aggrandizement via the 'carrot and stick' policy. But that had to wait for a long time since the Mughal Empire in India continued to expand during the 17th century and reached its zenith towards the end of the century.

The English merchants approached their Queen for a charter to trade with the East Indies. On December 31, 1660 the Company was granted exclusive rights to trade with India and other eastern countries. Their request was granted. Naturally the East India Company had to restrict its operations to mere trade only, and not to indulge in territorial aggrandizement. Nonetheless, soon they spread their roots in rural Bengal. A process of exploitation of existing discontentment amongst the poor peasantry provided the British fertile ground for settlement and expansion, besides a local militia to guard their assets, which in turn developed into a veritable force of arms. In the process this policy brought in handsome dividends to share holders of the trading company back home.

British Aristocracy's Failure in 1857

The British trading company had recruited a large army of native soldiers, nearly 2.5 lakhs of them, and established a network of military cantonments to retain tight control over the countryside. Every now and then there were rumblings of discontentment amongst the rank and file of what eventually evolved into a powerful Army of Indian soldiers under British officers. The first signs of resentment against the British came to the surface in 1824 when 47th Regiment at Barrackpur was ordered out to Burma. For a caste Hindu crossing the sea was sacrilegious carrying the stigma of loss of caste in the society back home. Religious sensibilities of sepoys who took part in the Afghan War were also seriously affected. On return home some of them were even not accepted in the caste fraternity, a sort of ex-communication from the community. Introduction of Enfield rifle led to the disbandment of a regiment besides execution of a sepoy, Mangal Pande, who fired at the Sergeant Major of his Regiment. No doubt the poor service conditions in the cantonments and religious beliefs and prejudices of upper caste Hindus who constituted the bulk of the Force contributed to rise of the Mutiny, later termed by nationalists as the First War of Independence, which brought the Company's rule to an ignominious end. By now British imperialism in India became an indelible fact of Indian political life.

The Revolt was crushed with an iron hand. Hundreds were butchered. Thousands were put behind bars. An uneasy peace and calm returned to the countryside. However, it was not long thereafter that the nationalist movements of various hues took shape in different parts of the country.

Yet another provocation was the otherwise well meant reforming zeal of British officialdom under the influence of utilitarianism, unfortunately leading to considerable opposition and resentment. The social legislation gave rise to suspicion that the foreign rulers were destroying local culture and religion with a view to aiding the missionaries' efforts towards evangelization. Several proclamations by the rebels expressed this cultural-religious concern in no uncertain terms.

The foregoing signs of an impending disaster were not paid any heed: a clear sign of systematic failure on the part of British aristocracy.

Shahenshah-e-Hindustan Failed his Subjects

Meerut was the epicenter of the first major challenge that came in May 1857. A group of discontented sepoys in the service of the British stationed at Meerut killed their European officers on 10th May 1857. During the early hours of next day they made their entry into Delhi, marched into the Red Fort through the Raj Ghat gate and approached the Mughal Emperor Bahadur Shah II. Although he was a mere figure head, a pensioner of the British East India Company but still carried the name and prestige of the great Mughals, of course without any authority worth the name. The rebels appealed to Bahadur Shah to take over leadership of the nascent freedom movement. He was not sure of the antecedents of the rebels, nor of his ability to provide an effective leadership to carry forward such a movement. Be that as it may, he appeared inclined to be persuaded to take up the new assignment. The crowd proclaimed him Shahenshah-e-Hindustan, the Emperor of India. The rebels then went ahead to take over the Imperial City of Delhi. They occupied, or caused extensive damage to public offices. In the process Mr. Simon Frazer, the Political Agent, and several other Englishmen were killed.

Approximately half of the total strength of rank and file joined the rebellion. The revolt spread like a wild fire engulfing practically the whole of North, Western and Central India. While South India remained quiet, Punjab and Bengal were marginally affected. The rebels did not have any outside support, nor supply of arms and ammunition. Communication equipment was non-existent. Leadership was at a premium. With the sole exception of Rani of Jhansi, there were hardly any outstanding leaders to take the movement forward. The rebels did show exemplary courage, determination and endurance in the face of heavy odds; but that was about all. Rani of Jhansi died fighting on 17 June 1858. Tantia Tope carried on guerrilla warfare until April 1859 when he was captured and executed. And that brought to end an exceptionally brave attempt to rid the country of English rule.

The sacrifices by employees of the East India Company totally failed to bear any fruit. Indian public was not organized for any such venture. The various rulers, rajas and maharajas were all on their own. Barring some exceptions, none made any serious effort to put up a united stand against foreign rule – a gross failure of Indian Polity. The Indian Polity, the prevailing nationalist political system failed the rebels who were fighting for freedom for the country.

Educated Middle Class Fails Indian National Congress

Bengal was the cradle of Indian nationalism. First it gave birth to British Indian Society of Bengal in 1843 followed by British Indian Association in 1851 which absorbed the earlier society in its folds. Concurrently, Bombay Society in 1832 was followed by the Sarvajanika Sabha in Poona in 1870. These regional organizations were the seedlings for Indian Association founded in 1876 which indeed turned out to be the Indian National Congress in an embryonic form founded in 1882 by a retired government official, A.O. Hume, nurtured by the then Governor General of India, Lord Dufferin. A conference attended by seventy-two educated middle class representatives from all over India met at Bombay on December 28, 1885 and formalized the Indian National Congress under its first President, W.C. Banerji, a Calcutta based barrister.

At first the line of action adopted by the Congress was not hostility towards the British Government of the day, more so since its infancy the Congress was a party of educated middle class. Instead, all it aimed at was piecemeal administrative reforms. It was a sort of moderate nationalism with faith in British sense of justice and generosity, besides secular nationalism far removed from doctrinaire liberty and equality. However, over a period of less than a century the objective of the Congress underwent an evolutionary process and gradually evolved into "Complete Independence" from British colonialism.

G.K. Gokhale was in the moderate faction of the Congress. He remained President of the Congress till the extremist faction took control when he resigned and founded the Servants of India Society for general welfare and good of the public at large. He died in 1915. Gandhiji regarded Gokhale as his 'political guru', while the Governor General Lord Curzon, the architect of British-India Expeditionary Force to Tibet in 1905, held Gokhale in great respect. Here it may be recalled that Abyssinia's defeat of Italy in 1894, Japanese defeat of Russian forces in 1904-05 and the hard time the British had at the hands of South African Republics exploded the myth of European invincibility giving a fillip to nationalist elements in India's struggle for freedom. Unfortunately, the faction ridden Indian National Congress was not in a position to derive any worthwhile benefit from these negative developments. Nonetheless, B.G. Tilak was the first Indian leader who, believing in the strength and superiority of ancient Indian culture unequivocally stated that the political goal of Indian National Congress must be 'Swaraj' and not mere administrative reforms. He went a step further by inaugurating Ganapati and Shivaji Festivals, the latter at Poona to celebrate killing of Afzal Khan by Shivaji soon after which Rand, the Collector of Poona and another officer, Lieutenant Ayerst were shot dead by Chapekar Brothers. Tilak was accused of instigating these killings and sentenced to 18 month imprisonment. Tilak's sacrifice and untiring efforts were contributory factors in revival of Hindutva. Young leaders like Swami Vivekananda and Dayanand Saraswati took up cudgels and gave a colourful lead to the nationalist movement.

Curzon's Perfidity in Bengal

As usual, Bengal was the breeding ground for any worthwhile freedom movement to take shape. Active politics took roots in Bengal and spread from there to other parts of India. No doubt Bengal which included Bihar and Orissa with its then population of 78 million (about a quarter of the population of British India) had indeed become much too unwieldy to administer. Lord Curzon therefore rightly decided to partition the Presidency into Bengal proper retaining Calcutta as its capital. This province had Hindu majority. The other Province was named East Bengal and included Chittagong, Dacca, Rajshahi, Hills of Tripura, Malda. Its capital was at Dacca. The other was Assam.

Besides the genuine administrative considerations, the Partition Plan had an ulterior motive, their own axe to grind in as much as Bengal was the nerve center of Indian nationalism that was gaining considerable strength day by day, and division of Bengal would weaken both the Bengalis and the national movement. The real intention of the then Viceroy, Lord Curzon (1899-1905) was to 'dethrone' Calcutta (to use his own phraseology) from its eminent position of leadership. Risley, the Home Secretary to the Government of India was more categorical in his expression on the subject: "Bengal united is Power; Bengal divided will pull in different ways".

The malafide intentions of the British did not end at that point; indeed they wanted the Bengalis to be reduced to a minority in their own homeland. Under the proposed dispensation Bengal proper was to have 17 million Bengalis and 37 million Oriya and Hindi speaking people! On the other side of the coin East Bengal formed a Muslim majority area having 18 million Muslims and 12 million Hindus thereby giving a communal colour to the entire plan for the benefit of Muslims thus winning over the Muslims all over India – killing two birds with one stone – an excellent strategy from the British political standpoint! The seeds of communal scourge that was to haunt India for a very long time to come had been surreptitiously sown.

The Indian polity, the nationalists, saw through the British perfidity, a clever trick indeed which in turn gave birth to anti-partition and Swadeshi Movements. The question arises: If the Indian polity adopted anti-partition policy with respect to Bengal, why did they not oppose the British policy to partition India? Had the Indian polity, the top political leadership of the country, opposed British partition plan for India, Pakistan would not have come into being, nor the mass transmigration of populations in their millions accompanied by murder, loot, rape, forced conversions, *et al.*, unheard of in the annals of civilization would have taken place. Communal riots became the order of the day all over the Indian sub-continent, and that meant rape, loot and murder *ad lib*. The sad and pathetic plight of millions of displaced persons, the refugees, is unimaginable even today. Our senior political leadership failed the people causing them untold misery.

The foregoing insidious plan led to widespread protests, demonstrations, mass-fasting, *hartal*, all in the name of extremist elements in the Congress Party. People were called upon to boycott all foreign goods leading to what may be described as an undeclared war between the people and the government. Brutal repression was let loose. Seditious meetings were banned. Newspaper presses were seized. Senior leaders of the nationalist movement like Lala Lajpat Rai and Ajit Singh were deported. Tilak was tried for sedition and sentenced to six years imprisonment and sent to Mandalay in Burma.

The repressive measures adopted by the Government led to formation of secret societies, violent revolutionary activities, assassinations, bombs and pistols took the place of non-violent agitations. Instigating revolts, disrupting communications, dacoities to raise money, and such other revolutionary activities became the order of the day. Another Chapekar brother murdered two police informers. All three brothers, three young men from the same family, were hanged, which in turn led to massive revulsion and nation-wide grief. After the Chapekar Brothers, the spirit of revolutionary terrorism was kept alive by Vir Savarkar.

In 1906 an unsuccessful attempt was made to assassinate Fuller, the unpopular Lieutenant Governor of East Bengal. A bomb factory was discovered in the garden of a house in Maniktola suburb of Calcutta. About the same time two English ladies were inadvertently killed by a bomb intended for the District Judge of Muzaffarpur. One of the accused committed suicide and the other was executed. About that time, the famous Alipore Conspiracy Case went to court. In the light of foregoing revolutionary violent activities the government resorted to a series of brutal repressive measures.

2

THE SWADESHI MOVEMENT : 1903-1908

The Swadeshi Movement had its genesis in the Bengal Partition Plan announced on 19 July 1905. Immediate and spontaneous protests followed all over Bengal and neighbouring provinces. The Swadeshi Movement was formally proclaimed in a meeting held in Calcutta Town Hall on 7th August 1905 when the famous Boycott Resolution was passed urging the country to boycott Manchester cloth and Liverpool salt. Bengal Partition became effective on October 16, 1905 and that day was declared a day of mourning and fasting throughout Bengal. Thousands upon thousands of people paraded the streets of Calcutta singing Bande Matram, which became the theme song of the Movement. The political objective now was Swaraj, complete independence. The British countered the Swadeshi Movement by helping in setting up of All India Muslim League. Maulvis and Mullahs were pressed into service. Soon communal riots broke out in Bengal. In other words, the British were the first to provide the initial spark to ignite the communal conflagration.

There were three main reasons for the Movement petering out:

- Repression by the Government;
- Internal squabbles and split in the Congress, the apex body;
- Lack of an effective organization.

The foregoing last two reasons for petering out of the Swadeshi Movement are a poor reflection on the leadership, more so when such a good cause existed for pursuing the objective. Internal squabbles indicate systematic failure on the part of senior leaders.

Returning Indian Patriotic Immigrants in the Blues

Gurdit Singh, an Indian contractor working in Singapore, chartered a ship to carry various Indians working in East and South-East Asia to Canada. The ship Kamagata Maru with 376 Indians on board arrived at Vancouver. The Press in Punjab had warned of serious consequences if the Indians were not allowed entry into Canada. Nonetheless, the ship was not allowed entry into the Port and was cordoned off by Canadian Police. It was then forced out of Canadian waters. Before the ship reached Yokohama, the port of its origin, World War I broke out. The British Government issued orders that no one shall be allowed to disembark en-route, not even at places from where they had boarded the ship! All passengers without exception shall disembark at Calcutta. This was a most unreasonable order depriving the people of returning to their homes and hearths.

The long and short of this episode was serious rioting and clashes between the passengers and Bengal Police near Calcutta when eighteen passengers were killed and 202 arrested. Some of them managed to escape. Meanwhile, the Indian Government issued an Ordinance under which severe restrictions were prescribed for the returning emigrants. An estimated eight thousand emigrants returned. All were thoroughly scrutinized and about 5000 were declared 'safe' and allowed to proceed to their villages in Punjab. Precautionary measures were taken for nearly 1500 men. By February 1915, 189 persons were interned and 704 were restricted to their villages. However, those who came via Colombo and South India generally reached their villages without being found out. It may be recalled that 40 Ghadarites (rebels) were sentenced to be hanged and more than 200 were sentenced to long terms of imprisonment with the result that bulk of the young educated secular nationalist leadership were decimated by their European masters in one stroke. Nonetheless, the surviving Ghadarites helped in laying foundation for a national secular peasant movement.

Here it may be recalled that the Congress was house divided from within. There were two major factions: the Moderates and the Extremists. Their objectives were identical but the methodology and approach were exactly opposite. The differences between the two exploded on the surface during the Surat session of the Congress which led to violent clashes between the two groups. The session was dissolved in chaos and the split in the Party was wide open. It remained so till 1916 when the two groups buried the hatchet and were reunited by Lucknow Pact for which Lala Lajpat Rai and Tilak made concerted efforts. The inability of the senior political leadership to reconcile the two groups for a long time was symbolic of systematic failure of India politics.

Revolutionary Terrorism

The extremist faction was not just a set of violent bands of vagabonds; far from it they were patriots of the highest order who were ever prepared to die for liberation of the motherland. Their efforts and sacrifices must not therefore be belittled. It was a son of Maharashtra, Vasudeo Phadke who is credited with making a start of revolutionary terrorism in India. He aimed at establishing a Hindu Raj in independent India by organizing secret bands of youth, collecting money through dacoities, disrupting communications, etc. Phadke's was an insignificant band which was easily crushed by British might. He was captured, sentenced to life imprisonment and sent to Aden where he died in 1883. The Chapekar Brothers' episode may be recalled in this connection. The spectacular bomb attack on Lord Hardinge on December 23, 1912, was yet another similar significant event. Of course the perpetrators of such patriotic acts were generally executed. Another daring act was the fatal attack on India House bureaucrat Curzon-Wyllie by Madan Lal Dhingra in July 1909. This brave son of the soil went to the scaffolding saying: "Neither rich nor able, a poor man like me can offer nothing but his blood on the altar of Mother's deliverance ..." — Unfortunately, the Indian political leadership failed to take advantage of such acts of individual heroism.

3

CIVIL DISOBEDIENCE AND NON-COOPERATION MOVEMENT

This long phase in the nationalist struggle for freedom, 1920-22 to 1930-32, had already seen many ups and downs. Bal Gangadhar Tilak had completed his six years jail term, mostly in Burma. Annie Besant decided to set up Home Rule League but Congress and the Muslim League declined to support her decision. However, Tilak went all out to support the Home Rule Movement and had succeeded in enlisting 14,000 members. Tilak was served a notice why he should not be bound over for good behaviour for a period of one year for which securities of Rs. 60,000 were demanded.

Jinnah Heads Defence Counsel for Tilak

Both Jinnah and Tilak belonged to the Congress. A team of eminent lawyers led by Mohammed Ali Jinnah defended Tilak. They lost the case in the Magistrate's court but he was later exonerated by the High Court. The Home Rule Movement continued to grow stronger, more so when moderate leaders like M.A. Jinnah, Madan Mohan Malaviya and Surendra Nath Banerji enlisted in the League as full members. By this time Mohandas Karmchand Gandhi[1] had tasted the traumatic treatment meted out to Indians in South Africa. It was a particularly nasty experience for a westernized Indian of whom Gandhi was the first one. Assumption of racial superiority by white rulers was the root cause. Gandhi adopted passive resistance as his *modus operandi* to fight this oppression before returning to India in January 1915. The brutality at Jallianwala Bagh was the last straw to draw Gandhi in the hot waters of Satyagraha in Indian politics. The Khilafat Movement in support of Turkey's

Caliph got a fillip when its Committee at its meeting at Allahabad on 9 June 1920 accepted Gandhi's suggestion of non-cooperation and also requested Gandhi to lead the movement. Hereafter he came to be called Gandhiji.

Lokmanya Tilak passed away on 1st August 1920 and that day of mourning was considered appropriate to launch the Non-Cooperation Movement on a countrywide basis. For such a movement to succeed it was felt that mass participation was a pre- requisite. The annual membership fee was therefore reduced to four annas (0.25 rupee) and village level committees were formed to organize and coordinate mass activities. Hindi was to be used as far as possible; thus Congress remained mainly a north Indian organization for the time being. However, Andhra Pradesh and Karnataka soon joined the mainstream movement.

Khilafat Episode

The Ali Brothers were the foremost leaders of the Khilafat Movement. They and many leading Congressmen toured the countryside and exhorted the public at large to join the boycott movement. A large number of students boycotted schools and colleges and instead joined the more than 800 national schools and colleges that had taken the place of official institutions. In the process the Swadeshi movement got a new lease of life. While boycott of law courts had a dramatic and inspiring effect, it was boycott of foreign cloth and goods that took the cake. Bonfires of foreign cloth and goods had a spectacular effect; so did the picketing of toddy shops. In July 1921, All India Khilafat Conference was held at Karachi in which one of the leading members declared on 8 July that "it was religiously unlawful for the Muslims to continue in the British Army" and this message be conveyed to every Muslim in the Army[2]. Mohammed Ali along with other leaders of the Conference was immediately arrested. As a protest against British rule in India, a *hartal* was observed all over India on 17 November 1921, the day the Prince of Wales landed in Bombay. Deserted streets welcomed the Prince and a huge bonfire of foreign cloth was lit in Elphinston Mill. Unfortunately as Gandhiji was addressing a big gathering at the site of the bonfire, clashes broke out between those who had gone to attend the welcome function and the crowd returning from Gandhiji's meeting. Parsis, Christians and Anglo-Indians became special targets of the irate crowd. There was Police firing. The turmoil lasted three days in which 59 persons lost their lives. Empty streets and downed shutters greeted the Prince wherever he went. Successful defiance of the Government acted as a heady wine and the non-cooperation movement became more and more aggressive. The Congress Volunteer Corps acted as a parallel police force, which became an eyesore for the authorities.

Chauri Chaura

Sooner than later it became difficult to draw a distinction between a Kisan Sabha meeting and a Non-cooperation meeting. Similarly, in Malabar region of Kerala Non-cooperation and Khilafat propaganda acted as a tonic in reverse in that it aroused Muslim tenants against Hindu landlords leading to communal riots with some fatalities (Mappilas Revolt). Repression was let loose all over the country to suppress the Non-cooperation Movement. The Congress was adamant on graduating to Civil Disobedience Movement, and so was the Viceroy. The finale came in Chauri Chaura in Gorakhpur district of U.P. on February 5, 1922 when a Congress and Khilafat procession got out of control in the face of Police behaviour. A section of the crowd attacked the Police who fired in return. This provoked the entire procession, who attacked the police force in return. The police took shelter in the Police Station. The crowd retaliated by setting the building on fire. Those who tried to escape the fire were caught, hacked to death and their bodies thrown into the fire. In this gruesome incident twenty-two policemen were brutally killed. On hearing of this extremely unfortunate incident Gandhiji decided to withdraw the Movement. Thus, the Non-Cooperation Movement came to an ignominious end on February 12, 1922.

However it would be a hasty conclusion to say that the Non-Cooperation was a failure. No doubt the battle was lost but the war was still on. A lot more was still in cold storage for Civil Disobedience Movement. Participation of Muslims in both Movements on an unprecedented scale was a positive outcome. May be the Caliph of Turkey was a contributory factor! Nonetheless, communal riots in Bombay during the visit of Prince of Wales as well as Malabar episode almost neutralized this positive trend. And to cap it all, the Chauri Chaura tragedy was a blemish which spoke volumes about the non-violent approach of Gandhiji. Or was it instigated against Hindu policemen? — — Symbols of Systematic Failures of not only the senior leadership but also of the rank and file, the public in general.

Civil Disobedience Movement: Salt Satyagraha

Civil Disobedience was not a mere slogan; it was the crux of a strategy taking India forward to elimination of English rule, the ultimate goal being complete freedom: SWARAJ. It was a complete programme by itself involving infringement of various public laws, rules and procedures enacted by the foreign rulers for their own convenience. Non-payment of taxes was a mere small part of the whole. Since the Viceroy, Lord Irwin, had ignored the demands contained in the memorandum of Eleven-Points put forward by the Congress towards partial settlement of public grievances, Gandhiji had no option but to resort to civil disobedience.

The first item on the agenda was to identify a simple straightforward issue that would be of common interest to the common man. The more the number of people involved, the better would be the action plan. Gandhiji appreciated that common salt was an essential requirement of every common person – man, woman or child; even an animal! Dandi March was the plan to initiate civil disobedience. It was so simple in concept and execution that few even amongst the intelligentsia and government officials grasped its long-term significance. Gandhiji accompanied by seventy-eight members of Sabramati Ashram representing various regions-religions marched from Ahmedabad through the villages of Gujarat covering a distance of 240 miles. Destination: Dandi village on the coast. Task: Collect salt from the beach. Effect: Breach of the Salt Act: A criminal offence!

Breach of Salt Act by various sections of the people had an electrifying effect all over the country. The movement, Salt Satyagraha, spread all along the West coast to the East, from Karachi to Calcutta, from Sylhet in Assam to Noakhali on the Bengal coast only to make salt. The Government was totally puzzled and perplexed. They just did not know how to handle a situation like that. But they refrained from arresting Gandhiji lest the conflagration spreads beyond control. However, Jawaharlal Nehru's arrest on 14th April for defiance of Salt Laws resulted in huge demonstrations and clashes with police in cities like Karachi, Madras, Calcutta, etc. About a week after that arrest of Congress leaders in North West Frontier Province (NWFP) led to huge unprecedented demonstrations in Peshawar. Khan Abdul Gaffar Khan had set up a formidable, well-disciplined, non-violent revolutionary organization called

Khudai Khidmatgars (Servants of God) popularly known as 'Red Shirts'. They were destined to play an extremely active role in the Civil Disobedience Movement. Their political and humanitarian work contributed to mass upsurge in Peshawar, which remained in the hands of revolutionaries for nearly one week. This period in NWFP was most significant in as much as that the soldiers of Garhwal Regiment belonging to northern mountainous belt refused to open fire on an unarmed crowd. That was not the only crowning glory of Salt Satyagraha – A police cordon had sealed off Dharasana Salt Works. A band of about two thousand volunteers under the first Indian woman president of the Congress marched towards the police cordon. As the protesters advanced, the police charged on them with steel- tipped lathis. The Satyagrahis did not offer any resistance whatsoever. The injured were carried away by their comrades on improvised stretchers. Column after column was meted out this treatment even though the Satyagrahis did not move forward but merely sat down awaiting the police blows. It was the month of May, very hot indeed by 11 am when the temperature in the shade was 116 degrees F. By that time 320 volunteers had been injured and two had died – all in the name of non-violent struggle. American journalist, Webb Miller's report of the incident carried the story of this non-violent heroism to all corners of the world. Needless to say this was not a solitary incident of its kind. Similar acts of non-violent heroism were reported from Bombay, Karnataka, Madras, various sites on the Orissa coast, besides coastal areas of Andhra and Bengal.

In order to boost the village level police force Chowkidars (village guards) were appointed by the administration. Their wages were to be paid out of funds specifically created for the purpose through chowkidari tax levied on the villages. In Bengal a no-tax movement was initiated with a demand for removal of these chowkidars. In Kheda district of Gujarat no-tax movement was in progress under which the villagers refused to pay land revenue. Another form of agitation in Maharashtra, Karnataka and Central Province was defiance of forest laws. Here the tribal population was deprived of their traditional rights on use of forest products without interference from the Government. A movement calling on the zamindars not to pay any "Land Revenue" to the Government, and a corresponding demand on the tenants not to pay any rent to the zamindars was an ongoing process. Since the zamindars were loyal to the Government it virtually boiled down to "No Rent" campaign by the tenants.

In short, various small-scale movements for redressal of local grievances had spontaneously mushroomed in rural areas in different parts of the country – all under the self assumed umbrella of Civil Disobedience Movement, the intention being to defy the government one way or the other. Circulation in urban areas of illegal newssheets (Patrikas) to defy the hated Press Act was yet another part of the Movement. So were the Prabhat Pheris in which men, women and children took to the streets early mornings, singing patriotic songs, *et al* ... It was a peoples' movement, by the people, for the people.

Indian Muslims Disinterested

In order to restore a semblance of normalcy Gandhi-Irwin Pact was signed on 5 March 1931. It was more in the nature of a 'truce', a 'provisional settlement' that included release of all political prisoners, return of confiscated lands, freedom to make salt in coastal villages, peaceful picketing, etc. Consequently, the Congress agreed to discontinue the Civil Disobedience Movement, it was a matter of truce and not a surrender. Moreover, of necessity mass movements have to be short-lived lest they die a natural death. Nonetheless, the Civil Disobedience Movement 1930-31 was a landmark in the history of India's struggle for freedom. However, it was very disappointing and unfortunate that participation in the movement by Indian Muslims, by and large, was on a much smaller scale than their numerical strength, besides being much less enthusiastic. The majority Congress Party had failed to carry the Muslim minority in their campaign(s). This Systematic Failure on the part of Indian Polity was to have catastrophic effect on later developments in India's struggle for freedom.

A failure is a failure and must not be condoned irrespective of the personalities involved. It is still more unfortunate that visible perceptible serious efforts were not made with the specific purpose of drawing a larger chunk of Muslim population. Of course the appeals of communal leaders, mullahs and maulvis, to stay away from active participation in the movement together with active encouragement by the foreign power to do so did have their desired effect. In the same vein it cannot be denied that the secular nationalist leadership failed to counter the insidious propaganda by the other side. In fact, Muslim representatives at the Second Movement (September-December 1931) were terrible religious fanatics[3]. "They were absolutely unwilling to discuss political problems on a non-theological basis". The Conference was a total failure. So was the third roundtable conference. In fact, Muslim delegates under the leadership of Jinnah took an openly communal stand in all the three conferences (1930, 1931 and 1932) leading to their failure to resolve the issues. Consequently, Gandhiji relaunched the Civil Disobedience Movement. The Government once again resorted to brutal repression. The brutality was so severe that public enthusiasm began to wane. Gandhiji decided to completely withdraw the movement in May 1934. It is note worthy that Civil Disobedience Movement of 1930-34 was the last mass movement launched by the Congress under the leadership of Mahatma Gandhi. Hereafter the initiative passed on to London where the British Parliament passed the Government of India Act of 1935 paving the way for elections to the provincial assemblies in the spring of 1937. The Congress won hands down and after some initial hesitation formed ministries in Assam, Bombay, Bihar, Central Provinces, NWFP, Orissa, and the United Provinces. However, all of them resigned following the outbreak of Second World War to which the British made India a party without consulting the popularly elected representatives of the people.

Here it may be recalled that there were serious differences within the Congress regarding acceptance of office under the Act of 1935. While Gandhiji favoured acceptance, other group which also included Jawaharlal Nehru was opposed to the Federal System as envisaged in the Act. However, Nehru soon fell in line leaving the field open to Subhash Chandra Bose who was re-elected as the Congress President defeating the Gandhian candidate. The senior leadership had miserably failed in maintaining cohesion in the Party. Soon Bose resigned and formed a new party known as Forward Block. Systematic Failures, one after another had overtaken the freedom movement.

Sikh Gurdwaras

The genesis of Akali movement lies in the tight control exercised over the Gurudwaras (Sikh Temples) by corrupt and ignorant mahants (priests) who enjoyed patronage of the Government. The Sikh Sangat wanted to wrest control of Gurdwaras from the mahants and managers appointed by the colonial regime. An agitation was started with this end in view. The control of Akal Takht (Golden

Temple) was a sensitive issue. A number of meetings were organized. Finally, the Government wanting to play safe asked its appointed managers to resign so that the control passed effectively in the hands of the reformists. The Shiromani Gurdwara Prabhandak Committee as central body having 175 elected Sikhs took charge.

All went well except at Gurdwara Nankana Saheb, the birth-place of Guru Nanak. Narain Das, the mahant of Gurdwara Nankana Saheb refused to surrender control peacefully. He organized a mercenaries force of 500, armed them with guns, swords and *lathis*. On 20 February 1921 an Akali *jattha* entered the Gurdwara to pray. The mahant's party opened fire on the *jattha* killing nearly 100 persons. The tragedy acted as a spark. The mahant was arrested. Gandhiji, Maulana Shaukat Ali, Lala Lajpat Rai and other national leaders visited Nankana to show their solidarity.

The "Keys Affair" in October 1921 added to prestige of the Akalis. The Government had taken charge of *toshakhana* of the Golden Temple. The Akalis reacted immediately and sent jatthas to the Temple. A *hartal* was observed. The Government arrested the Akali leaders like Baba Kharak Singh, Master Tara Singh and many others. This led to further unrest among the Sikh populace of Punjab and that was likely to spread to the army. So the government decided to play safe again, released the leaders and handed over the keys of the Toshikhana to Baba Kharak Singh. The Government bowed to the peoples' will in the case of Gurdwara Guru-Ka-Bagh also in village Ghokewala. By and large, the Akali movement made substantial contribution to the political development of Punjab besides furthering the nationalist objectives.

Untouchability and Temple Entry

Eradication of untouchability was an important appendage of social reform agenda of the Congress. Gandhiji gave top priority to this item of the agenda, so did Lokmanya Tilak. Two famous struggles in Kerala inspired the nationalist movement in this direction:

The *avarnas* (those without a caste, later known as the Harijans) the depressed classes, were subjected to de-grading and de-humanizing social treatment. The Ezhavas and Pulayas could not come within 16 and 72 feet respectively of the higher castes. Struggles against these disabilities was one aspect;

There was a major temple in village Vaikom in Travancore. Its four walls were surrounded by temple roads, which were out of bounds to all avarnas.Kerala Provincial Congress Committee decided to launch a Satyagraha by defying the un-approachability rule. A procession of *savarnas* (caste Hindus) and *avarnas* was organized to march on the Temple roads on March 30, 1924. The authorities put up barricades on these roads, imposed prohibitory orders, arrested the Satyagrahis and sentenced them to imprisonment. The Maharaja of Travancore died in August 1924. The Maharani as Regent ordered release of all Satyagrahis.

Gandhiji did not enter a single temple in Kerala during his tour of the region in order to register his protest over the inhuman restrictions. In continuation of struggle for eradication of untouchability, the KPCC initiated a Temple Entry Satyagraha at Guruvayur on November 1, 1931. It aroused countrywide response and the day was observed as All Kerala Temple Entry Day. However, the Temple authorities did not take kindly to the Satyagraha and called for police protection. The Temple staff came out to challenge the peaceful Satyagrahis. They were beaten up mercilessly while the police stood by watching the *tamasha*, ready to intervene if situation so demanded. The Satyagraha continued and most Congress leaders were imprisoned. The popular campaign for eradication of untouchability and for temple entry continued unabated, well after even the Civil Disobedience Movement had been called off. Finally, in November 1936 the Maharaja of Travancore issued a proclamation under which all Government-controlled temples were thrown open to all Hindus irrespective of caste. Nonetheless, untouchability and restrictions on entry into some temples continued even long after the Maharaja's proclamation. It was only after the Constitution of Republic of India as passed by the Constituent Assembly was promulgated that untouchability became an offence and caste inequality was abolished, at best legally only, guaranteeing equal rights to all citizens irrespective of caste. Nevertheless, it must not be assumed that the evil of caste system or untouchability has been totally eliminated from the Indian society. It is unfortunate, but true that Indian polity continued to tolerate these evil practices, besides some other social evils like dowry system, child marriage, etc had continued for centuries. This entire scenario represents systematic failure of Indian social system on a gigantic scale, the sole exception being the practice of *sati*, which the social reformers succeeded in eliminating totally.

Bhagat Singh and Sukhdev Executed

Bhagat Singh, Sukhdev and Rajguru were executed on March 26, 1931. The youth of India were seething with anger, further aggravated by the Congress meeting at Karachi to endorse Gandhi-Irwin Pact. For the first time Gandhiji was greeted by black flags all the way to the Congress session in Karachi. And it was also the first time that Congress enunciated in clear terms what so far had been mere rhetoric:

- Basic civil rights of free speech; free press; free assembly; freedom of assembly and association;
- Equality before the law irrespective of caste, creed or sex;
- Neutrality of the State towards all religions;
- Elections on the basis of universal adult franchise;
- Free and compulsory Primary Education;
- Just and equitable labour laws — in short, Fundamental Rights and Economic Freedom.

The concept and content of Swaraj as well as political and economic programme of the Congress got defined for the first time. The political prestige and morale of the Congress was now at its zenith. The bureaucracy was seething with anger, gunning for revenge for its loss of prestige. Gandhiji requested for a meeting with the Viceroy for 31st December 1931. He declined. Instead, Gandhiji was arrested on January 4, 1932. The Government also promulgated various ordinances and assumed draconian powers to rule the country. The situation in general deteriorated to more like a "Civil Martial Law" as described by a historian of the time. Civil liberties disappeared into the blues and the authorities could seize persons and property at their sweet will. Most Congressmen were put behind bars. In the first four months over 80,000 Satyagrahis, mostly urban and rural poor were jailed. No-Tax-Campaigns were treated with great severity. Whipping of prisoners was often resorted to, so was beating the people in public. For some reason or no reason at all! Freedom of expression was given a go by. Action was taken against

109 journalists and 98 printing presses. In the face of relentless repression by the authorities, despair and despondency was in the air all the time. Once again Muslims were conspicuous by their absence, or extremely small presence.

The public at large woke up to the reality of the situation. Gandhiji became the target of adverse criticism all round. Subhash Chandra Bose and Vithalbhai Patel in Europe were sharp critics of Gandhiji's methodology and leadership of the Freedom Movement. In 1933 they said: "Mr. Gandhi as a political leader has failed" and went on to add "a radical reorganization of the Congress on a new principle with a new method, for which a new leader is essential".

Communal Vote Bank

The Communal Award of August 1932 added fuel to the fire. It conceded to each minority community – Muslims, Sikhs, Christians and "Depressed Classes" – a certain number of seats in the legislatures to be elected by separate electorates, voters of their own community only. A sort of Vote Bank for each community was thus created. The colonial power thereby added another class of people as the minority community, thus separating the Scheduled Castes from the main stream Hindus. Eradication of Untouchability as a measure of reform would thus come to an end. The Award, if implemented *in toto*, made sure that an untouchable would remain untouchable forever. India's unity and social integrity were indeed at stake! The evil designs of the colonial rulers were partly negated with the signing of Poona Pact under which the idea of separate electorate for the depressed classes was abandoned. Nonetheless, Muslim communal politics got a big boost in the process, albeit Sikhs in general did not fall a prey to British machinations. The Congress as far back as 1916, as part of a compromise with the Muslim League, had already accepted the genesis of the idea of separate electorate, a sort of reserved vote bank, for a part of the nation. Those seeds of dissension had now grown into a full-fledged tree, standing upright in its own right. You cannot undo the past; it goes into oblivion to become history.

It was a Systematic Failure of Himalayan proportions by the Congress magnitude of dire consequences of which could not be gauged by the Indian Polity at that point of time.

Notes

1. Tendulkar D.G.: *Mahatma, Life of Mohandas Karamchand Gandhi,* 8 volumes, New Delhi, 1969, Reprint Vol. II, p. 52.
2. The foregoing comments are not to belittle the contribution of NWFP, parts of East Bengal, Tripura and the poorer sections of the Muslim community at large.
3. Sitaramayya Pattabhi: *Report of the Linguistic Province Commission, 1948;* p. 942.

4

DEMAND FOR MUSLIM HOMELAND

India has been a multi-religious multi-ethnic society from times immemorial, and continues to be all the more so till today. India has given shelter to whichever religion or community who sought refuge in this country for whatever reason. In the process we became a multi-ethnicity country having pockets of diverse racial and cultural groups of people spread all over. These groups often interacted closely resulting in socio-cultural-economic diversity on a wide scale besides some mixed racial-blood too. Such a situation is eminently conducive to competition for grabbing the limited resources available to satisfy all demands. It is here that religion and religiosity comes into play for the simple reason that followers of the same religion have common economic, social, political and cultural interests. Therefore it becomes imperative for that community to stand together to obtain their rightful share of the spoils, the common denominator being the commonality of religion — the bedrock of communal ideology. Indian soil was more than fertile in which this ideology could grow in abundance.

Safeguarding Community's Interests

With multiplicity of religious faiths there was a natural divergence and dissimilarity of interests amongst them. Every faith had its own belief system with emphasis on safeguarding the community's interests, material and spiritual. It is the materialistic aspect that led to antagonism and mutual hostility since they had to share the same cake. Secular interests of one community were incompatible with those of the other resulting in hostility in pursuit of which violence was often resorted to. This is precisely how the situation developed between the Hindus and Muslims over a period of centuries, more like an evolutionary process than merely an abrupt eruption. Communal ideology thus became the breeding ground for communal violence on a mass scale between Hindus and Muslims. This scenario could be taken forward to relationship between the other communities following different religions – the Sikhs and Christians for example, albeit there were practically hardly any violent clashes with Sikhs/Christians on one side and Hindus/Muslims on the other. Fear and hatred were absent from the communal syndrome prevailing in the 1920's and the 30's. However, this happy state of communal harmony lasted till about 1937 after which it took an altogether different turn. Muslims came to believe, to be more precise they were made to believe – that their faith, culture and life styles were incompatible with those of the Hindu majority. They belonged to two different nations. It was the birth of "Two-Nations Theory".

It is generally believed that Indian communalism had its roots in the medieval period. It is a hangover of past deeds and misdeeds, acts of omission and commission by our forefathers. That may be right to an extent only. On the other hand, in its subsequent form it is the byproduct of modern politics, technological advance and economic boom. The "Revolt of 1857" was a turning point in as much as both Hindus and Muslims fought shoulder to shoulder against the colonial imperialist power. It was a break with the pre-1857 medieval years. The fresh start happened to usher in communalism of a new kind wherein social, political, cultural and economic issues were on top of the agenda. This ideology of communalism could take shape only because of popular participation by the people on a large scale that could take place through means of mass mobilization and mass media. Indian society had gone through a process of transformation under the impact of colonialism leading to integration of various regions of the country, transforming India into a nation, which earlier on it was not thereby providing new means of individual identity. In the process religious consciousness was transformed into communal consciousness in certain parts of the country amongst certain communities.

Muslim Madrassas

Indian economy was essentially colonial in character. There was economic stagnation that gave rise to antagonism and divisive forces. Unemployment or underemployment was an acute problem, particularly for the middle and lower middle classes who could not possibly go back to land to earn a living. They fell back on narrow short-term solutions by way of regional, communal or caste based reservations of government jobs. The net result was communalism of the worst kind since religious distinction coincided with social, class and caste distinction. For example: Conflict between tenant and landlord in East Bengal and Malabar was represented as struggle between Muslims and Hindus. Similarly, the communalist forces portrayed struggle between peasant-debtor and merchant-banker as oppression of Muslims by the rich Hindus. Yet another factor that goes back to the 19th century, and still continues to be in operation is the educational backwardness of Muslims. Their "madrassa" style education, far removed from English education is hardly conducive to professionalism or job capability. That is where Hindus score much better giving rise to jealousy and inimical feelings.

Wahabi Fundamentalism

The 19th century added yet another negative element in the communal cauldron – the revivalist movements amongst the Muslims and Hindus alike added to mutual suspicions and tears. The Wahabi was essentially fundamentalist and aimed at restoring the pristine purity of Islam[1]. Syed Ahmad Khan's reformist movement was founded on the principle that Hindus and Muslims are two separate nations and their interests are mutually antagonistic. His movement essentially had the same objective and characteristics as that of the Wahabis. Appreciating the value of English education he established the Muhammadan Anglo-Oriental College at Aligarh in 1877. It was later upgraded to a full fledged Muslim University. His Aligarh movement added to the already full basket of plethora of mutual distrust and differences resulting in further widening of the gulf. On the other side Swami Dayanand Saraswati founded the Arya Samaj in 1875 calling the Hindus back to the Vedas, with a view to inculcate pride in the ancient Indian cultural values.

Cow Slaughter

Killing of cows was strictly banned in Punjab under the Sikh rule. But with the arrival of British administration this prohibition was lifted. However, with the founding of Arya Samaj the demand for cow protection gained ground. The agitation spread to UP where the cow protection was not merely a religious question but also had economic justification for the agrarian people. This question further accentuated the differences between the two communities. Whichever way you looked at the problem, it boiled down to communalism, in one form or the other providing the British a convenient handle for furtherance of their rule over Indian Empire. And Indian polity cooperated with them whole heartedly!

Direct Action Day by Muslim League

A most terrible outcome of this policy of communalism occupying a supreme position in Jinnah's politics was the holocaust that resulted from the Direct Action launched by the League on August 16, 1946 in furtherance of their demand for Pakistan. Communal riots instigated by Muslim League engulfed the entire country on an unprecedented scale. The riots started at Calcutta where the League Ministry headed by Chief Minister Suhrawardy declared the Direct Action Day as a public holiday so as to give the menacing mobs a clear hand to loot, burn, rape and murder ad lib for the simple reason that the Chief Minister had promised that the police and the army will not interfere in observance of Direct Action Day. The Government of the Day abdicated its primary duty and did nothing to prevent the massacres. In the face of Government's deliberate policy of inaction, the Hindus and Sikhs also retaliated. Thus, it became free for all. At least 4,000 had been killed and 10,000 injured many very grievously. Soon the riots spread to many other parts of the country, more so since the same Muslim League was responsible for Direct Action Day. The list is long and heart rending in its details. The main victims of this holocaust in Muslim dominated areas were the Hindu merchant class and moneylenders.

British Divide and Rule Policy

The British policy was crafted and implemented in a manner that it encouraged divisive tendencies among various sections of the society. The internal social and political conditions in India were such as to encourage the British in their evil designs to cause mutual disaffection. They consistently treated Hindus, Muslims and Sikhs as distinctly separate social and political entities, and pretended as if there was nothing in common between them. In course of time they started including the depressed classes, the untouchables also in the same bracket. In British eyes Indian society was comprised of mutually exclusive, antagonistic religion-caste based communities. They went out of their way to reward, favour one community or another causing further dissentions. Even criminal activities by persons, agitations and communal press were tolerated beyond limits of transgression. The Viceroy readily gave appointments to communal organizations and accepted their demands while the nationalist elements were totally denied audience, or their demands were rejected out of hand. Going a step further, in 1932 the Communal Award accepted all the communal demands put forward by the so-called representatives of the community, whose credentials were accepted without question while the nationalists were made to wait in the wings to prove their representative character. The Communal Award was announced on August 10, 1932 by Ramsay McDonald and gave recognition to the following minorities:

Muslims;

Indian Christians;

Anglo Indians;

Europeans;

Depressed Classes;

Backward Classes;

Commercial and Industrial Classes;

Landholders;

Labor;

Universities;

Sikhs.

The mischief did not end at that point! A fixed number of seats were allocated to each group. The instrument of 'separate electorate' was wielded so cunningly that the minorities relished the fruits procured by their self-appointed representatives. By not taking action against the excesses committed by the communalists, the British encouraged growth of this scourge. Similarly, they turned a blind eye towards communal riots and the atrocities committed on innocent people. However, communalism was not the only bane of modern Indian society. The colonial power encouraged conflict between regions, caste against caste, province against province, language against language, and so on and so forth. It was a powerful instrument to assist in keeping the country divided. As long as the colonial power was in control, it was virtually impossible to eliminate communalism and its all-pervading powerful influence; under the circumstances the communal imbroglio could not possibly be resolved. Overthrow of the colonial regime was perhaps the only possible solution. Here we must not lose sight of the pronounced Hindu tinge in the philosophy and practice of nationalism. Ancient Indian culture had an upper hand in national thought and propaganda to virtual exclusion of medieval Indian culture wherein Muslim influence was predominant. This gave rise to Muslim fears that success of the Movement would lead to Hindu supremacy in the country.

The history taught in schools and colleges was somewhat distorted and had a communal bias, especially in respect of ancient and medieval periods. This formed the basis of communal propaganda by many Muslim intellectuals as well as semi-educated maulvis. To cap it all, a British historian described the ancient period of Indian history as the "Hindu Period" and the medieval period as the "Muslim Period". One fails to understand why he did not describe the modern period as the "Christian Period"! By implication it means that basic character of Indian polity was identified with the religion of the ruler(s) at the time. The result was that all communal historians as well as imperialist historians saw the medieval period as one long story of Hindu-Muslim conflict. Of course their view was distorted through coloured glasses! Religion is not the cause of communalism, but religiosity was certainly a major contributory factor. After all, religion is a belief system, a matter of personal belief. By itself it is not communal; it is the ideology of a religion based socio-political identity that indeed is communalism.

We in India have come to think that Divide and Rule policy was adopted by British imperialism in India only; or for that matter, greater autonomy or full independence by constituent units of the country was restricted to Khalistanis, Nagas, and Manipur etc., in India only. No, it is not so. We in India were not an exception to this historical evolution. Conflicts in Turkey between the Republicans' secularism supported by the Turkish Army and Khalifat's religious fanaticism; between ethnic Slovaks and ethnic Hungarians, Racism, anti-Semitism, Catholic-Protestant conflict in Northern Ireland, Christian-Muslim conflict in Lebanon, *et al ad infinitum*, are outstanding examples of similar circumstances producing identical results amongst societies geographically so much apart.

Xinjiang (Sinkiang) : China's "Kashmir"

Besides the foregoing instances, it is not widely known that China too has problems with Islamist separatists identical to our Kashmir problem. Xinjiang of Aksai Chin notoriety is "China's Kashmir". But unlike our Kashmir it is not a small area. Its size is 1.8 M sq km almost one sixth of China, about half as much as India. Our Kashmir measures some 2,65,000 sq km, of which some 8,600 sq km is under Pakistan's illegal occupation, some 37,500 sq km under China and the remainder 1,41,000 km^2 is with India. The so called disputed part of Kashmir, some 45,000 km^2, is less than one hundredth of Xinjiang. So China's Kashmir problem is 100 times bigger than that of India! But how did China resolve a problem of such gigantic proportions? – Certainly not the way Mr. Jawaharlal Nehru did!

India's then Prime Minister, Pandit Jawaharlal Nehru, voluntarily made our Kashmir into an international issue that was well within our own capability to resolve, all because he stood on an elevated pedestal of world statesmanship. On the other hand, China kept its Kashmir problem under wraps, securely within its own domain.

In 1949, Xinjiang had a majority of Turkish Muslims (Uighurs), under a short-lived state of East Turkestan. China invaded it, crushed it, and won back its territory. The name Xinjiang literally means "Old Frontier returns to China". China integrated its "Kashmir" with its mainland which, now has a population of 20 million plus comprised of 45% Uighur Muslims, 12% other Muslims, and a whopping 41% Hans Chinese, against 6% in 1949. China did not trust the original local population; it trusted its own racial stock. It is noteworthy that the 41% Hans did not include either the PLA or the Chinese migrant workers.

Rhetoric-Idealism is one thing; statesmanship comes from an entirely different breed.

Economic cost of India's Kashmir is sky-high. It receives a per capita Central Grant of INR 8,092, while for the rest of India it works out to a mere 1,137. This is the Nehru-Gandhi "Minority Card" playing, to benefit the Congress Vote Bank—A short term Party-

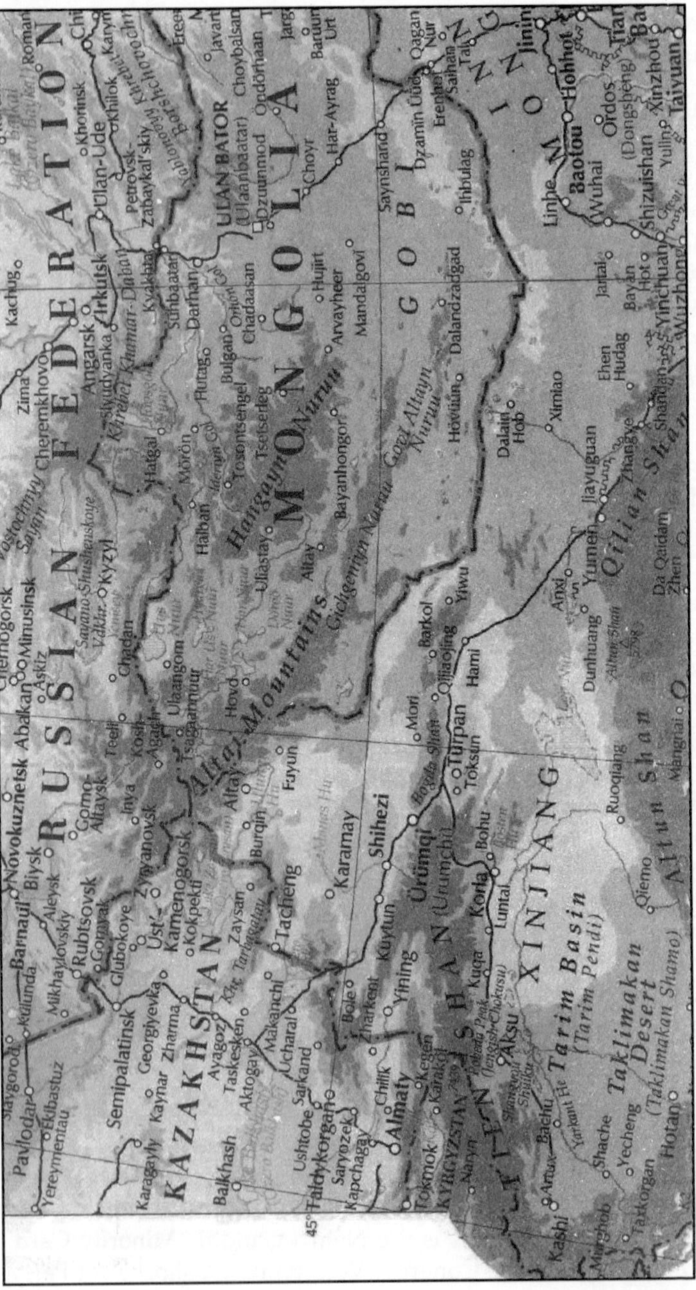

Map: PART CHINA-INNER MONGOLIA

benefit *but a long term disaster for the country!* My apprehension is that overplaying the minority card by the ruling party might lead to another partiton of India after about half a century. This is all the more so since the "Congress Party played religious politics after 26/ 11 attacks". According to the US envoy the "Party accepted Hindu terror angle to allay minority fears."[1] Moreover, while there has not been a single terrorist attack in the United States since 9/11, we in India have been subjected to terror attacks from across the border as well as the LOC, day out and day in. This aspect needs rational analysis by you, the reader.

Incidentally, if the Indian grants to Kashmir were directly remitted by money order, each Kashmiri family of five would receive INR 40,460 every year. Now multiply this by 60, it comes to a staggering amount without considering the compound interest! Just imagine how rich and prosperous every Kashmiri would have been today but for the great "Indian Political System", imposed in the garb of distorted democracy and pseudo-secularism. And where has all that grant-money disappeared? You, my dear reder, knows as well as I do!

Uighur Muslims, like their Kashmiri counterparts, continue to fight for freedom. Violence and terror are as widespresd in Xinjiang, albeit at a much lower level than our Kashmir, thanks to Pakistan ISI, China and to a lesser degree large scale armament aid by the "Human Rights Champions", the Unitrd States Administration. Militancy in Xinjiang keeps growing. For instance: On August 05, three days ahead of the Beijing Olympics, a terror strike killed 16 policemen; on August 11 when the Olympics were in progress, terror attacks near Beijing killed eleven people. Again, on July 6 next year there were huge riots between Uighur Muslims and Hans Chinese in the capital Urumqi (also spelt as Urumchi), resulting in 184 deaths and over one thousand injured, most of the casualties were Hans. In the wake of these developments, Chinese President attending the G-8 meetings flew back immediately. His Government declared war on three fronts; Separatism, Extremism and Terrorism. Friday prayers in Urumqi mosques were banned. The Muslims were told to pray from their homes.

Instead of working to change the political and communal demography in favour of rest of India, (as China did), the Indian Government did not even have the courage to prevent the expulsion of lakhs of Hindus, the Pundits, from the valley where they were the intellectual elite for centuries. Instead, the Indian Government went in for Article 370 that prevents Indians from other parts of the country even to migrate to Kashmir, let alone buy land there, their own country. Once again the minority card of the Congress Vote-Bank left behind a trail of politIcal and communal disaster. Consequently, India has to defend Kashmir with the help of its Army rather than in cooperation with the local population – all this as the bane of Indian democracy![2] And in the bargain, bring a bad name to Indian army. Thanks to Pandit Nehru's statesmanship!

Map : PAKHTOONKHWA (Pakhtoonistan)
NWFP-Baluchistan-Part Afghanistan

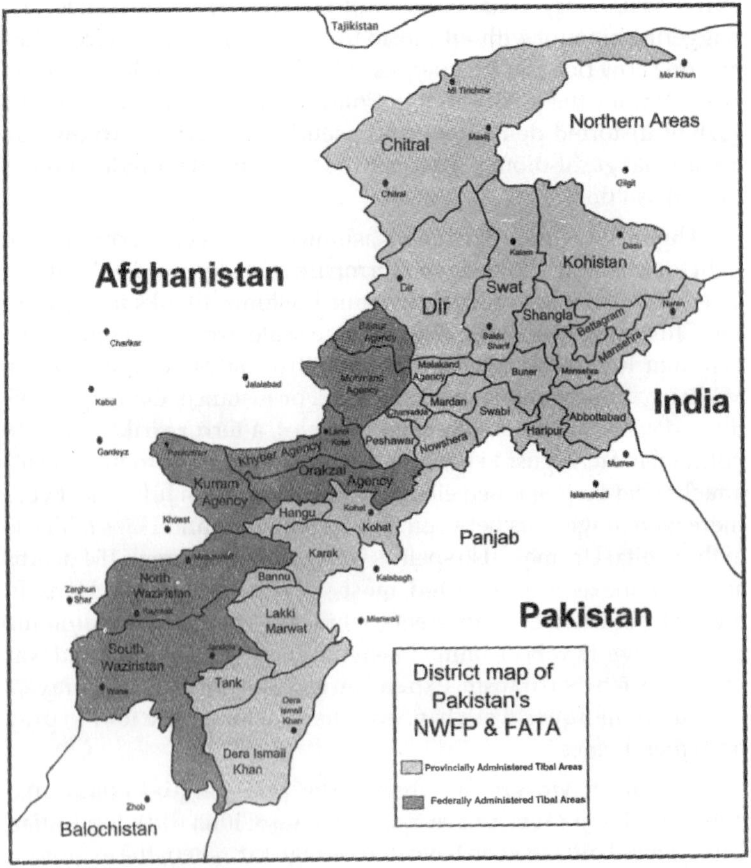

Pukhtoonistan-Baluchistan-Sind

Sind, Baluchistan and Pakhtoons are eminent examples of application of the afore-mentioned evolutionary development practiced nearer home by British imperialism, besides some in China, Tibet, Mongolia, Soviet Empire, and many others farther away where imperialism of a different hue played a major role. Constraints of space restrict me to briefly mention in outline those nearer home. **Pukhtunistan** (Pukhhtoonkhwa) Demand for Pukhtoon homeland has a strong historical backing in as much as when the British started taking over Pukhtoon areas in the nineteenth century, the Pukhtoon people were living as one nation with the rest of Afghanistan. When some elements of occupied areas became restive, the British sent large number of troops to maintain law and order and thereby perpetuated their rule. Drawing lines on maps is old British habit, a technique to resolve knotty territorial issues (as they did in respect of China, Tibet and Aksai Chin). So in 1893 they created the Durand Line to divide the Pukhtoon people into two: roughly one half remained in Afghanistan and the other half in the then expanding British- Indian Empire. At present this line marks the border between Pakistan and Afghanistan much to the chagrin of Afghanistan and inhabitants of NWFP. The situation was further complicated when Pakistan came into being and some Pukhtoons found themselves under Baluchistan. This gave rise to a Pukhtoon nationalist demand for creation of a unified Pukhtoon homeland which would include entire NWFP, those areas of Afghanistan and Baluchistan populated by Pukhtoons. In other words, they demanded restoration of status quo ante. Afghanistan claims that Durand line is totally arbitrary, and has no historical or geographical validity, besides depriving Afghanistan of its territory that was traditionally Afghani. In any case it was never meant to be an international border line. To cap it all, Khan Abdul Gaffar Khan, "Frontier Gandhi", leant his full support to the nationalist movement backed by his quazi-military organization known as the 'Red Shirts'. Gaffar Khan's organization was the strongest nationalistic movement amongst all the provinces that were going to form part of the new State of Pakistan. Jinnah's Muslim League was no match for Gaffar Khan.

Shortly before their final departure from the Indian sub-continent the British had to decide the fate of NWFP amongst other provinces of British-India. They decided to hold a referendum in NWFP offering a choice to the people to choose between India and Pakistan.

However, Gaffar Khan asked the British to give the people a third option as Pukhtoonkhwa while Afghanistan wanted another option as union with Afghanistan. The British Viceroy of undivided India, Lord Mountbatten, rejected both new proposals and stuck to the original offer. As a protest, Gaffar Khan boycotted the vote and 99% of those who voted opted for Pakistan. Nonetheless, Gaffar Khan continued his campaign for Pukhtoonkhwa for which the new government of Pakistan put him behind bars for decades.

Baluchistan

"I have been a Baluch for several centuries. I have been a Muslim for 1400 years. I have been a Pakistani for just over 50 years"[4]. Nawab Akbar Bugti Khan, a tribal chief in Baluchistan, runs a state within State. He runs his fiefdom from his heavily guarded mud fort deep in Baluchistan desert. He has no love for Pakistan, nor for its troops whom he does not wish to see anywhere in the vicinity of his Fort. For him ethnic ties are more important than religious affiliation. Same is the case with many in rural Sind, NWFP and small parts of southern Punjab. While Jinnah preached loyalty to Pakistan alone, he as well as successive Governments in Pakistan have shown little regard for the ethnic/cultural/linguistic diversity of the country. No wonder therefore that they lost East Pakistan in 1971 War of Liberation and have not yet succeeded in emotionally integrating Sindhis, Punjabis, Pakhtoons, Baluch and the incoming Mohajirs, the refugees from India who migrated in the wake of Partition in 1947. This is symbolic of Systematic Failure of Pak Polity. Unless these divisive tendencies of provincialism are eradicated from the ethos of those who govern Pakistan, a strong nation-state cannot be built.

It should be borne in mind that while the migrants from East Punjab came to West Pakistan to save their lives, the Mohajirs from UP, Bihar and other parts of India came to Pakistan in search of a new and more prosperous future, perhaps with an eye on the bureaucratic cake of the new government who would need the services of Muslim intelligentsia from India. And till lately they have succeeded in grabbing the major portion of that cake occupying high positions in the government and the defence services, besides holding political appointments as Presidents, Prime Ministers, governors, etc. Unfortunately for Pakistan, the new elite has not learnt its lesson from 1971-breakup of the country. The governing leaders, mostly Punjabis and Mohajirs, continue to ignore nationalistic sentiment of constituents units. Sindhu Desh is still an active movement, howsoever suppressed. Autonomy for Baluchistan is a live wire. Punjabi arrogance and Mohajirs sentiment continues to prevail over other ethnic minorities. A strong Pakistan shall remain a distant dream unless ethnic diversity is accorded its rightful place in the hierarchy of Pakistan. A Systematic Failure by Pak Polity, to say the least....

Sindhi Nationalism (Sindhu Desh)

The Mohajirs assumed, albeit erroneously, that they had made sacrifices towards creation of Pakistan and therefore had a right to reap benefits accruing therefrom. They did not fit in the traditional power structure of their newly adopted country, more so since they are comparatively much better educated. So they turned their attention to bureaucracy, business and the military. The impact of Urdu-speaking Mohajirs on Sindhi cities like Karachi and Hyderabad was immediate and enormous. They made deep inroads in the Sindhi culture and language besides their life style. They soon linguistically outnumbered Sindhis in Karachi by 58% to 14% while in Hyderabad over 66% of the population was Urdu-speaking Mohajirs. They rarely mixed with the local Sindhi population, socially or otherwise.

In the wake of Partition and communal riots bulk of the Sindhi middle class abruptly left for the safety of India. The consequent vacuum was promptly filled by the Mohajirs who occupied homes and businesses abandoned by the departing Hindus. There was no Sindhi middle class left behind to come in their way. Mohajirs initial success acted as a heady wine. The local Sindhi population was no match for the ideologically driven and highly motivated Mohajirs who also took over many chairs in the administration earlier held by the Hindus. In the process the Mohajirs became politically and economically much stronger than the local population. To cut the long story short, Karachi was declared the Federal Capital Area under the control of Central Government of Liaqat Ali Khan, another Mohajir. He had full support of Jinnah, yet another Mohajir. This came as a shock to Sindh Chief Minister Ayub Khusro as well as Sindhi rank and file. But in 1948 they were not organized or strong enough to offer any resistance to these sinister moves.

However, destiny was in favour of the Sindhis. The death of Jinnah in 1948 and assassination of Liaqat Ali Khan removed two top Mohajirs from the scene. The 1955-One Unit Plan to balance West against East Pakistan was another positive development. Since Punjabis accounted for nearly 40% of population of West Pakistan they started asserting themselves against the Mohajirs who lost many jobs to Punjabis both at the provincial and federal levels, besides in Sind of course. The One Unit Plan was implemented to weaken the nationalistic movements in the constituent units of Pakistan; but instead it strengthened those movements in NWFP, Baluchistan and in Sind, particularly against the Mohajirs' undue interference in Sindhis internal matters. For instance: the University of Karachi forbade the students from answering questions in Sindhi[3]. This discriminatory approach added to high degree of resentment the Sindhis felt against the intruding Mohajirs, which in turn led to Sindhi nationalists joining hands with Pukhtoons, BalOchs and Bengalis in 1948 to form the Peoples' Organization. But the name, its objectives and methodology made little impact on the national political scene.

Pakistan army has been dominated by Punjabis from day one. (So had been the Indian Army). "It is estimated that 65% of officers and 70% of other ranks are Punjabis" against their 56% share of the population. Pukhtoons from NWFP with 16% of population constitute an estimated 22% of officers and 25% of other ranks". The BalOchs and the Sindhis have always remained severely under represented. General Yahya Khan replaced Ayub and reversed the One Unit plan which action went in favour of Mohajirs' rivals in the provinces. Yet another blow for Mohajirs was the loss of Bangladesh shaking the ideological foundations of Pakistan, more so since a large number of Biharis had migrated to East Pakistan who were now politically isolated and have been placed by Bangladesh in cramped refugee camps for decades with no future in sight. Their miserable plight is akin to Bhutanese refugees of Nepali origin living in refugee camps.

After the 1971 fiasco, Zulfiqar Ali Bhutto took charge of the country. He was a Sindhi – a Sindhi for the first time had reached the highest executive office in Pakistan. He introduced a quota system applicable only to Sind under which 40% of government jobs and educational places were reserved for urban areas and 60% for rural areas where the native Sindhis generally lived. Consequently, many lower and middle level jobs went to the Sindhis at the expense of Mohajirs who were further hit by Bhutto's' nationalization program. The language controversy added to Mohajirs' woes, and in turn Bhutto's too. Sindhi used to be a compulsory language in Sind. During Ayub's Martial Law regime many officers complained that learning Sindhi for the duration of their short term posting in Sind was a waste of time. So the requirement was dropped. After Bhutto came to power he restored status quo ante by passing the Language Bill to which there was sharp and swift reaction by the Mohajirs on July 08, 1972, when the Mohajirs took to the streets of Karachi causing all round havoc leading to police firing in which twelve persons were killed. Next day's demonstrations were equally violent and ten more were killed in police firings. Eventually, Bhutto climbed down and passed an ordinance whereunder no one would lose job merely on account of not knowing the Sindhi language. General Zia's coup came as a welcome relief to the beleaguered Mohajirs. The execution of Bhutto added oil to the fire. MQM (Mohajirs Quami Movement) launched agitation(s) for restoration of democracy and general elections. Nevertheless, conditions in Sind remained disturbed for quite some time.

An analysis of the foregoing episodes, their genesis and handling would clearly show that the polity of the entire subcontinent was susceptible to a series of systematic failures from which it learnt lessons, too little, too late, at considerable cost.

Safeguarding Muslim Interests

Hindus were, and still are, in overwhelming majority in India. The Muslim leaders feared that in the event of British Colonial withdrawal from the sub-continent they would be left high and dry. The British readily agreed with the Muslim leaders. The latter felt that they needed the former for safeguarding them as a minority community. Meanwhile Sir Syed Ahmed Khan of Aligarh Muslim University fame made a 'U turn' and said that the British were the best guardians of Muslim interests. In his view Congress was a Hindu body political and social objectives of which were anti-Muslim. In his perception Hindu and Muslim interests were on a permanent crash-course. He further objected to Congress demand for democratic elections based on universal adult franchise that in turn would put power in the hands of staunch Hindus. Even though this premise was not valid, nonetheless, this situation was not acceptable to Muslim leaders.

The All India Muslim League, a conservative political organization, was founded at the end of 1907 by a group of upper class rich Muslims like the Aga Khan, the Nawab of Dacca, the Nawab Mohsin-ul-Mulk, some big zamindars and ex-bureaucrats, etc. It was a totally communalistic organization of Muslims formed to look after Muslim interests against the Hindu majority. Its agenda did not include nationalistic or patriotic themes, or elimination of colonial rule from the country. The League did not think the ethnic minorities like Pukhtoons and Balochs worth consideration either. The League demanded separate electorate for the Muslims. Syed Ahmed had already gone a step further when he reiterated demand for reservation of government jobs for Muslims, seats in legislative assemblies, district boards, *et al.* The British were quick to recognize the inherent logic of official protection for the minorities and actively promoted and supported Muslim brand of communalism. The Muslims refused to see that not one of the demands put forward by the nationalist movements launched by the Congress was pro-Hindus. But logic generally fails in the face of emotional communal outbursts. A major objective of the League was to see that Muslim intelligentsia did not join the Congress, or take side with the colonial regime. Muslim League wanted to make sure that Urdu was recognized as the language of Muslims while their Hindu counterparts were out to safeguard the place of Hindi, particularly in UP and Bihar. Anti-cow slaughter movement was not directed against the Muslims but was so portrayed by the vested interests.

Separate Electorate

The Minto-Morley Act of 1909 created separate electorate for the Muslims. A Muslim elector was enrolled if he paid income tax on an annual income of Rs. 3,000 only while his Hindu counterpart could be enrolled only if he paid one hundred times that amount i.e. Rs. 300,000/- per year. While a Muslim graduate of three years standing could acquire the right to vote, a Hindu graduate required 30 years standing to get the same right. Muslim representation in the legislative councils was also increased well beyond their fair share, all at the expense of Hindu majority. And the so called 'Hindu Congress' remained a mute spectator of trampling of Hindu rights. This gross injustice against Hindu majority was perpetuated by the British Government in the face of top Congress leaders who did not have the guts to protest against such disparities. The so called Hindu Congress failed miserably to get equal treatment for the Hindu majority as opposed to the Muslim minority, all in the name of a false sense of secularism, pseudo secularism indeed! It was a loud and clear sign of Systematic Failure of Indian Polity which strengthened the foundations of Two Nations Theory and subsequent trauma of partition of India leading to Independence. Now, it has become second nature to Congress to play the 'minority card' to secure their vote bank. Yet another sign of Systematic failure of Congress – Old habits die hard!

The infamous Rowlett Act (1919), Jallianwala Bagh Massacre (1919), Fatwa declaring India Dar-ul-Harb, the Khilafat Movement, Chauri Chaura episode, etc., further complicated an already complex issue.

Till early 1920's two issues kept the peace between the two communities. First was the non-cooperation movement during which Hindus and Muslims stood together with common objective of dealing with British colonialism and imperialism. Once this key stone was removed, they were again at each other's throat. The second issue was Khilafat. In 1922 Turkey was declared a Republic and the country came under the rule of Kamaal Ataturk. The Khalifa, the Sultan of Turkey was deposed and in 1924 the institution of Khilafat was abolished. Thus, another corner stone of unity between the two communities got displaced. The vacuum was filled with virulent communalism of the kind in which the Muslim League excelled. It came as a boon to the League which had been lying dormant for so long.

Jinnah Leaves Congress, Joins Muslim League

Mohammad Ali Jinnah of Bombay was a secular leader and a member of the Congress. However, he was opposed to the Non-Cooperation Movement of Mahatma Gandhi and in protest resigned from the Congress in 1920. The inability of the Congress to keep its flock together, and nip the divisive tendencies in the bud has brought many misfortunes to the country. Finding the right opportunity, Jinnah once again moved to the forefront of middle class Muslim politics giving a go bye to the secular principle of the Congress. He went all out to revive the League as an active organization in opposition to the Congress. The British too gave a helping hand in as much as they encouraged separate electorate, reservation of seats and jobs for the Muslims thereby giving a push to the policy of 'Divide and Rule'. The relations between Hindus and Muslims were further embittered by untimely murder of a famous Arya Samaj leader, Swami Shradhanand by a young Muslim fanatic. This tragic event further widened the already wide deep gulf between the Congress and the League.

Attempt at Unity

Unfortunately for India of the future, Congress did not learn any lessons from the past, or the ongoing mistakes. The Lucknow Pact of 1916 is a glaring example. When the First World War broke out in 1914, Turkey allied itself with Germany against Britain placing the Indian Muslims in a dilemma. This proved to be blessing in disguise, albeit very short term, in that efforts at unity between the Congress and Muslim League took shape. Both the parties held their 1915-annual session at the same place (Bombay) and leaders joined the session of one another. Again in 1916 both parties held their sessions at the same time in Lucknow. They accepted the Lucknow Pact that embodied immediate and definite self government as the minimum common demand, but not as the final distant objective.

As usual, the Congress played its minority card and accepted separate electorate in all provinces including Punjab and Bengal, further agreeing to 50 per cent seats in Punjab and 40 per cent in Bengal, well above their fair proportionate share. The agreement also provided that no bill or resolution concerning a community shall be passed if 3/4th of that community was opposed to it. Again, this was Congress playing the minority card with expertise! Continued Systematic Failure by the Congress leadership ... Incidentally, at the same time the Moderate and Extremist factions of the Congress also buried their hatchet and came together on a single platform. This facilitated Tilak's entry back into Congress fold. Concurrently, Mrs. Annie Besant founded the All India Home-rule League in September 1916 which worked hand in glove with

Tilak's Home rule League. The objective of the two Leagues was less radical and all they asked for was self government within the British Empire.

Notes

1. Islam is the second largest religion of the world after Christianity having 1.57 billion adherents constituting 23% of world population against its share of less than 5%. At the time of Partition in 1947 India had the second largest Muslim population in the world (140 M) after Indonesia. However, as on 08 Oct. 2009, Indian Muslim number 160,945,000 while Pakistan's are 174,082,000 and Indonesia's are 202,867,000. The Sunnis are the dominant sect while the Shias are only 10-13%. of the total Muslims in the world.
2. ToI dated December 12, 2010.
3. Courtesy: Vivekananda Kendra Arun Jyoti, and Brigadier P.S. Kulkarni, AVSM, who sent the text to the Author (and modified by the Author).
4. Jones Bennet Jones Owen Bennet: *PAKISTAN, Eye of the storm*; Yale University Press, USA, 2002; Interview with Jones in 1999 and p. 137 of the Book.

5

ROAD TO FREEDOM

"Just as it is impossible to know when a swimming fish is drinking water, so it is impossible to find out when a government servant is stealing money." —Kautilya's Arthashastra (Science of Wealth) written around 300 BC.

Our road to freedom finally ends with freedom to indulge in all sorts of machinations to make money by hook or crook, rampant corruption at all levels of politicians and bureaucracy, high or low; only those at the lower levels are convicted and punished; the rich and high ups cannot be caught, let alone punished. Criminalization of politics is the first fruit of our free-democracy. *Mera Bharat Mahan!*

The withdrawal of Civil Disobedience Movement left the Congress no meaningful issue on the strength of which the freedom movement could be accelerated forward. A feeling of despair and despondency filled the air during 1934-35. The Congress leadership then reviewed its working strategy, performance and achievements during the past few years from which three streams of thought emerged:

- Going back from revolutionary to reformist approach, the pre-1919 moderate phase;
- Council-entry and forming provincial ministries to resolve peoples' day to day grievances through efficient public administration;
- Pursue constructive programmes along with social reforms to eradicate well-known chronic social evils.

Leftist Faction in Congress

None of the above was acceptable to leftist-minded younger generation who were forcefully pulling on the leash to be allowed to take up revolutionary activities, violent or otherwise. Jawaharlal Nehru was in the forefront of Gandhiji's critics along with other socialist-communist ideologues. He challenged the basic Gandhian non-violent philosophy and his strategy of starting a movement, calling it off when repression by the authorities, or violence by the agitators, crossed the line he had set in his mind as the limit. After a pause the struggle was resumed, possibly with altered objectives. This strategy came to be known as Struggle-Truce-Struggle (S-T-S). Notwithstanding the validity of criticism, it stands to reason that no movement, political or radical-social, can last over a long period of time, more so when it is being met with severe repression. Nehru also agreed that any such movement has of necessity to go through ups and downs but that does not mean that a passive phase or compromise should be accepted to call off the movement. He was of the opinion that by late 1930's a stage had been reached when it had become necessary that conflict and confrontation become permanent features against colonial-imperialism till they are totally eliminated from the soil of our country. Permanent hostility and confrontation were *sine qua non* for success against colonialism. Aggressive direct action was the key element; Interposition of a constitutional phase was a blemish. By this time stage seems to have set in for a possible split in the Congress, the only political party in the forefront fighting for freedom.

That is when Gandhiji stepped in to diffuse the breach. He decided in favour of the council-entry faction and permitted them to enter legislatures. Of course he continued to believe that freedom could be won only through Satyagraha, and not via the parliamentary politics. Since mass movements could not be a permanent feature of the struggle, of necessity therefore a pause was called for so that those who could not give vent to their patriotism during active period of the Movement could do so during the passive phase. Moreover, a large section of the intelligentsia of the country appeared to believe in parliamentary democracy.

Congress Assumes Power

So far the history of the Congress was replete with launching mass movements that sometimes turned violent resulting in casualties, or were crushed through severe repression by the authorities, again resulting in casualties, more often than not some fatal ones too. The assumption of power by Congress Ministries transformed the entire psychological outlook of the country. Congress prestige went up sky high. The public at large came to realize that the Congress could also wield power for their benefit, albeit within the limited powers and resources, which the imperial power had delegated to them. Thousands of political prisoners were released as a first gesture. Deportation and internment orders against political detainees were cancelled.

The new ministers set a personal example in plain living and voluntarily reduced their own salaries from Rs. 2000 to Rs. 500 per month, besides taking immediate steps to pass legislation to ameliorate the condition of the peasantry as promised in their election manifestos. Concurrently, Congress ministries all over the country repealed all emergency powers acquired by the Colonial power in 1932 through draconian laws like the Public Safety Acts etc. Bans on illegal organizations such as Hindustan Seva Dal and Youth Leagues as also on political books and journals were lifted. Although Communist Party was banned under orders of the Central Government, they could function more easily in Congress ruled provinces. Press freedom was restored. Securities taken from newspapers were refunded. Pending prosecution cases were withdrawn. Black listing of newspapers for purposes of official advertising was cancelled. Confiscated arms were returned and forfeited arms licenses were restored. Police powers were curbed. CID agents were prohibited from shadowing political workers and reporting their speeches-activities etc. However, some right wing Congress Ministers proved to be exceptions and continued to use CID for shadowing communists and Congress extremists.

The British were well aware of ultimate objective of the Congress. They knew that the Congress policy was to confront colonialism-imperialism, and not to cooperate with them, their rulers. The Congress ministries therefore knew that time period available to them was indeed limited. With the war clouds looming large over the horizon in Europe, the ministries had therefore to act rapidly to achieve as much as was possibie. This was particularly so regarding agrarian reforms, which take exceptionally long time to conceive and implement, more so since the agrarian structure in India is extremely complex and complicated. It varies in different parts of the country and is not easily susceptible to reforms. Its various components like land rights, debt, money lending, share cropping, etc. further complicated matters. For all practical purposes no progress could be made in this direction due to time constraint and complexities of the problem. However, certain aspects of debt relief were satisfactorily resolved in some provinces.

Peasants Long March: 1500 miles

The provincial Kisan Conference of Andhra organized a truly long march in 1938 in which more than 2000 peasants marched over 1500 miles in 130 days. They had started from Itchapur in the North and reached the Madras Legislative Assembly on 27 March 1938 to present over 1100 petitions for debt relief and redressal of connected grievances. The Congress Ministry was sympathetic and expressed their appreciation of the physical efforts. They appointed a Zamindari Enquiry Committee but the legislation could not be passed before the Congress ministries resigned. In this connection clash between *jotedars* and *bargadars* of Bengal Provincial Kisan Sabha in early 1947 under Muslim League Ministry of Suhrawardy is noteworthy. The peasants were subjected to severe repression and at Khanpur twenty peasants were killed

The Congress Ministries were pro labour and set up a Labour Enquiry Committee under Rajendra Prasad. The Committee recommended:

- Labour Wage to be minimum Rs. 15 per month;
- Formation of an Arbitration Board;
- Labour recruitment for all mills by an independent board;
- Maternity benefits to women workers;
- Recognition of Mazdoor Sabha (Left dominated Union)
- Strengthening of Trade Union rights;
- Improvement in labour conditions;
- Compulsory conciliation-arbitration before resorting to strikes.

The management refused to accept these recommendations. However, after considerable pressurizing, some of the recommendations were accepted and implemented. Certain social reforms and welfare measures were also part of the Congress agenda. Prohibition was introduced in certain areas. Laws were passed to enable untouchables (*Harijans*) to enter temples, free access to government offices, free access to public sources of water, wells, ponds, roads, hospitals, educational institutions, restaurants and hotels etc. The Congress governments paid special attention to primary, technical and higher education as well as to public health and sanitation. Education facilities for Harijans and girls were expanded. Emphasis was laid on manual and productive work as part of educational setup.

Continuation of mass political activity was the basis on which Congress leadership had accepted formation of ministries in the provinces. The question arose as to what should be the attitude of popularly elected Congress administrations towards popular agitations, especially those which crossed the bounds of existing laws laid down by the Imperial Power? Unfortunately, this subject had not been given due consideration, perhaps none whatsoever, before the decision to enter legislatures was taken. Political work outside the legislature would naturally involve organizing popular protests. And those protests might as well be against its' own actions and decisions! How could a political party running a government organize popular movements and simultaneously enforce law and order? The situation would turn out far more complex if the protests took a violent turn. Here it needs to be clearly understood that the existing laws were in fact colonial laws, formulated by the colonial power to safeguard its position, while the party running the government of the day was committed to overthrow the same laws. It was a totally incongruous situation for which there was no historical precedence.

Congress ministries did not know the answer. More often than not, the ministries treated all militant protests and trade union agitations as a law and order problem taking recourse to Section 144 of the Criminal Code. In the process trade union leaders, agitating protesters defying the prohibitory orders and the peasants of Kisan Sabhas were arrested. And that is what happened even in Kanpur! In order to resolve the built-in contradictions, The All India Congress Committee met in September 1938. A resolution was passed condemning all those who advocated class-war, murder, loot and violence in the name of freedom struggle. The Congress ministries had a number of positive achievements to their credit, the most important one being their tight control and firm handling of communal riots.

A simple scapegoat-way out of a complicated difficult situation was the mistaken belief that passing of resolutions could resolve such complex issues! The systematic failure had reached its zenith ... The outbreak of World War II on September 1, 1939 generated a political crisis in the country. The Congress ministries resigned in October 1939. That day was celebrated by Muslim League under the aegis of Jinnah as a day of liberation from the majority Hindu rule. Such was the poison of communalism in the minds and hearts of Muslim League. The byproducts of this development were:

- Coming closer together of the Left and the Right factions in the Congress;
- Muslim League passed the famous Pakistan Resolution in 1940.

The Idea of Autonomous Muslim Homeland

The very idea of a separate homeland for Muslims was first mooted on December 29, 1930 by India's most popular poet, Sir Muhammad Iqbal.-In his Presidential address at the Allahabad session of All india Muslim League he suggested that Punjab, NWFP, Sind and Baluchistan be constituted into a single self governing unit. By implication he seems to have meant a semi-autonomous territory that would be a homeland for Muslims of North West India. It could be a part of the British Empire, or even out of jurisdiction of the Empire, but it should be constituted as as a single self governing geographical unit. However, Iqbal did not use the word 'Pakistan' as the name did not exist at that time.What exactly he meant is not clear. However, scholars believe that Iqbal was not thinking in terms of partition of India, but in terms of a federation of autonomous states within India.

The name 'Pakistan' was coined in 1933 by a young student of Cambridge University, Choudhry Rahmat Ali (1897-1951). He published a pamphlet 'Now or Never' in 1933 in which he called the proposed State as Pakistan, the "Land of the Pure". While Iqbal's idea had four provinces, Rahmat Ali wished to amalgamate five by including Kashmir also. The etymology of the name is quite interesting: It was created by using the first letters of the five constituting units – 'P' for Punjab, 'A' for Afghania (NWFP), 'K' for Kashmir, 'S' for Sind and the final part of 'stan' as part of Baluchistan. 'PAKSTAN' did not pronounce well. So he added an 'I' as in Afghan-i-stan. The concept and the name started taking concrete form in 1937-39 when the Muslim League started a poisonous baseless propaganda against the Congress whom they called "Hindu Congress". Muslim League advocated partition of the country on religious lines and the British Government supported the stand taken by Muslim League right from the beginning.

Most Muslims were reluctant to join the Congress or the Freedom movement, for that matter. In the elections for the Provincial Assemblies 90.2% of Muslim voters from all over India voted for Muslim League which campaigned for formation of separate sovereign Muslim homeland, Pakistan. And Pakistan did become a reality on August 14, 1947. After the boundary lines were drawn the irony of fate for Indian National Congress's secularism was that out of all those who voted for Pakistan, a mere about 7,226,000 Muslims actually migrated to Pakistan. Of these 5.3 million Muslims migrated from India to West Punjab. Thus, the bulk of population of Pakistan was already residents of that geographical area. In other words carving out Pakistan, with all its catastrophic consequences, did not bring any worthwhile benefits for Indian Muslims. On the contrary those whom Jinnah left behind became victims of suspicion and disloyalty. Moreover, both communities suffered nearly 500,000 to one million casualties besides the innumerable rapes, tortures, cruelties, forcible conversions, *et al.*

The number of Hindus and Sikhs who had no option but to migrate from West Pakistan to India was slightly higher; it was 7,249,000 making a total of 14.5 million people who crossed the border into what was perceived as relative safety of religious majority. Of these, 3.4 million Hindus and Sikhs moved from Pakistan to East Punjab in India, besides a further 1.2 millions migrated in each direction to and from Sindh. However strangely enough, the net flow of Muslims since partition is from Pakistan to India. It is indeed a strange irony of political reality that more Muslims chose to come and live in India than Indian Muslims (excluding DPs) chose Pakistan as their permanent homeland. The woes of displaced persons need hardly any elaboration.

Needless to say that none of the two governments was prepared to deal with transmigration of populations on such a gigantic scale, indeed staggering in its complexity and magnitude. Estimates of the number of deaths range around 500,000 to as high as one million. Obviously, these figures are mere guesstimates only. The massive violence and slaughter that occurred on both sides of the border is indeed mind boggling. Can humans behave in such a ghastly manner? Besides the killings, rapes and injuries are beyond estimation.

Areas in West Punjab such as Lahore, Rawalpindi, Multan and Gujarat had a large Sikh population and many of them were killed by radical Muslims. On the other side in east Punjab, Amritsar, Ludhiana and Gurdaspur had a majority Muslim population in which many of them were wiped out by Sikh guerrillas who launched an all out war against the Muslims. In the partition plan of Bengal the Muslim majority district of Murshidabad came to India while Hindu majority district Khulna and Buddhist majority Chittagong division went to Pakistan under the Radcliffe Award. Perhaps, geographical contiguity was the major factor in this apparent contradiction.

Sindhi Hindus (Sindhu Desh)

At the time of Partition there were 1,400,000 Hindu Sindhis, though most were concentrated in main urban centers like Karachi, Hyderabad, Shikarpur and Sukkhur. Relations between Hindus and Muslims in Sind were cordial and neighbourly. Therefore Hindus and Sikhs were expected to stay in Sind following the Partition. However, because of an uncertain future in a Muslim country, a sense of better opportunities in the new emerging India, and most of all because of sudden heavy influx of Muslim refugees from various parts of Northern India, many Sindhi Hindus decided to leave for India. Moreover, many Muslim immigrants instigated violent incidents in Karachi and Hyderabad resulting in about 776,000 Sindhi Hindus moving out to India. That was the first wave from Sind, and the trend of migration continued for the next more than fifty years. According to Pakistan's 1998 census, around 2.28 million Hindus continued to live in Sind while the number of Sindhi Hindus in India was 2.57 million as per the Census records of 2001.

Since 92.2% of Indian Muslims were clamouring for Pakistan, why did they not go to their cherished homeland when it was created for their benefit? Since Jinnah had said Muslims were not safe in 'Hindu India' and Islam would be decimated in Hindu India, why did he not collect his flock and move them to the safety of his Pakistan? That would have been the logical outcome of Muslim League's agitation for a separate homeland for South Asian Muslims. Obviously, that would have been the rational conclusion of the preceding developments. My remarks should not be misconstrued as anti-Muslim and I don't mean that Muslims have no place in India; far from it. But those guilty of treason against integrity of the country have no place here; it is those elements who should have been the first to be sent to Pakistan for which they were fighting for. And why the Congress leadership did not take any steps to send them to the land of their dreams? But Congress had got so used to playing the minority-card, their safe vote-bank for all the years to come with the result that they continued to enjoy the fruits of land of their forefathers, the land towards whose integrity and honour they had no regard, let alone reverence. Alas, the Congress leaders showed no remorse for betraying their Hindu majority which made personal sacrifices for the cause propounded by the Congress! The Partition and its catastrophic consequences speak volumes against the Congress minority-card. Indeed a profound Systematic Failure of Congress! What type of secular-democracy the Congress had in mind? — a democracy in which the majority is reduced to a secular minority while the minority is accorded the benefits of a communalistic non-secular majority — Totally irrational to say the least...

The right and rational course of action by the great Congress Party was to send all those who sought Pakistan as their dreamland, and allow only those Muslims to stay on in India who had impeccable credentials of having been nationalists/non-Muslim Leaguers throughout the struggle for independence. That would have been systematic success story to teach Mr. Jinnah a lesson of a lifetime by having his flock together. He had neither the land nor the economic infrastructure to support such a huge mass of population. About 50 million additional mouths to feed, house and clothe would have been impossible for Mr. Jinnah. Considering the awesome burden of the consequent situation, it is well on the cards that, perhaps, Mr. Jinnah would have sought reunification with India! But it was not to be a success story for India; instead it remained a Systemic Failure of Indian polity. Yes, the 'ifs' and 'buts' of history ....

Quit India Movement (1942)

Complete failure of the Cripps Mission (March 1942) was the signal for Gandhiji to launch the next phase of offensive. The proposals put forward by this Mission did not actively encourage the formation of a separate state of Pakistan but nor did it actively discourage it. Jinnah rejected the proposals out of hand while the Congress rejected the same primarily because *de facto* power would still remain in British hands; and secondly, because of unrealistic provision for non-accession. Failure of this Mission created a sort of moral crisis for Gandhiji and his methodology to attain complete independence for free India. The war situation had taken a serious turn for the worse. Japanese attack on India was imminent. Gandhiji was aware that Japan was not at war with India, and therefore will not invade India if the British left the country in an orderly manner as opposed to what had happened at Singapore, Malaya and Burma. Therefore, a resolution was passed at the All India Congress Committee meeting held at Bombay on August 08, 1942: "An immediate ending of British rule in India is an urgent necessity both for the sake of India and the success of United Nations."[1]

Immediately thereafter all the senior leaders of the Congress including Gandhiji, Nehru, Patel, Azad, Rajendra Prasad were arrested. The Congress was declared an illegal organization. Gandhiji was lodged in Agha Khan's palace in Poona while the Working Committee members were imprisoned in Ahmednagar Fort. A large number of Congressmen were arrested all over the country and put behind bars. Violent protests shook the country all over the place. The atrocities inflicted on the people were brutal to the extreme. By the end of 1943 the movement had fizzled out.

According to the official records of the Central Legislative Assembly, 60,229 persons were arrested, 18,000 detained under the Defence of India Regulations, 940 were killed and 1630 injured during police-military firings in which sometimes even machine-guns were also used. It is noteworthy that a significant section of the population did not take part in this Movement. The Communists and Muslims had openly opposed it while Hindu Mahasabha and the Liberals remained silent spectators. The British did not budge at all. The Congress organization had disintegrated and disappeared from the scene at a critical moment in its history. Instead, Muslim League with active support of the British-Indian Government consolidated its position. It emerged as a formidable force to reckon with. The League followed the lead of the Congress and declared their membership open for a mere two annas. Hordes of Muslims soon swelled the ranks of regular members of the Muslim League. There was no doubt that the people were no longer committed to

Gandhian methods of non-violence to gain independence. So much was sacrificed and so little achieved! It was a clear cut case of Systematic Failure at the highest level. Howsoever high sounding it might have been the "Quit India Movement" was a total failure.

Indian National Army

Subhash Chandra Bose, ex President of Indian National Congress, disappeared from his house in Calcutta on January 17, 1941. He reached Moscow via Kabul and flew from there to Berlin where he was well received by the German Government. He contacted Indian soldiers who had been taken prisoner by the German Army and organized them to fight for India's freedom. The legion soon grew to its full strength of three thousand. He also set up Free India Centers in Paris and Rome.

In December 1941, the war broke out in the East. Japanese forces overran the whole of South East Asia. An old revolutionary, Rash Bihari Bose who was living in Japan called for a conference of Indians held at Tokyo March 28-30, 1942. It was decided to organize an Indian National Army (INA) that would conduct operations under direct command of Indian officers to liberate India from British colonial rule. The INA was formally established on September 01, 1942. Concurrently, Indian Independence League was established covering the region under occupation of Japanese forces. This was followed by a conference at Bangkok June 15-23, 1942. It was a fully representative conference attended by Subhash Bose and about one hundred delegates from all over South-East Asia and the Far East. In June 1943, Bose reached Tokyo where he was received by Japanese Prime Minister Tojo who approved of Bose's plan of forming a Provisional Government to take charge of Indian Territory as the Japanese forces move on. Bose reached Singapore on July 02, 1943 to a grand welcome by the Indian residents there. Two days after that Rash Bihari Bose handed over charge of Indian Independence League to Subhash Chandra Bose. The formation of Azad Hind Fauj (INA) was announced the next day. A conference attended by delegates from all over East Asia was held at Singapore in October 1943. Netaji Subhash Chandra Bose read out the famous Proclamation on October 21 in which he announced setting up of the Provisional Government for India at Singapore, Bose became the head of the State as well as its Prime Minister and Supreme Commander of the Army.

Provisional Government of Free India

The Provisional Government was soon recognized by Japan, Germany, Italy and six other countries. Its first action was to declare war on Britain and USA. At first the expenses of the Provisional Government were met by voluntary contributions and Japanese aid, but later through levies on Indian properties. Hindustani was declared the national language. 'Jai Hind' was to be the formal greeting, Congress Tricolour the national flag and Tagore's poem as the National Anthem. The Japanese Government handed over the Andaman Islands to the Provisional Government of free India. Netaji visited the Islands in December 1943 and shifted his headquarters to Rangoon.

INA soldiers first set foot on Indian soil when they captured Mowdok, about 80 km to the East of Cox Bazaar in a night surprise attack. However, Japanese main drive was for Imphal, the capital of Manipur. Three special units of INA were attached to the Japanese forward troops. On March 19, 1944 they planted the Tricolour Flag for the first time on the liberated soil of India. Same day Tojo declared that Provisional Government of free India would administer the territory so liberated. By then INA troops had advanced about 150 miles into Indian Territory.

The American atom bombs closed the final phase of Japanese offensive in the East. The British forces occupied Rangoon in May 1945. Netaji left Burma and flew to Singapore via Bangkok and reached Saigon where he was offered two seats on a Japanese plane bound for Tokyo. The plane landed at Toihoku in what then was called Formosa (Taiwan) at about 8 pm August 18, 1945. The plane took off for Tokyo but was reported to have caught fire immediately after take off. Subsequent events are surrounded in mystery. Netaji's badly burnt body is reported to have been shifted to a hospital where he died that very night between 8 and 9 pm.

Mass demonstrations of sympathy were held all over India. There was large scale fraternization between the INA soldiers and the local population. People at large blamed those senior Congress leaders who had earlier declared Netaji as some sort of *persona non grata*. All this sympathy and enthusiasm shook the British to the bone. This was indeed a contributory factor for their early departure from India.

Trial: INA Personnel

The government decided to try several hundreds of the 20,000 INA prisoners on trial in public, for charges of waging war against the King and for using brutal methods in inducing other prisoners to join them. The first trial was held in Delhi's Red Fort in November 1945. One Hindu (P.K. Singh), a Muslim (Shahnawaz Khan) and a Sikh (Gurbux Singh Dhillon) were in the dock. A military tribunal was set up for the trial. The Congress set up a Defence Committee comprising Bhulabhai Desai, Tej Bahadur Sapru and Jawaharlal Nehru. The trial caused great excitement in the country, more so since name of Subhash Chandra Bose who had become a national hero was associated with the INA prisoners. Large demonstrations were held and funds were collected for the benefit of the prisoners. Fiery speeches applauding the role of INA became a daily routine. The police and the army were deployed to maintain law and order. Hundreds were killed in the process. The intensity of mass demonstrations, immense outpouring of sympathy for the INA soldiers, their patriotism and fighting spirit, shook the Congress leadership and allied parties who had earlier condemned Bose as a collaborator of fascism, a sort of *persona non grata*. They felt ashamed of their past actions with regard to Netaji Subhash Chandra Bose and regretted their systemic failure in this unworthy episode.

Indian Naval Mutiny

The Government was scared that the INA spirit might percolate down to the regular forces. In fact it did. And the Naval Mutiny (February 18-23, 1946) was the first open defiance of military discipline. This was the greatest threat to British imperialism in India. The ratings of the Signal Training Establishment INS Talwar of Royal Indian Navy in Bombay went on a hunger strike on February 18, 1946 protesting against bad food and racist humiliations. By the next day the protest had spread to all 20,000 ratings in 18 shore-establishments in Bombay besides the twenty ships in the harbour at the time. The Union Jack was removed from Ship's masts. Instead, Congress and Muslim League flags were hoisted. The Ratings also elected a Central Naval Strike Committee with MS Khan as the President. Their demands included better food and equal pay with the white ratings. National/Political demands like release of all INA prisoners and withdrawal of Indian forces from Indonesia were tagged on to their basic grievances.

As usual the British resorted to violent measures of suppression. While Bombayites brought food and water to the striking ratings, the authorities deployed British troops to quell the rebellion. A seven hours gun battle ensued outside the Castle Barracks on February 21, 1946. However, by next day the strike had spread to Naval Vessels all over the country as well as to some ships in the open sea making a total of 78 ships, 20 shore-establishments and 20,000 ratings. At Karachi, INS Hindustan surrendered after a gun battle while the students and public demonstrated support through violent clashes with the police and the army. On the advice, and promise of no-victimization by Sardar Patel, the Strike Committee surrendered on February 23, 1946. Mr. Khan declared: "We surrender to India and not to Britain." The strong man of India, Sardar Vallabh Bhai Patel could not keep his promise to the strikers. Yet another High Level Failure!

Muslim League Consolidates

During the War Years, Muslim League had consolidated its position considerably. Inaptitude of Gandhiji and covert, if not open support of the British Government, helped the small minority League to match its strength with the majority Congress. As already mentioned, the League imitated the Congress to introduce two-Anna-membership to swell its rank and file. Insidious propaganda against the Hindus was spread *ad lib.* Hindu merchants, zamindars and money-lenders were particularly targeted to derive maximum advantage out of popular discontent against these classes of Hindus. The rising tide of virulent communalism swept aside even the die-hard Muslim secular nationalists. Jinnah's position became one of crowning glory, totally unassailable as the sole spokesman of all Indian Muslims – this was the situation in which Lord Wavell took over from Lord Linlithgow in October 1943. The new Governor General released Gandhiji, but other members of the working committee remained behind bars. Immediately after release, Gandhiji announced that Civil Disobedience portion of the 08 August, 1942 stood automatically cancelled. But the Governor General refused to initiate talks till the resolution was withdrawn. He also refused to order release of other members of the Working Committee. Thus Gandhiji was left alone to face the music in the aftermath of fizzled out Quit India Movement.

Rajagopalachari prepared the ground for a meeting between Gandhiji and Jinnah. The talks were extended over a period of time. Gandhiji virtually conceded Jinnah's demand for a separate state for the Muslims of India. Rajah's formula made considerable concessions to Jinnah. However, ultimately, the talks broke down since Gandhiji did not have any official status in the Congress. To cap it all, the High Command members did not approve of Gandhiji agreeing to partition of the country. In their view the unity of the country could not be sacrificed besides agreeing to other concessions.

Princely States (Nizam of Hyderabad)

The pattern of British conquests of Indian sub-continent created two types of India: British India and the Princely States, the latter forming nearly two-fifths of the sub-continent. Some states like Mysore, Nizam State (Hyderabad) and Kashmir were bigger than even many countries of Europe, while others were mere estates counting their population in thousands. However, all Princely states recognized paramountcy of the British Crown, which in turn guaranteed protection to the autocracies, wielding absolute power concentrated in the hands of the ruler, against any internal or external threat. Land tax was higher than that in British India; civil liberties were correspondingly less. The State revenue was used at the personal discretion of the ruler, often for personal ostentatious living. Rule of law was what the ruler prescribed at that point of time. Consequently, most of the states suffered under heavy load of economic, social, political and educational backwardness. Of course there were some notable exceptions like Baroda and Mysore states. Nonetheless, the fact was that all the Indian States under their respective rulers were legally independent entities.

The rise of nationalism and nationalist movements in British India under aegis of the Congress had a direct impact on the peoples of the Princely States. It was inevitable, whether the British or the Princes liked it or not. The peoples of the Princely States breathed a whiff of fresh air blown over from British India, charged with aroma of civil liberties, political consciousness, fundamental rights and responsible government. Mark you, it was just the stale whiff, and nothing in original. Nevertheless, it did make the states' peoples conscious of what to them at that time were mere abstract concepts.

Soon a number of organizations mushroomed under the generic name of Praja Mandals demanding responsible government and rule of law. Some agitations and protests were indeed inevitable. The Congress responded with restraint. World War II brought about a distinct change in the political environment of both British India and territories under the Princely States. Defence of India Rules was promulgated giving the Government unfettered authority. The political leadership responded with "Quit India" movement in August 1942. This time the Congress made no distinction between British India and the States' jurisdiction, inter alia, demanding merger of the States in the mainstream India. Failure of Satyagraha launched by Rajkot Pratinidhi Sabha was at one end of the spectrum. Nizam of Hyderabad was on other. His dominions comprised of three distinct linguistic groups: Marathi-speaking 28 per cent, Kannada-speaking 22 per cent, and Telgu-speaking 50 per cent. Osman Ali Khan ruled this conglomeration as a personal autocracy of which he became the head in 1911 and continued till 1948 when he was forced to merge his State in the Indian Union. The Nizam's own estate, Sarf Khas, constituted ten per cent of the total area of the State. Its income went directly to the Nizam to meet his personal royal expenses. About thirty per cent of the area of Nizam State was held as jagirs by various categories of rural population where illegal levies, exactions and forced labour (*vethi*) were the rule.

Rajkot was a small princely state in the Kathiawad peninsula. Its representative assembly consisted of ninety members elected on the basis of universal adult franchise — quite an unusual occurrence in a small enclave having a population of barely 75,000. While the ruler was a staunch Muslim the overwhelming population was Hindu speaking three distinctly different languages. On the other hand, in the Nizam State of Hyderabad cultural, linguistic and religious suppression of Hindus by Nizam was such that Urdu was made the court language and all efforts were made to impose this 'foreign' language on South Indians who belonged to a different ethnic and linguistic stock. Osmania University was a symbol of Nizam's neglect of the majority of his subjects. Osman Ali Khan kept up his campaign to project Hyderabad as a Muslim State, more so after 1927 when Ittehad-ul-Muslimin emerged as an organization that projected the Nizam as the "Royal Embodiment of Muslim Sovereignty in the Deccan". However, the "Quit India" movement got good response from Hyderabad. The peasantry agitated for abolition of forced grain levy, practice of *vethi*, exactions and illegal seizures of land. The peasants' movement was brutally crushed through large scale arrests, beatings and severe repression by the police and armed forces of Nizam State. Thousands were beaten black and blue, hundreds died and many leaders languished in jails.

Lord Mountbatten announced in a press conference held on June 04, 1947 that the British would leave India for good on 15th August 1947. Nizam Osman Ali Khan lost no time and announced on 12 June that on the lapse of British paramountcy he would become a sovereign monarch. In other words he would not accede to the Union of India. Hyderabad State Congress held its open session June 16-18 to demand accession of the State to Indian Union and formation of a responsible government. The State Congress had full support of the National Congress. After consultations at Delhi it was decided to form a Committee of Action, which was to function from Bombay, outside the Nizam State, to avoid arrest. The Committee was to have subsidiary offices at Sholapur, Vijayawada and Gadag. The struggle was formally launched on 07 August, to be celebrated as "Join Indian Union Day". The proposal received overwhelming response. As usual repression was set in motion with beatings and arrests. On 13 August the Nizam banned ceremonial hoisting of Indian National Flag. This caused great resentment. Protests and demonstrations were held all over the State. The storm troopers of Ittihad-ul-Muslimin, the Razakars, were armed by the State Force and let loose on the people for dacoity, looting, murder and rape. The raids were intensified on the villages. The State Congress was the main vehicle for organizing mass movements and over 20,000 Satyagrahis were in jails.

The writing on the wall was large and clear. The Nizam was not going to sign the instrument of accession in a peaceful manner. The Indian army moved in on 13 September 1948. The Nizam and his Razakars surrendered on the 18th. The accession and integration of the Indian Union was now complete.

The inordinate delay in resolving the Hyderabad crisis resulted in untold misery for the people of the State. The decision to send in the Army was a foregone conclusion since the Nizam had repeatedly made it more than clear that he would not accede to the Indian Union. The writing on the wall was loud and clear. Then why this vacillation in taking the bitter pill! Same old story of systemic failure of Indian polity! On the other hand, Pakistan, having perceived that Maharaja Gulab Singh was in no mood to accede to Pakistan, sent their raiders into Kashmir well before the date of Independence. By preempting the issue they gained much ground and strategic advantage for all times to come.

Indeed, political objectives are achieved by timely application of military strategy.

Note

1. Tendulkar, D.G.: *Mahatma, Life of Mohandas Karamchand Gandhi*, 8 volumes, New Delhi, 1969, Reprint Vol. 2, p. 52.

6

PARTITION-INDEPENDENCE

With the end of the War in Europe and subsequent General Elections, Labor Party assumed power in London on July 26 under Prime Minister C.R. Atlee. A marked shift in British policy towards India took place. Soon after that the Americans dropped two atomic bombs on Japan: one at Hiroshima on August 06 and the other at Nagasaki on August 07, 1945 bringing the Second World War to an abrupt end when the Allies celebrated August 15 as Victory Day.

The foregoing developments led to the visit of Cabinet Mission from England comprising of Secretary of State for India Pethic Lawrence, President of the Board of Trade Sir Stafford Cripps, and the Lord of Admiralty Alexander. They, along with Lord Wavell carried on extensive negotiations with various Indian leaders from March 24 to June 1946. At the outset the Mission rejected Jinnah's demand for Pakistan since it would include a large number of non-Muslims. Since the Congress and the League could not agree to a common plan, the Mission presented its own plan in the vain hope that it would break the deadlock. But nothing worked. So on July 04, 1946 Lord Wavell formed a caretaker government of officials alone. However, Wavell felt the need to bring in at least the Congress alone in the caretaker government if the League persisted in its refusal. Ultimately, an interim government dominated by the Congress was sworn in on September 02, 1946. It was headed by Jawaharlal Nehru. In order to prevent the Congress from enjoying the fruits of power, Muslim League also decided to join the Interim government. The League continued to attend the Constituent Assembly which had started functioning effective December 09.

Meanwhile back home Gandhi-Jinnah talks had failed. In fact none expected them to succeed. So did the Bhulabhai Desai-Liaqat Ali parleys fail to yield any result. In the meantime the War came to an end in Europe on May 07, 1945. The Japanese had been driven out of Burma. By now the main base for operations in the East had shifted to India. Lord Wavell ordered the release of all Congress Working Committee members on June 14, 1945 and proposed talks on formation of a new Executive Council. All members would be Indians except the Viceroy and the Commander-in-Chief. Caste Hindus and Muslims would have equal representation. The Viceroy called for a Conference at Simla to work out the nuts and bolts of the proposal.

The Conference opened on June 25 and lasted till July 14. The Congress strongly objected to being reduced to a party of Caste Hindus and parity with Muslim League. Jinnah insisted that Muslim League alone would have the right to choose all Muslim members of the proposed Council and that there should be a sort of communal veto in the Council and decisions opposed by the Muslims would require 2/3rd majority. Jinnah's demands were patently absurd. Maulana Abdul Kalam Azad was the Congress President at the time and Congress should not be allowed to nominate him to the Council! Stupid absurdity, to say the least! In the face of Jinnah's intransigence, Wavell dissolved the Conference thereby indirectly conceding Jinnah's demand for a communal veto. No attempt was made to call the League's bluff. Yet another dead-load in the box of systematic failures of Indian polity! In other words Jinnah wished to have all Muslims of India to be citizens of proposed State of Pakistan besides exercising the communal veto. The two propositions read together should have opened the eyes of the pseudo-secular Congress to the realities of prevailing politics of Jinnah under the patronage of British-Indian Government. Therefore when partition did come through, Congress should have taken action to meet Jinnah's ambition of having all Muslims of India under the benign rule of his cherished new sovereign state. But the Congress allowed Jinnah to have the cake and eat it too! It was indeed another serious error of judgment and failure of policy on the part of Gandhi-Nehru combine piling up in a heavy mass.

"My description of the partition as the greatest blunder in the history of the mankind is an objective assessment based on the bitter experience of the masses. ... Had the subcontinent not been divided, the 180 million Muslims of Bangladesh, 150 million of Pakistan and about 200 million of India would together have made 530 million people and, as such, they would have been a very powerful force in undivided India."[1]

Similar views were expressed by two other staunch supporters of Muslim League who had played critical roles in the creation of Pakistan: H.S. Suhrawardy of Bengal Muslim League and one time Chief Minister of that Province, and Chaudhry Khaliquzzaman, Head of the Muslim League in United Provinces. On second thought perhaps, they too felt that their demand for Pakistan was a serious error. Hardly a month had passed since the creation of Pakistan when, on September 10, 1947 Suhrawardy wrote to Khaliquzzaman that "Muslims in the Indian Union have been left high and dry." Sober thoughts came to these two leading figures of Pakistan rather late in the day. Of course now they couldn't have gone back to Jinnah to undo the past; it had already slipped into history; nor could they ask that the Muslims left behind in the Indian Union be evacuated to the new State of Pakistan. That too was not at all a workable proposition. However, they were happy to share their mutual concerns and regret that "the partition of India proved positively injurious to the Muslims of India and on a long term basis for Muslims everywhere." Suhrawardy got Gandhiji to endorse a "declaration of cooperstaion and mutual assistance between the two Dominions" committing both to protecting their minorities and not to make provocative statements against each other, but to his great horror and astonishment Jinnah refused his consent. Suhrawardy begged him to do so in the interest of Indian Muslims for whom they all had struggled together, "for sake of the helpless and hapless Muslims of the Indian Union."[2] But Jinnah did not relent. No doubt Muslims everywhere in India in those critical times were beset with fear and suspicion. This episode goes to show how deep and serious was Jinnah's feigned concern for Indian Muslims while demanding a separate homeland for their safety and protection against the so called 'Hindu-India'. And that is precisely what the British Imperial Power wanted at that point of time from their London trained westernized barrister—The Indian Nationalist Polity was totally powerless to counter this insidious irrational development.

Obviously Sardar Patel was right that you cannot ride two horses at the same time, nor can you have the cake and eat it too. The intellectual elite of UP had laid the foundations of Two-Nation

Theory claiming that the Muslims of India were a separate nation. For all the rank and file who had chosen not to go to Pakistan, mere verbal or written loyalty to the Indian Union would not suffice. They would continue to be considered as spies and disloyal citizens. Perhaps some of them from UP still are. "They would have to give practical proof of their loyalty." To make it worse: The Government servants were the worst hit; they were under a cloud of suspicion, right or wrong, and many had to shuttle between chairs. And woes begone to those who had relatives in Pakistan in those early years of Independence. In fact, practically every family in UP was divided. It was the same with Hindus in Pakistan who had not migrated in the early waves, more so amongst the Sindhis, of course at a much lower level since their numbers were microscopic. By now it would have been obvious that, in addition to the foregoing negative syndromes, communal and linguistic riots were always dangling as the Swords of Damocles over the Muslims the heads being left behind in the Indian Union, Most of UP Muslims fell in this category. Their cheirished dreamland of Pakistan turned out to be their misfortune of their own making!

The end of World War II was an event of great significance for Europe and Asia alike, more so for India since that brought the Labor Party to power in England. A similar major political event occurred in India too. The 1946 elections marked a turning point in India's struggle for freedom. The Congress won in the Central Assembly in the general (non-Muslim) constituencies with 57 out of 102 seats in the bag. In the provinces it got 91.3 per cent of the non-Muslim vote resulting in its securing majority in all the provinces except Bengal, Sind and Punjab. Congress won alright; but it also went a long way to prove the Muslim League charge that Congress was a 'Hindu Congress' and Muslim League represented all Muslims of India. However, Gandhi-Nehru combine could not perceive what was in store for them after partition. Congress success in 1946-elections was in reality a signal of failure of ideological basis of Gandhi-Nehru Party.

The Muslim League success was more spectacular. By that time Muslims constituted about 25-30 per cent of India's population... The League won all the 30 Muslim-seats in the Central Legislative Assembly securing 92.2 per cent of the Muslim votes. And Muslim League was hell-bent on partition of India to create a safe haven for Muslims of India. In other words, by implication, 92.2 per cent of Indian Muslims wished to live in their new homeland, Pakistan. But when Pakistan was created, courtesy the Nehru-Gandhi duo and the British Imperialists, only a microscopic minority of Muslims went to their cherished new homeland! Irony of fate for India's secularism! In the provinces too the League's performance was equally successful where it won 425 out of 496 Muslim seats. However, the League failed to secure majority in the key province of Punjab despite all the advantages it had. Further, both the parties were surprised by Congress winning in NWFP and Assam, the two provinces constantly claimed for Pakistan while in Bengal and Sind it was at the mercy of British in as much as the League ministries had to depend on European and official support.

Lord Mountbatten announced in a press conference held on June 4, 1947 that the British would leave India for good on 15th August 1947. The Nizam of Hyderabad, Osman Ali Khan, lost no time and announced on 12 June that on the lapse of British paramountcy he would become a sovereign monarch.

On the question of partition of Bengal and Punjab, Gandhi said that he preferred united India and a united Bengal, yet India's Hindu majority did not have the right "to keep everyone united by means of compulsion", and Bengal Muslim majority could not compel the province's Hindu population. Gandhi was as much against forced Partition as against forced Unity[3]. Mr. Jinnah is on record: on "the question of division of India into Pakistan and Hindustan Mr. Gandhi does not accept the principle of division. He thinks division is not inevitable, whereas in my opinion, not only is Pakistan inevitable but this is the only practical solution of India's political problem." The Congress Working Committee met on May 31 and June 01 and 02 to consider the Partition-Independence Plan. Gandhi told the committee that he disagreed with it but would not stand in the way. Gaffar Khan, JP and Lohia also expressed unhappiness, but everyone else was in favour. The Plan was approved. Gandhiji was aware that desire for power had influenced their decision, but he did not wish to be an obstruction in their way. Be that as it may, since there was no meeting ground between the Congress and Muslim League, partition was inevitable. Nonetheless, Gandhiji having been the undisputed leader of the Congress between 1919 and 1945, had to share, at least partly, some of the blame for the lawlessness and violent crimes and severe atrocities committed before, during and immediately after partition.

The results of the 1946-elections clearly pointed towards impending break up of India and carving out a separate Muslim homeland out of united India – Pakistan. But did the 92.2 per cent, or whatever percentage, of Indian Muslims who were clamouring for Pakistan go to their cherished homeland! A Himalayan systematic failure of India's top political leadership – the Gandhi-Nehru combine. By this I do not wish to imply that Muslims have no right to live in India; far from it. Every Muslim in India has the same rights and priviliges as any body else. India is a secular country. However, what I do mean to say is that having voted for Pakistan, those persons had themselves forfeited their right to continue to live in the so called "Hindu India". Further, my remarks are directed against the Indian Muslims who voted for Pakistan; the present generation of Indian Muslims is a different matter altogether. They are part and parcel of Indian democracy.

By June end voting in the provincial assemblies was complete. Sind Assembly decided to vote for Pakistan by 33 to 20. However results of the referendum in NWFP and Sylhet were still awaited. Nevertheless, Cabinet Partition Committee was disbanded and replaced by Partition Council comprising of Mountbatten as Chairman, Patel and Rajendra Prasad for the Congress with Rajagopalachari as alternate member, Mr. Jinnah and Liaqat for Pakistan with Abdul Rab Nishtar as their alternate member. Any disputes that the Council could not resolve were to be referred to an Arbitral Tribunal chaired by Chief Justice of India, Sir Patrick Spens, though in the end his services were never called upon.

The Council was to work through a Steering Committee of two officials: Chaudry Mohammed Ali of Finance Department and H.M. Patel, Cabinet Secretary for India. Both were distinguished ICS officers of good standing and had known each other for long. Both got on the job efficiently and quickly. They set up ten expert committees on various matters of nuts and bolts of governmental functioning, the most important of which was Armed Forces Reconstitution Committee. These Committees were assisted by a mushrooming network of departmental committees, each balanced by equal number of Muslim and non-Muslim members while the Armed Forces Committee was augmented by a number of British officers.

India Office in London expected Nehru and Jinnah to write to Mountbatten requesting him to be their first Governor-General. While Nehru had already asked Mountbatten to be the first Governor-General of independent India, Jinnah remained conspicuously silent. After prolonged procrastination Jinnah finally answered

Mountbatten that he, Jinnah himself, would like to be the first Governor General of Pakistan which came as a personal shock and humiliation to the Viceroy.

Process of Division

The Joint Defence Committee to monitor division of armed forces and their assets was set up on June 30. This job required a man of great sensitivity, tact and firmness. V.P. Menon suggested Sir Chandulal Trivedi, then Governor of Orissa and soon to become the first Governor of East Punjab, a most difficult of all the new appointments in India. Trivedi had been Secretary War department until 1946 and probably knew more about the administration of armed forces than any other official. He was lifelong friend of Liaqat. He could therefore deliver the goods successfully and amicably. Initially, the soldiers were to be allocated to each dominion with religion as the criterion. But the sub-committee entrusted with job soon realized that this was not acceptable to one and all, particularly the Muslims who did not want to give up their homes and hearths in India and migrate to Pakistan to be labeled as refugees.

Captain (later Lieutenant General) L.S. Menezes commanded a rifle company at Thal in Kurram in NWFP. He was a Christian and his men were Muslims. They wished to return to India, and were therefore replaced by two companies of Dogras who had chosen Pakistan. While en route to their base in India, Menezes Company was forcibly taken off the train at Lahore, because Pakistanis were suspicious of a company of Muslim going to India.

Both sides accused Auchinleck of partiality. He therefore resigned (or was asked to resign) as Supreme Commander of the two armies. The supreme Headquarters was closed down by the end of November 1947.

Boundary Commissions

Punjab and Bengal had voted for partition. Two Boundary Commissions, each of four high court judges as members, two nominated by India and two by Pakistan, were set up to demarcate the boundaries. The Bengal Commission was based in Calcutta and the Punjab one at Lahore, both under the chairmanship of Sir Cyril Radcliffe having a casting vote. Since Radcliffe could not possibly be present at both places, he based himself at Delhi with everyday's record of proceedings being flown to him in Delhi. The member-judges were so partisan and antagonistic that they would hardly talk to each other, let alone discuss harmoniously. Radcliffe had never been to India, had not been exposed to Indian-communal divide; hence his objectivity was impeccable. And he would not accept any payment for his services either.

Radcliffe's job: Separation of 88 million people most of whom were all out to be on each others' throats, and for dividing 175,000 sq miles of territory between the two warring communities as equitably as possible. And for this stupendous task all he had was a mere five-week period! Above all, his terms of reference were also vague in as much as demarcation was to be done on the basis of ascertaining the geographical contiguity of majority areas of Muslims and non-Muslims, and in so doing take into consideration all other factors. The 'other factors' were never defined.

Division of Bengal and Punjab was a hard nut to crack. In both provinces any dividing line was bound to cross through heavily populated areas, rail and road communications, power lines, irrigation schemes, even individual land holdings. The line might separate a peasant from his lands while a factory may have its warehouses on the wrong side. So on and so forth. The Bengal Commission was also responsible for Sylhet district and other Muslim majority areas in Assam while in the hill tracts around Chittagong the tribal population was Buddhist. To cap it all, the big question was who should get Calcutta in Bengal and Lahore in Punjab. Without Calcutta the Muslim East Bengal would degenerate into a rural slum. And Calcutta, without its riverine hinterland which would fall in Muslim East Bengal, would find it difficult to survive. However, Muslims were merely a quarter of its population; therefore it should go to India.

Punjab Commission faced similar problems. Both sides laid claim to Lahore. Lahore had a slight Muslim majority while Sikhs in particular and Hindus generally had their holy shrines, historic sites and pilgrimage centers in and around Lahore. The dividing line would in all probability deprive the Sikhs of their heartland. The Sikh shrine of Nankana Sahib, about 12 miles north of Lahore was a serious bone of contention. If it was not given to East Punjab, the Sikhs intended to wage what may amount to a 'communal war', for which the martial Sikhs were well prepared, organized and armed, rather than a mere communal riot. The Sikhs were high strung on this issue. So V.P. Menon came out with a brilliant idea that

Jinnah should be approached to declare Nankana Sahib as Vatican of the Sikhs and thus assuage the Sikh sentiment. However, nothing came out of this although Sikhs had warned as early as March 1947 that they would set up an independent Sikh-State by force if their demands were not conceded. Shiromani Akali Dal added fuel to the fire by declaring that Pakistan would mean death to Sikh Panth, as had happened during the Moghul period, particularly under Aurangzeb. Briefly, the Sikh demands were:

- They must have their holy shrine at Nankana Sahib;
- At least one canal system;
- Arrangements to bring at least three-quarters of Sikh population from West to East Punjab;
- In the exchange, property must be taken into account since Sikhs were much better off than their Muslim counterparts.

Giani Kartar Singh once again warned that if their demands were not conceded in the Boundary Commission Award, they would be obliged to fight on revolutionary lines, murder officials, cut rail lines, destroy canal head works, and so on. Their tentative plan was to start trouble around August 07, 1947.

The Punjabi Hindus and Sikhs had contributed to development of irrigation-system and had some of the richest lands in the country. The Sikhs owned about 40% of fertile land in the area and the Muslim peasantry worked the lands for them. The latter outnumbered the Sikhs by a majority of four to one. Coupled with this was Muslim majority tehsils of Ferozepur and Zira which legitimately fell in the sphere of influence of Pakistan. This area formed a salient[4] north of River Sutlej whose significance lay in:

- Head waters of the canal which irrigated the Princely State of Bikaner that was acceding to India;
- One army arms-depot was located in the Salient. This would give Pakistan virtually its only source of weapons and major part of its military stores and equipment.

In this connection it is noteworthy that Montgomery district had a population of nearly a million Sikhs while the Muslims numbered a mere one quarter of that, but surely Montgomery could not possibly be given to India; it had to be part of West Punjab.

In view of the prevailing tensions in Punjab it became imperative to position a strong Boundary Force to maintain some degree of law and order after the Award was announced. It was decided to set up the Punjab Boundary Force with 4 Infantry Division as the nucleous. This Force was to be about 50,000 strong with a high proportion of British officers, but no British units, under overall command of Major General Pete Rees, GOC 4 Infantry Division. The Force was to be in position in the 12 disputed districts by August 01, 1947. Brigadier Digambhar Singh from India and Ayub Khan from Pakistan were to be the two advisers to the Force Commander. By the time the Boundary Force was in place, the casualties in Punjab were estimated at 4,632 killed and 2573 seriously wounded. Over 77% of casualties took place in rural areas while in urban areas twice as many victims were wounded. At that time the dead included three times more non-Muslims than Muslims, notwithstanding the Sikh's loud militancy.

Independence Day

Mountbatten was sworn in as the first Governor-General of India at 8:30 am August 16, 1947 by an Indian Chief Justice before an audience of former freedom fighters. The crowds outside the Council Chamber were so dense that even the 400-strong bodyguard could not clear the way for His Excellency to reach his carriage. However, Nehru climbed up the roof and waved back the crowd, and they obeyed him as they would have obeyed no one else that day of intense rejoicing.

The rest of the day was one vast unending party culminating in the evening as the main event of the Day: Hoisting the new India's National Flag at India Gate. Military bands including that of INA were in place. Once again the throng was so thick, so enormous that the carriages carrying Nehru and Mountbatten found it extremely difficult to get through. The planned parade and speeches had to be abandoned. Nehru gave the signal for flag to be raised and the guns to boom out their salute. As the flag broke at the top of the pole, a beautiful rainbow appeared behind it as if the gods of Indian pantheon were welcoming the new and saying farewell to the old. However, in the words of a brave real soldier: "it is sad but true that when India attained independence, there was no meeting ground or contact between the Politician, the Civil Servant and the Soldier – there was in fact a little more of distrust."[5]

The far reaching effects of this deficiency were perceived only after the Sino-Indian War of 1962 when the Government of India committed Himalayan Blunder at all levels of governance.

Radcliff did not attend and left the same day. So did the Governor Jenkins and all the ICS officers. Gandhi too did not attend the celebration; for him it was no celebration at all to see India divided and in communal frenzy unheard of in history of civilization.

Notes

1. Muttahida Quami Movement (MQM) leader Altaf Hussain; October 2000.
2. Noorani, A.G. ed., *The Muslims of India: A Documentary Record* (New Delhi, Oxford University Press, 2003) pp. 40-52; and Chaudhury Khaliquzzaman, *Pathways to Pakistan*(Lahore, Longmas, Green, 1961) as quoted by and based on *INDIA After Gandhi* by Rama Chandra: Guha; pp. 366-67.
3. Gandhi Rajmohan: GANDHI The Man, His People, and The Empire; University of California Press, Berkley, 2007, 2008; p. 574.
4. Grigg John: Myths about the Indian Independence; Austin University of Texas Press 1998, p. 211, Jinnah, M.A.: Speeches and Writings; edited by Jamal-ul-Din, Vol. I, Lahore 1960, pp. 243 & 248.
5. Dalvi, J.P. Brig.: *Himalayan Blunder*, Natraj, Dehradun 1969/1997/ 2010; p. 400.

7

CONSTITUTION AND SYSTEM OF GOVERNMENT

Although socialism as such was not fundamental to Indian Constitution, establishment of a socialistic pattern of society was guiding principle of the Congress right from day one of Independence. The principal means of production to be brought under social ownership so that equitable distribution of wealth could be achieved were its cardinal principles. The Finance Commission was incorporated in the system to ensure equitable distribution of revenue between the Centre and the States.

The Constitution stipulates that the Indian State shall be a liberal democratic state in which rule of the people shall prevail. By implication, it means that the government machinery is run by the people to attain greatest good of the greatest number. But in actual practice who runs this monolithic system? The bureaucracy: a legacy of the British system which was designed for furtherance of the colonial power.

India's Constitution was meant to be federal in character. However, when it came to brass tags, a number of unitary features were incorporated in the interest of unity and defence of the country with the result that the Constitution was so diluted that it turned out to be more unitary than federal. It would therefore be more appropriate to classify our Constitution as "quasi-federal". As for the interstate water disputes the Constitution provides for the Parliament to make laws for adjudication. Such disputes may be excluded from the jurisdiction of Courts. The Zonal Councils and Inter-States Council play a vital role in inter-state relations as well as river-waters and other disputes between the states. It will not be out of place to mention that the Planning Commission—notwithstanding its importance or useful work in development of the country—has resulted in erosion of powers, rights and jurisdiction of the States in the sphere of their own activities.

The Constitution provides for a President to be appointed by indirect election. He is the nominal head of the State with no direct executive powers. But all executive actions are done in the name of the President. However, the President is not a 'cipher'. He has certain rights and discretionary powers as became evident when Gianni Zail Singh as President of India appointed Mr. Rajiv Gandhi, a working pilot and not even a member of the Parliament, as the Prime Minister of India ignoring the traditional procedure of appointing the deputy Prime Minister/senior most Cabinet Minister as the interim Prime Minister pending election of the new Prime Minister by the majority party in the Lok Sabha. Relationship between the President and the Prime minister is a delicate issue to be handled tactfully in a matured judicious manner; the personalities and temperaments of the two plays an important role in developing this relationship.

According to the Constitution the authority of the government is not absolute; it is limited by legal and moral laws. But is that so in practice? Today, in the first decade of the 21st century we find that the Indian State is "centralized in nature, bureaucratic in form, and capitalist in context". Sarkaria Commission Report provided the necessary guidance for smooth running of Centre-States relations. Furthermore, "the Constitution is a dynamic document". Therefore it stands to reason that as opposed to the rigidity of a Federal Constitution it should be susceptible to change to meet changing circumstances. However, it must not be allowed to be amended at the whims and fancies of the political party in power to meet its vested interests. The Indian Constitution has been amended ninety-three times since its inception.

We are supposed to be a liberal democracy with more than one political party, each competing with the other for power, in open but not secretive competition. The media is again open and objective and not a tool in the hands of the government of the day, not to be monopolized by the party in power. Is that so in reality?

Our forefathers who wrote the Constitution visualized a State where freedom of speech and expression, open discussion and expression of views, universal adult franchise with free and fair elections were to be the ruling principles. Unfortunately, vote bank politics, defections, "*ayaram gayaram*" syndrome, *et al*, have perverted the liberal democracy concept to the point of absurdity. Power at any cost, by hook or crook, is the order of the day. The chaotic scenes witnessed in the sacrosanct Lower House of our Parliament and in various state assemblies are outstanding examples of how democracy should not be practiced. It is this degradation of the system that has alienated the decent peace loving people of Kashmir, besides many others. It is a top example of systematic failure of the Indian State and its Constitution. Misuse of Article 356 to impose wherever non-Congress governments rule the state has been a constant irritant to the opposition parties. The party in power at the center, usually the Congress, passes a hint to the Governor who sends a report to the President. The latter is advised by his Council of Ministers to impose President's rule in the state. The rest is history ...

Incorporation of the highly controversial Article 370 in the Constitution providing for special treatment for Kashmir turned out to be a catastrophic provision for the unity and security of the country. It forbids Indian nationals from settling down in Kashmir, or to buy/own property in that State. By implication, it meant that Indians were foreigners in Kashmir while Kashmiris were at full liberty to live and own property in the rest of India. The Congress had overwhelming majority in the Constituent Assembly and must be held culpable for this major error of judgment. It was yet another serious failure of Indian National Congress. However, the present prevailing situation in Kashmir does not warrant abrogation of Article 370 *in toto*; that would only make matters worse. What is required at present is an amendment of constitutional provisions so that Kashmiri women who marry a non-Kashmiri man and Indian citizens are free to buy/own landed property in Kashmir, and are also free to settle down therein. The internal autonomy aspect should not be tinkered with, Never.

Bureaucracy is an essential component of modern state. It is expected to interpret and implement State policies and laws without prejudice or external pressures. In practice, the government policy is implemented and its authority administered by the archaic bureaucracy in conjunction with the police and other law enforcement agencies, most of which are totally oppressive, utterly corrupt, regionalist, parochial, using third degree methods in crime investigation and using fake documents as well as fake encounters besides false and fake evidence. Of course all this is done with knowledge and concurrence of the government of the day, albeit complicity of the government may only be assumed as such. Over-centralization has come into being in the name of development. The Center has abrogated to itself all the powers of economic, social, agricultural and industrial development. Public sector has taken over what should have been rightfully in the domain of private sector. And public sector means state control on finance, production and distribution – inefficiency, cost-escalation and corruption galore.

Since the political parties indulge in playing the minority-communal-caste cards, bureaucracy goes a step ahead to further the objectives of the party in power. Objective approach and impartiality are lost in this muddle. Furthermore, bureaucracy means red-tapes, a technique for self preservation through file pushing, abrogating personal responsibility in decision-making process. The net result is delay and cost over-runs.

India claims to be a secular state, but it is so in favour of Muslim communalism – Like during the cold war period, India was neutral on the side of Soviet Union! So it would be more appropriate to categorize India as a secular state on the side of Muslim communalism, rather than just a secular state. Of course this is the result of policies adopted by our own polity. I agree that the amended Preamble to the Constitution proclaims India's resolve for "Secular Sovereign Democratic Republic". Certainly a high sounding noble resolution! But what we have in practice is merely a Sovereign Republic which is neither truly secular nor is it democratic in true sense of the word; being more dynastic and bureaucratic. It would have been secular if there was no communal card attached to it primarily for vote-bank politics. The special treatment reserved for Haj pilgrims is an outstanding example of non-secular working of Indian Republic. So is system of special grants to Madras as to finance their activities - a step-motherly treatment to the majority and other communities.

India may not have a State Religion but there is no denying that most official functions are inaugurated with Hindu rituals. Of course Hinduism is not a State religion of India, far from it.

The foregoing shortcomings and failure of the governing polity have come to occupy a permanent place in the system, systematic indeed!

Political Party System

Howsoever the party system may be imperfect, in democratic parliamentary system as adopted by India there is no alternative to multi-party system. It is life blood of democracy. Moreover when the suffrage is large and wide ranging, political parties are bound to mushroom. The power must therefore be entrusted to the majority party to form the government irrespective of whether it emerged as the majority party in a straight forward manner, or if it was contrived via coalitions, defections, etc. The mere fact that the majority party is communal in character or name is no excuse to deny it the privilege to form the government and nominate the Prime Minister.

Regional parties in India are a recent phenomenon. They have hardly any ideological basis, and are controlled by power-hungry politicians hankering for the fruits of power via exploiting regional, communal or caste sentiments. Unfortunately, our politics is over-dominated by religion and caste considerations, a shortcut to arouse the people to gain their support. No doubt the party system is the bedrock of parliamentary democracy promoting legislative excellence, the disagreement by the opposition are artificial in as much as they are expressed for the sake of opposition irrespective of merits of the case. Similarly, in some cases the apparent unity of thought and action may also be contrived artificially through the whip system, private cliques, or otherwise by suppressing truth and encouraging falsehood. Whip system itself is contradiction of democracy. These two last characteristics are indeed the bane of party system in Indian politics which keeps many intellectually qualified persons away from public life – loudly proclaiming systematic failure of our polity.

Loyalty to the party rather than to State is another major drawback of party system. The political parties in India face problems of media hostility, trade unions, student organizations, cultural, religious and linguistic groups, indiscipline, defections, splits, regionalism, finance, and above all the nuisance of pressure groups of one kind or the other, *et al*. Of late, coalition politics in India have come to occupy an important slot in our body-politics. The primary cause of rise of this new phenomenon has been erosion of strength and moral standing of the once upon a time dominant party. Instability in government has come to be the major negative feature of this type of politics, besides of course defection-politics, money-power, lure of office and lust for power adding to the damage done.

However, coalitions based on pre-electoral alliances overcome much of the likely damage while post-electoral coalitions are the worst scourge when horse-trading dominates ministry making. The President and the Governors must crush this systematic pest.

8

FIRST INDO-PAK WAR 1947-48

Pak Invasion of Kashmir

Kashmir will fall into our lap like a ripe fruit.

– M.A. Jinnah, August 1947

But it did not; and could not have. The Kashmiris knew their beans!

KASHMIR AND SURROUNDINGS

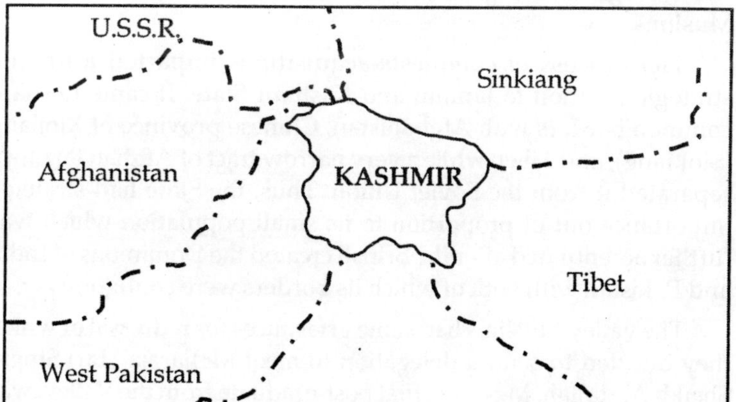

Historical Background

Gulab Singh was born in 1792, son of Mian Kishore Singh, in a *jagir* near Samba, about 24 miles south of Jammu. He was good at horse riding and wielded his sword effectively. He distinguished himself in the Battle for the defence of Jammu against attack by the Sikh forces. Maharaja Ranjit Singh was so impressed that he took him in his service. By dint of personal valour and loyalty to the Sikh cause, he was made a general in the Sikh army. The Maharaja was highly impressed by Gulab Singh during the sieges of Multan and Jalandhar. His success in subjugating the tribes of Yusafzai in 1819 resulted in capture of Peshawar. In recognition of his services the Maharaja made him the Raja of Jammu.

Gulab Singh moved out of Jammu and conquered Ladakh in 1930's and acquired the 'Valley Beautiful' from the British in 1840's. The State of Jammu and Kashmir had been established in the first half of the nineteenth century. His successors added Gilgit and frontier areas in the extended State. Thus, the State covered an area of 84,471 sq miles with a population of four million only. It had five distinct geo-cultural regions: province of Jammu having marginal Muslim majority (53%); the Valley of Kashmir in the north with substantial Muslim majority; Ladakh to the east of the valley bordering Tibet had Buddhist population; further west were the frontier regions of Gilgit and Baltistan where the people were mostly Muslims.

The process of conquests-acquisitions imparted a unique strategic position to Jammu and Kashmir State. It came to share common borders with Afghanistan, Chinese province of Xinjiang (Sinkiang), and Tibet, while a very narrow tract of Afghan territory separated it from the Soviet Union. Thus, the State had strategic importance out of proportion to its small population which was further accentuated after the British created the Dominions of India and Pakistan with both of which its borders were contiguous.

The valley Muslims had some grievances for redressal of which they decided to send a delegation to meet Maharaja Hari Singh. Sheikh Abdullah, M.Sc., the first post-graduate from the Valley, was denied a government job, a major error by Dogra aristocracy turned out to be a historic blunder. He was one of the members of the delegation. Well before the meeting one of the activists, Abdul Nadir was arrested and put on trial in 1931. A clash between the protesters and police ensued in which twenty-one persons died. Next year All Jammu Kashmir Muslim Conference was formed to guide and direct growing opposition to Maharaja's rule. After a year Sheikh Mohammad Abdullah transformed the organization into National Conference open to Hindus and Sikhs. This new organization asked for representative government based on universal suffrage. It was around this time that the Sheikh and Jawaharlal Nehru met, more by chance than by deliberation. The acquaintance instantly turned into friendship, the common denominator being socialism and Hindu-Muslim harmony which, in turn, led to close relations between the Indian National Congress and the National Conference. Thereafter Abdullah was frequently in and out of jail.

The Mountbatten Plan for partition-independence for India provided for lapse of British paramountcy over the princely states numbering more than 545. The states were expected to sign a declaration of accession to the Union of India/Pakistan before August 15, 1947. Most of the states complied. Amongst the diehards was the Jammu and Kashmir state under Maharaja Hari Singh. On 03 June 1947 it was announced by the Viceroy that the British would leave India for good on August 15, 1947. Hari Singh's Prime Minister, Ramachandra Kak, encouraged the Maharaja to think in terms of independence after the lapse of British paramountcy. Then the Maharaja would be free to align with any power, not excluding Russia.[1] Soon after the decision to partition India was made, he visited Kashmir and met Kak. He told Kak to advise Maharaja Hari Singh to accede to either Dominion, but accede he must. However, Kak informed the Viceroy that Kashmir intended to stay independent. The Viceroy then asked for an appointment with Hari Singh who at the last moment feigned illness and declined to meet the Viceroy. And as on 15 August 1947 Hari Singh had not acceded to either Dominion reiterating his intention to remain independent, and that he would change his mind only if one of the two parties decided to use force. Within days of these prophetic words were spoken, a force of several thousand armed men crossed the border from the north on October 22, 1947. Tribal invasion of Kashmir had begun.

"The Mother of All Raids": Preparations in Pakistan

Right from day one, in fact well before even the date of partition of India was finalized, pro-Pakistan Muslim League had set its heart on the 'Beauty Queen', the Vale of Kashmir, then part of the virtually independent state of Jammu & Kashmir under Maharaja Hari Singh. Pakistan's initial plan ("Operation Gulmarg") was in two phases: Phase 1 starting in September 1947 involving numerous small scale and fifth columnist activities aimed at shattering the State Forces to be followed by Phase 2, "The Mother of All Raids", in the second half of October 1947. The organizational structure of Op Gulmarg had its roots in the North Western Frontier Province (NWFP) which was virtually pushed into the lap of newly created State of Pakistan. As a result, Khan Abdul Gaffar Khan, the "Frontier Gandhi", was in Pakistani prisons for nearly three decades

The Pathan Lashkar of one thousand tribesmen was the key stone of their future military operations. Every Pathan clan was required to raise one *lashkar* of tribesmen – Pakistan fights for Kashmir by proxy. The Deputy Commissioners and political agents of the government were made responsible for recruitment. The leadership of Lashkar Force was in the hands of Pak regular Army: one major, one captain and ten Junior Commissioned Officers (JCOs), all Pathans dressed and lived like other tribesmen.

JAMMU AND KASHMIR

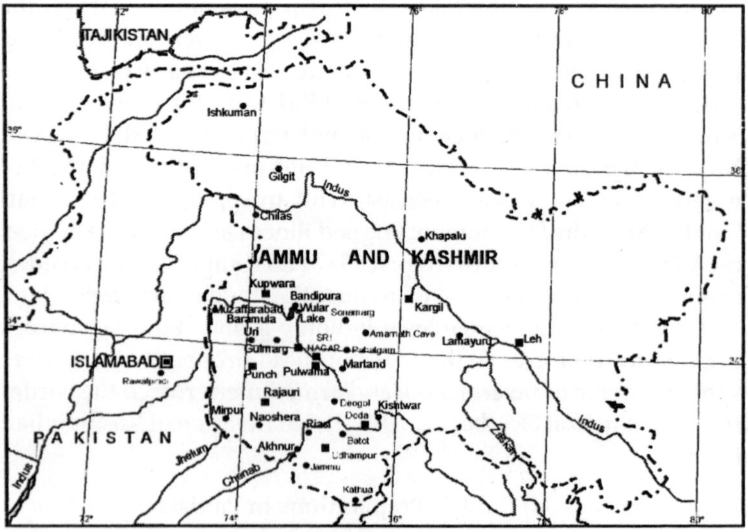

A lashkar was divided into ten companies each about 100 strong under the JCO. Major General Akbar Khan DSO, with self assumed title of "General Tarique" was in overall command and Brigadier Sher Khan was the liaison officer for Pak Army with the Lashkar Task Force. General Tarique's HQs were in the same building in Rawalpindi as that of Pak Army Commander-in-Chief. In other words, Pak Army and the Lashkar Task Force were hand in glove relationship. When the Governor of NWFP, George Cunningham first told Jinnah about the tribesmen, he said: "Don't tell me anything about it. My conscience must be clear."[2]

Lashkar Force concentrated at Bannu, Wana, Peshawar, Kohat, Thal and Nowshera by first week of September 1947. The Brigade Commanders at these locations provided basic military hardware and administrative support to the tribesmen. The Task Force concentrated at Abbottabad by 18 October 1947 in a specially demarcated security zone about ten miles outside the garrison town. Once in the security zone, no one was allowed to go out, nor any visitors allowed in. The tribesmen were given their final orders and briefing in this security zone.

The British civil and military officials turned a blind eye to all these preparations for the raid, "Mother of all Raids", besides giving active administrative assistance. By now, all was set for Pak invasion of Kashmir. General Sir Frank Messervey C-in-C Pak Army informed his Indian counterpart, General Sir Rob M. Lockhart of the impending invasion, but the latter did not pass on the information to the Indian Government in whose service he was. This led to an acrimonious exchange between Nehru and Lockhart in late January 1948 after which the latter was unceremoniously packed off to Britain - too little, too late!

'Op Gulmarg'

- Main force of six lashkars to advance from Domel to Uri-Baramula;
- Capture Srinagar airfield;
- Secure Banihal Pass;
- Secure Haji Pir Pass with a view to facilitate advance of two lashkars direct to Gulmarg so as to secure the right flank of the main force;

- Two lashkars to secure Tithwal, cross over to Nastachun Pass and capture Sopore, Handwara and Bandipur;
- A force of ten lashkars to operate in Poonch, Bhimber and Rawalkot sectors with Jammu as the final objective;
- Administrative and back-up support by 7 Infantry Division;
- D-Day: 22 October 1947.

The foregoing bold and ingenious plan for capture of J&K using Pathan tribesmen in conjunction with Pak regular army troops was the brain-child of British officers then serving with Pak Army.

And the Plan Unfolds – 4 JAK Battalion commanded by a Jammu Dogra, Lieutenant Colonel Narain Singh, was one of the crack battalions of JAK State Forces. The battalion was half Dogra and half Poonchi Muslims. It was responsible for defence of borders in Muzaffarabad-Domel sector. Unfortunately, Muslim troops in the Frontier Illaqa in the north to Poonch-Mirpur area proved untrustworthy while the Commanding Officer kept up his trust and faith in his comrades in arms, in true spirit of an infantryman. And that was his undoing! Every single Muslim of 4 JAK Battalion, without a single exception, defected to the enemy on night 21/22 October 1947. That fateful night about five thousand heavily armed tribesmen crossed the border. They were guided through the town areas of Domel and Muzaffarabad by the Muslim defectors. The Poonchi Muslims themselves struck in the early hours of October 22 killed the Commanding Officers and most of the Dogra troops: an internal coup in the State Forces of J&K had taken place – A systematic failure of Indian Military tradition, blind faith and trust on one side, treachery and deceit on the other.

"Tribal Invasion of Kashmir" had now begun in full force. Road to Srinagar was now open. It was barely 100 miles away, just a few hours of car drive. The glittering prize of 'Valley Beautiful' was right there to fall in the lap of Mr. Jinnah, for grabbing by Pakistan without any further ado, more so since the vital Domel-bridge had fallen intact in the hands of the raiders. The first serious clash between the State Forces and the lashkars took place about half a mile short of Garhi on the morning of October 23. The tragic news of decimation of 4 JAK Battalion reached acting commander of State Forces, Brigadier Rajinder Singh who collected a couple of hundred men and swiftly moved towards Uri, a town nearly half way between Srinagar and Muzaffarabad. He reached there before the invaders.

As a first precautionary step the Brigadier got the steel girder bridge that linked the town to the north demolished, thereby holding up the advance of the tribesmen. But they could have advanced to Srinagar if they wanted to. But it was a big 'if'; and they did not want it! They had not come all that way to gain any territorial gains for Pakistan; they came for love of plunder and the beauties of Vale Beautiful! And that is what they went all out for.

GENERAL MAP OF KASHMIR VALLEY

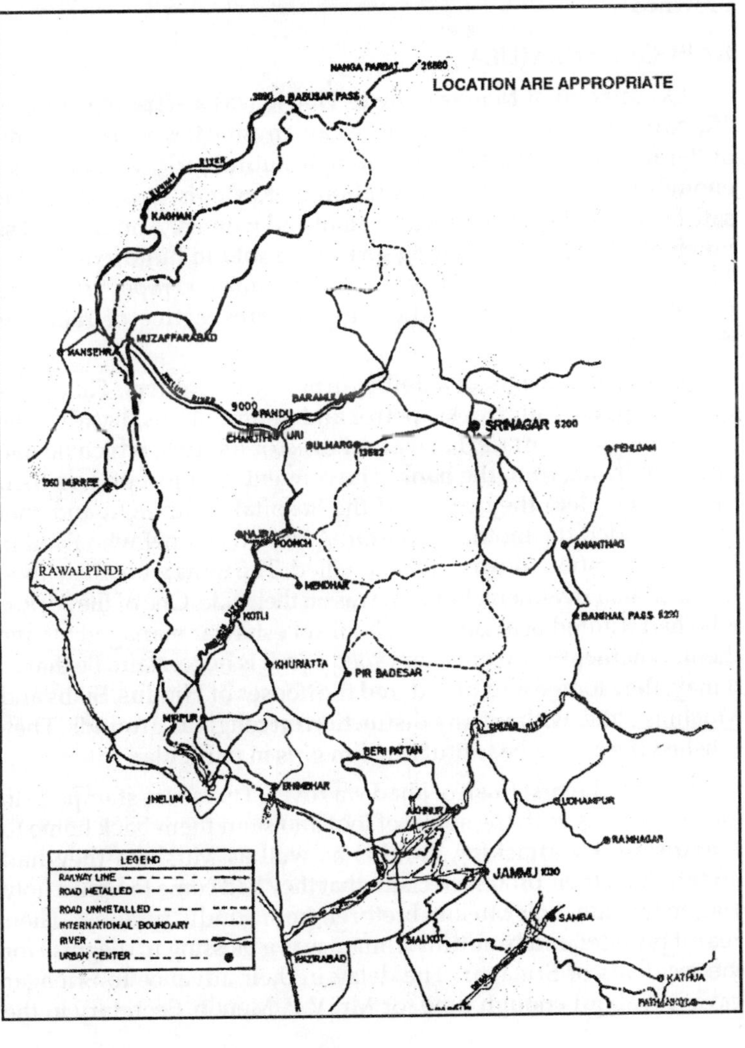

The raiders outflanked Uri. Soon it became untenable, and was abandoned by the State Forces. The tribal advance continued to next objective, Mahura Power House. The delay imposed at Uri gave enough time to the management to put the power house out of action, may be out of sheer panic, thereby plunging the entire valley including the capital Srinagar in darkness. There was great panic amongst the Hindu and Sikh population of Srinagar resulting in a vast multitude of refugees making their way down to Banihal Pass onwards to Jammu which now turned into a Hindu majority province.

RAPE OF BARAMULA

Occupation of Mahura Power House was a stepping stone to "Rape of Baramula". The horrors of Pathan atrocities on the residents of Baramula, particularly the young beautiful girls, was evidence enough that the so called liberation of Kashmir was indeed the satisfaction of tribesmen's lust for loot and women. And they got so much of the latter that young girls were sold in hundreds for Rs. 150/- each back home! They carried on murder, rape, arson and plunder for three long endless nights irrespective of religious affiliations.

A British manager of a timber firm saw the raiders. They were well equipped with trucks, petrol and ammunitions, besides two and three inch mortars. He was relieved of Rs. 1500 which he had just withdrawn from the bank. The convent of St Joseph was their next target. Here they smashed the hospital equipment and shot and wounded the mother superior. A retired colonel who lived in the same compound was shot and killed. The nuns were then lined up for similar treatment. But God was on their side. One of the Afridis who had studied in a convent school at Peshawar managed to save them. Whether they were later raped or not is not certain. Be that as it may, they looted and plundered the houses of Hindus, Sikhs and Muslims alike, without any distinction on religious grounds. They relished the young beautiful Muslim girls in particular.

By now the first flush of jihad was over. There was stampede to load the trucks with the spoils of loot and send them back home to Waziristan. By attacking Hindus as well as Muslims they had undermined their professed claim that they had come to fight a holy war, to liberate their Muslim brethren from Hindu 'tyranny'. Their zeal at plunder and beautiful women was a blessing in disguise for the residents of Srinagar. The delay in their advance to Srinagar gave just about enough time for Mr. V.P. Menon, Secretary in the

State Department of which Sardar Vallabh Patel, the strongman of India was the Minister in charge. V.P. Menon had to commute twice between Delhi and Jammu to get the accession formalities completed as a pre-condition laid down by the British Governor General of India, appointed by kind courtesy of Mr. Jawaharlal Nehru, to enable military intervention by India.

Kashmir is nagging India *ad infinitum, ad nauseam*. However, it is India that is the creator, and also the victim of this sordid affair. There would have been no Kashmir problem if only we had matured experienced political leadership at the helm of affairs. The 'ifs' and 'buts' of history come to fore only well after the event when damage has been done!

Plan and administrative structure of partition of India had many self- inducted, self-destructive incongruities built into the system. Right from day one, the two new Dominions were at loggerheads over the fruits of Independence, each vying for the largest possible slice of the cake. As ill luck for India would have it, Field Marshal Sir Claude Auchinleck was the Supreme Commander of armed forces of both India and Pakistan with headquarters at Delhi, while General Sir Frank Messervey was Commander-in-Chief of Pakistan Army. These two generals were in constant communications on all military developments in the region. The plot for inducting thousands of tribesmen in the guise of raiders as saviors was hatched in Pak Army headquarters at Rawalpindi. Sir George Cunningham, the then Governor of NWFP was destined to play a major role in recruiting, organizing, arming and making administrative arrangements for putting this gigantic plan into action. This trio of British top generals acted in a manner that was most astonishing, professionally dishonest, treacherous and deplorable. Ultimately, they proved to be the villains of the piece, with top honours going to Auchinleck who did not take the trouble of apprising the newly installed Indian Government of ominous developments taking place across the still un-demarcated border.

Indian Military Intervention

Towards the end of October 1947 Srinagar was on the verge of falling in Qabaili hands — to suffer the same fate of loot, plunder, rape and murder that had befallen Baramula and all other towns. At this point of time when the situation was in a 'touch and go' state, India decided in favour of military intervention to save the "Valley Beautiful" from the wild tribal Lashkars. The first contingent of Indian Army, 1 Sikh, (Battalion less two companies), was ordered to concentrate at Palam Airport by 04:00 am October 27, 1947 ready to be flown in to Srinagar airfield (Badgom) for an operational mission. The so-called Srinagar airfield was nothing more than a dirt strip indeed, without any communication, navigational, refueling facilities whatsoever. Present at Palam were Commanding Officer 1 Sikh, Lieutenant Colonel Dewan Ranjit Rai to receive "Op Instruction" at the airfield just before takeoff. The Op Instruction was completely silent on information about the enemy so much so that it enjoined on the Commanding Officer to divert to Jammu if no signal was received to land at Srinagar – This type of instruction was not expected from a General Officer Commanding-in-Chief of the caliber of General Russell, more so when it was quite clear over the past 3-4 days that military operations were imminent.

While Indian military intervention was a foregone conclusion on October 25, it became a certainty the next day. It was therefore a matter of simple military prudence that at least on the 26th fighter reconnaissance mission(s) should have flown over the Valley. C-in-C ® IAF Air Marshal T.W. Elmhurst should have ordered such a mission. General Lockhart should have insisted on this elementary military action before permitting his troops (so what if they were Indians!) into battle zone. All else having failed to do their bit, last but not the least, General Russell should have got this done early morning on D-Day. It was a serious lapse on the part of higher echelons of military hierarchy, the highly decorated experienced British Generals in the service of Government of India. It was a glaring case of systematic failure in the Military High Command, perhaps it was by deliberation.

Brigadier Hiralal Atal had been personally selected and briefed by Prime Minister Nehru as Liaison Officer to Kashmir Government. The first Dakota flight had Brigadier Atal, Lieutenant Colonel Dewan Ranjit Rai, and leading elements of the Sikh battalion on board. The DC3 aircraft piloted by a young Flight Lieutenant took off at 6:30 am October 27, 1947. It was indeed a historic flight that landed at Badgom airstrip at 9:00 am! On landing they were greeted by an Indian army officer whose services had been lent to the State Government. He and the acting Chief of Staff of State Forces briefed C.O. 1 Sikh. Immediately after the aircraft was unloaded, Atal directed the pilot to fly over Baramula for a quick aerial reconnaissance. On landing back the pilot reported that there was no movement on the Srinagar-Baramula Road. Baramula was burning at places, and smoldering at others. Hardly any human movement in the town was seen. What the British Air Marshals should have done 3 days earlier was now done by Brigadier Atal within minutes of landing.

About 300 troops with their arms, ammunition and personal equipment were airlifted that day in twenty-eight Dakota sorties. In the following days more than one hundred planes, some commandeered from private carriers and the rest of the ® IAF ferried troops and military supplies to Srinagar airfield, which otherwise was an apology for an airfield. The planes landed in Srinagar mostly to the sound of small-arms fire, in the haze of clouds of dust left behind by the departing planes. On the return trip they carried casualties and some refugees too.

Indian army intervention came just in the nick of time. Concurrently, Lord Mountbatten went on a peace mission to Lahore on November 01, 1947. His meetings with Jinnah were contentious. Jinnah described Kashmir going to India based on fraud and violence. The fact of the situation was that violence had come from the tribal Lashkars who were Pakistani citizens and accession of Kashmir to India was the consequence of the tribal invasion; otherwise Hari Singh was interested only in independence.

SKETCH MAP: BATTLE OF SHELTANG[3]

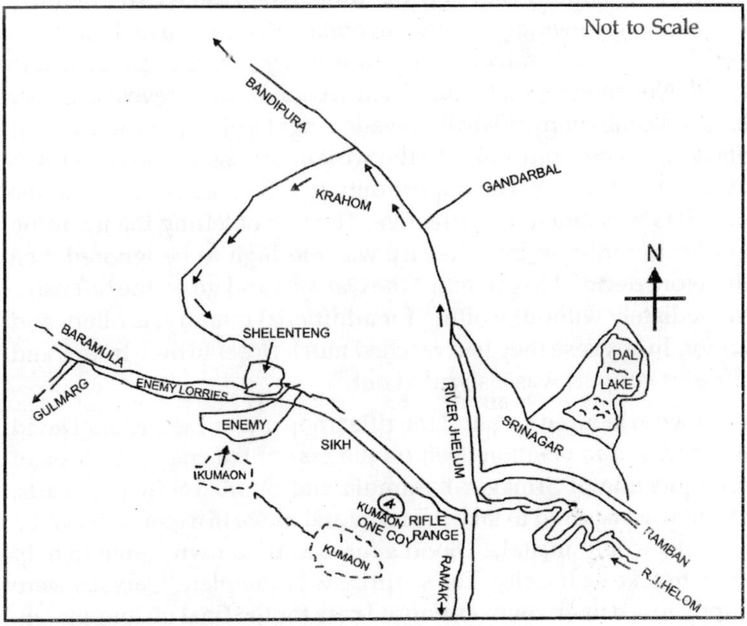

There were numerous skirmishes; however, the outcome of these skirmishes was not of much consequence from the higher perspective. After 161 Infantry Brigade had concentrated in and around Srinagar, Brig. L.P. Sen took steps to strengthen his hold on the city and its surroundings by redeploying his battalions of which he had four by now besides a squadron of Daimler armoured cars supported by a rifle troop. Initially he had positioned 1 Sikh at Pattan. A minor unfortunate incident led to his withdrawing from the strongly held defended positions at Pattan without giving a hint of his proposed action to his superiors and New Delhi. This caused furor amongst the political leadership in the State, in the Divisional HQs at Jammu, and above all in the circle close to Pandit Nehru. All wondered how a temporary Brigade Commander could muster the temerity to take such unilateral action. Pandit Nehru issued instructions for his immediate replacement before he could do any further damage. However, Sardar Patel, the strong man of India had recently visited the Brigade and was impressed by Sen's military credentials. He came to Sen's rescue and orders issued by Pandit Nehru were reversed. Thank the Lord for small mercies!

Major Rikhye of 7 Cavalry Regiment with one troop of four Daimler Armoured cars and the Rifle Troop joined 161 Infantry Brigade in the evening of 5th November 1947, a "virtual gift from gods". Further reinforcements promised by Sardar Patel fetched in on 7th November, as scheduled. Air reconnaissance revealed a very large concentration of Qabailis invaders right in the open, near village Sheltang, about four miles to the west of Srinagar. The target was much too tempting. The opportunity to inflict heavy losses on the invaders was much too attractive. The risk of letting the invading hordes to infiltrate into the city was too high to be ignored. Sen therefore decided to pre-empt the Qabailis and go on the offensive immediately without waiting for additional infantry, artillery and armor. In any case they had reached much closer to own troops and close air support was also ruled out.

Two armoured cars and the rifle troop under Lieutenant David was ordered to position itself on the rear of the enemy in Area of road junction of Srinagar-Baramula and Sumbal-Srinagar roads. David was required to take the route and move in a manner that the Qabailis would mistake David's force as their own, come to help them to take on the city. The surprise was complete. Qabailis were happy to see their 'own' armoured cars for the final victory march.

As soon as David's force was at the right place, Sen gave the code word 'Go' when all hell broke loose on the unsuspecting Qabailis who were dreaming of a victory march to the city and all the 'perks' that went with that prize. They were shot up by their 'own' armoured cars from the rear, by the Sikhs in front, and bayoneted by the Kumaonis from the right. Confusion galore! The Sikhs also joined the assault, so did the reserve company of 4 Kumaon on the right flank of 1 Sikh. Qabailis fled westwards towards their favourite haunt of Baramula. The Air Force Spitfires strafed the fleeing enemy from above. In matter of just about twenty minutes from the word "GO", a major disaster like a thunderbolt had struck the Qabaili raiders. And they fled, fled back at high speed to the safety of Muzaffarabad leaving behind 472 dead counted on the battlefield plus another 146 between Sheltang and Pattan. They also left behind 138 civilian trucks and buses which was welcome gift to the Emergency Government's fleet of vehicles. The battle field was littered with large number of weapons of all types and makes besides rations, medical stores and ambulances etc.

The Battle of Sheltang proved to be turning point in the fortunes of India. It was an unmitigated disaster for Pakistan and a magnificent victory for Indian troops in their first battle in defense of their own country led by their own officers. Brigadier Sen's plan was indeed brilliant in concept and glorious in execution. Its success went a long way to vindicate his stand in the eyes of Sheikh Abdullah and Pandit Nehru both of whom were gunning for his skin, besides many other doubting Toms of course.

Advance Resumed

The rot had set in within a few weeks of Independence. May be, it already had even before Independence was ushered in. To be more specific, it started exactly on 13th November 1947. Indian forces re-occupied Uri on that fateful day. While it should have been the harbinger of total elimination of the so called 'raiders' from the soil of Kashmir, it was not to be destiny? No. It is so easy and simple to blame destiny for our failures but we must not fall victim to that cowardly escape-goat. Intelligent and analytical approach in the light of historical data is the answer.

Pursuit of enemy after success in a defensive battle is an essential part of battle procedure, a military doctrine, a cardinal principle. And Commander 161 Infantry Brigade was no exception. Within minutes of enemy withdrawal he ordered advance to Baramula to start around midnight 07/08 November. Baramula was retaken around 7:30 am 8th November. Bakshi Gulam Mohammed was in Baramula within an hour of its falling back in the lap of Kashmir Government. By this time additional reinforcements had arrived from India and the restructured 161 Brigade was straining on its leash to push forward to Uri-Domel-Muzaffarabad. By this time Major General Kalwant Singh with his TAC (Tactical) HQ had moved from Jammu to Srinagar — a most unfortunate development, if ever there was any!

The restructured 161 Infantry Brigade left Baramula at 7:00 am November 18 for advance to Uri. Unfortunately, Sen's brilliant plan and magnificent success in the Battle of Sheltang did not go down well in Kalwant Singh's throat! His attitude and some of his unprofessional actions appeared totally irrational bringing to surface a heavy dose of jealousy. Small minds, big jobs! 161 Brigade had hardly advanced a few miles beyond Baramula when Kalwant Singh ordered Sen to shed 1 Para. Sen tried, but the General refused to see reason. The advance was halted to comply with an absurd irrational stupid order. It was a flagrant violation of a cardinal principle of war in as much as instead of reinforcing success in fast moving operations the General did exactly the opposite. The System became a stumbling block to success — a serious and severe Systematic Failure in military command and control — a proverbial case of two swords in one scabbard!

By 13th November 1947 the invading hordes had been decisively defeated. There were hardly any raiders, or enemy troops, or their accomplices beyond Uri; none left between Uri and Muzaffarabad. They were safely ensconced in Muzaffarabad, enjoying the comforts of their loot and the beauties abducted from the Valley Beautiful.

Nehru's Folly: Victory India, Advantage Pakistan

Uri was a small town on the bank of River Jhelum, a convenient halting place half way between Domel and Srinagar on the main road. It had a number of cafes, restaurants, teashops, wayside eateries, etc. It was reoccupied on November 13, not recaptured since there were no enemy troops in and around Uri at that time. Immediately after JAK Div HQs got this good news, Kalwant Singh ordered to cease further advance to Domel. This was most unfortunate for India in as much as a golden opportunity to resolve the Kashmir imbroglio for-ever, once and for all, was deliberately let go. LOC to become the *dejure* boundary between India and Pakistan was the real solution, and remains so till today.

Brigadier Sen vehemently protested against this order. He explained to the General that he had the enemy on the run. Unless pressure was maintained against him, he would recover and come back to fight another day. Instead of being on the attack mode, Indian Army would have to be on the defensive. This is precisely what happened in the end.

General Russell, the Western Army Commander under whose overall command Kashmir operations were being conducted, was extremely keen to exploit success right up to Domel and Muzaffarabad, more so since the invaders had been decisively defeated. The Qabailis were on the run and must not be given an opportunity to regroup, no respite whatsoever. He wanted hot pursuit right up to the Pak border. He recommended: "... we should continue our advance right up to Pakistan-Kashmir border, demolish the two bridges over the Kishenganga at Domel and Kohala. Our troops should withdraw immediately thereafter, leaving the Kashmir Police to take over border policing duties at Domel and Kohala." His plan further envisaged retaining one brigade group in the Valley as a mobile reserve to deal with any serious border violations or incursions. The crux of Russell's plan was to seal off the Valley as one time permanent solution of the Kashmir problem. That was the higher strategic objective — that is what real generalship and statesmanship is all about.

Lieutenant General Sir Dudley Russell, KBE, CB, DSO, MC, was a notable exception amongst the British top brass, perhaps the only one of his kind who rendered honest, bold and militarily correct advice besides making positive efforts to steer India to complete victory. However, when he was snubbed in his efforts by inexperienced political leadership who would rather not accept advice from a military man, he like a good soldier obeyed the political directive without any reservations. No doubt Nehru had steered India to freedom significantly well under Gandhi's guidance. He had created a wide niche in international field in a remarkably short time, bringing name and fame for himself and his country. To stand on an international pedestal is one thing; military strategy and tactics fall in a totally different field of which he had neither the knowledge or training, nor the inclination. But still he spurned sane advice from a high level expert thereby leaving an extremely thorny problem for posterity. Mere Nehruvian idealism and rhetoric do not go a long way; indeed they do not go anyway at all, certainly not in the domain of military strategy. Idealism and rhetoric are no substitute for sound military strategy.

By that time all the Qabaili invaders had fled to the safety of Domel-Muzaffarabad. It has been personally confirmed by Colonel Akbar Khan, DSO, (later Major General) who had assumed the grandiose pseudo-title of "General Tariq" on taking over command of all operations in the Valley, that there were no Qabailis (or Pak Army troops) between Uri and Muzaffarabad to stop the Indians. But the Indians managed to halt themselves! In his Book[4] Akbar Khan is quite candid about the absence of any organized opposition in this stretch of 75 miles to Indian advance to Domel, if it did come about. But India managed to halt itself at Uri with one full brigade twiddling their thumbs for good seven days and let the golden opportunity go past. They could have moved forward in their trucks and jeeps and reach Kashmir-Pak border in less than four hours! A top level Systematic Failure indeed – India's victory turned out to be Pakistan's success story!

No doubt Jawaharlal Nehru made significant contributions – personal, financial and family sacrifices ... there is no doubt that, but for Pandit Nehru's intervention in day to day military operational details for which he had neither the background nor training, or inclination, and if 161 Brigade under Brig L.P. Sen had been permitted to continue the advance from Uri to Muzaffarabad, there would have been no Kashmir problem at all today. There would have been no "Azad Kashmir" either. No POK ... The 'ifs' and 'buts' of history ...

Nehru Regrets his Second Folly

A Foray in the UN: While the war was over for all practical purposes, on January 01, 1948 India decided to take the Kashmir issue to the United Nations. This was done on the advice of the Governor General, Lord Mountbatten. The argument put forward by India was that since Jammu and Kashmir State had acceded to the Union of India, the northern portions which were still under illegal occupation of Pakistan, or its affiliates, should in all fairness be handed back to India. India plea was for UN help towards clearing this illegal occupation by Pakistan. What was well within your own grasp, you did not seize it yourself, and now you wanted a third party to do the dirty work for you. How naïve, and immaturish approach to international military matters! Of course, our Prime Minister committed a blunder in approaching the UN for what we could have, or should have, done ourselves. In return, we the victims of aggression were placed on equal footing, the same pedestal, as the aggressor, perhaps worse.

Pakistan suggested withdrawal of all armed forces in the state and holding of a plebiscite under an "impartial interim administration". Pakistan's contention was vigorously supported by the British. The Americans also supported Pakistan's stand to ascertain the wishes of the people. Sheikh Abdullah in his speech at the UN Security Council on February 05, 1948 was quite blunt without diplomatic niceties when he said that "no power on earth can displace me from the position which I have as long as the people are behind me I will remain there."[5] By now Nehru bitterly regretted going to the United Nations where he complained like an innocent novice that power politics, and not ethics, played a dominant role. Whoever heard of ethics in international diplomacy (!), where deceit, beguile and delusion is practiced by expert diplomats for politico-military gains. This was our world-level statesman! The Indian politicians blamed Mountbatten for dragging India to the UN. The psycophants had a knack of finding a scape goat for their revered hero.

War Recommences

The snows melted during May 1948. The weather conditions were just about right for hostilities to commence again where they had halted in November of last year. With Uri as the secure base, an infantry brigade advanced north and west. It took the town of Tithwal but met with sharp resistance on its drive to the key objective of Muzaffarabad. Brigadier Sen was absolutely correct in his assessment in October-November 1947. So was General Russell. Instead of attack mode, Indian Army was now on the defensive mode!

The LOC on the other side was frequently shifting. Kargil and Drass fell to the enemy which posed a threat to Leh, the capital of Ladakh. The enemy forces which received arms shipments via covert means gave advantage to Pakistan. However, the IAF came to the

INDIAN ATTACKS TOWARDS MUZAFFARABAD

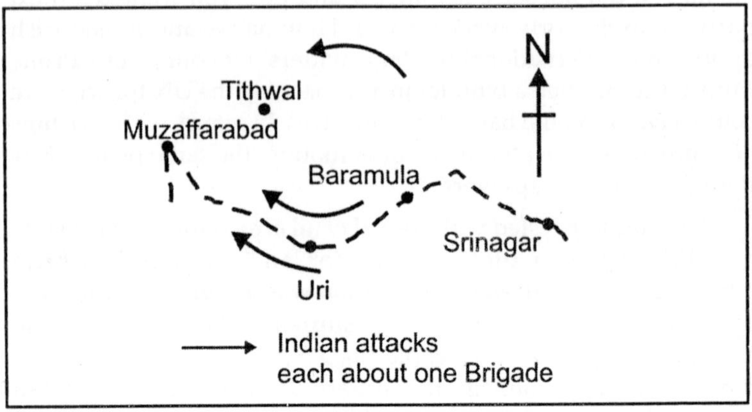

rescue of Indian Army. In November 1948 both Kargil and Drass were recaptured by Indian forces thereby ensuring the security of Leh. Meanwhile, hostile hill-positions around Poonch were also cleared. However northern and western parts of Kashmir continued to remain in possession of Pakistan. Now that winter was once again about to set in, it was considered prudent not to undertake further advance to those areas.

Meanwhile, the UN had appointed a Special Commission which made extensive tour of the region besides visiting Delhi and Karachi. The Sheikh had a long talk with one of the members, Joseph Korbel, the Czech member and a scholar of repute. He dismissed the idea of a plebiscite as well as independence and suggested that the only solution was partition of Kashmir. Otherwise India and Pakistan will continue fighting *ad infinitum* bringing more suffering to the people of Kashmir. And that is what precisely has been happening ever since.

By March 1948 Hari Singh had been divested of all his authority and retained as a ceremonial head of State with the title of Sadr-i-Riyasat. In April 1949 Hari Singh was replaced by his eighteen year old son, Karan Singh as the Sadr-i-Riyasat. Concurrently, Sheikh Abdullah and three other men of the National Conference were chosen to represent the State in the Indian Constituent Assembly thereby affirming the accession of the State to the Indian Union.

Pakistan was carved out of India as a separate homeland for the Muslims of not only India but of the entire South Asia. Islam was the basis of its birth. Its first Governor General was a Gujarati who had married a Parsi Lady, and enjoyed his scotch and soda. The Prime

Minister was an aristocrat from the United Provinces of India who had married a Christian Lady. Neither of them was practicing Muslim in the true sense of the word. And that partially held good for a majority of top civil servants too in the newly formed State of Pakistan — they were mostly Mohajirs, the migrants whose ancestral homes were on Indian soil, as were many of their relatives. In other words, the ruling class of Pakistan had no roots in the country they craved for. This also raises the question: how many Muslims who agitated for creation of a separate homeland left India to go and live in their cherished new homeland? Why not all the 92.2% who voted for a separate homeland for themselves to be carved out of India? That should have been the logical rational outcome of a separate Homeland!

India went to UN when its army was on a winning spree with the raiders running helter skelter. Systematic Blunder of Himalayan proportions by Mr. Nehru for which the posterity can never forgive

MAP : CEASE FIRE LINE 1949

him. Ironically, subsequently India has been consistently rejecting "third party" involvement in the dispute. Again, a totally irrational approach! Plebiscite in Kashmir remains buried under the debris of systemic failures of Indian Polity, perhaps a blessing in disguise!

The present ratio of soldiers to civilians in Kashmir is extremely high: population of eight millions has 450,000 Indian soldiers and Para-military troops. In the aftermath of 1857-Mutiny even British India had merely 100,000 soldiers against a population of 200 million! Obviously, India has not been able to win the hearts of Kashmiris despite the initial euphoria of November 1947 when Indian troops were seen defending Srinagar after the "Rape of Baramula" by Pakistanis. A conspicuous systemic failure of Indian polity to derive full benefit from a positive situation ...

Conclusions

Pakistan came into being purely on the basis of religion, as a home-land for South Asian Muslims. Pakistani elite, largely the intellectuals who migrated from India to their cherished homeland, felt that their new nation was incomplete without full integration of the Muslim majority State of Jammu and Kashmir. It is a different matter altogether that most of the Indian Muslims who voted in favour of Pakistan, after all the havoc that came as backlash of Partition, did not move to their cherished dreamland but continued to live comfortably in their homes in India. It is therefore difficult to understand the rationale behind their obsession with Kashmiri Muslims most of whom were firm believers in Sufiism, and its mysticism? On the other hand, India was not prepared to compromise on its secular foundations and remained determined to hold on to that ideology. Muslims have every right to live an equal honourable right to live in secular India; but not those treacherous elements which created havoc while demanding a separate homeland. Jinnah should have taken his flock to the Islamic safety of his new creation; why Kashmiris Muslims alone! That did not happen, nor was it expected to. However, while the Muslim citizens of free India have complete freedom to live anywhere in India, they also have a moral obligation to "remove the doubts and misgivings entertained by a large section of the people about their loyalty founded largely on their past association with their demand for Pakistan..."

besides some of their unfortunate activities like supporting anti-Indian movements emanating from Pakistan by organizations like Lashkare-Toiba and their many ancillaries, both in Pakistan and in India. To make matters worse for themselves, the same Muslims who voted for Muslim League (i.e. Pakistan) in 1946 elections formed the same Muslim League with a cosmetic change in the name, implying thereby continuation of the same ideological divide against the majority. 92.2% of Indian Muslims wanted Pakistan. They got it. Having got what they wanted, they did not want to go there. On top of that Mr. Nehru felt it was the responsibility of the Home Minister, Patel, and the Government of India, and people of India, to make Muslims feel secure in India. How irrational!

Pakistan just could not reconcile to the idea that Muslim majority State of Jammu and Kashmir should form part of the Indian Union, like millions of other Muslims continued to be citizens of the Republic of India despite their earlier slogan-shouting demanding Pakistan. Obviously, Pakistan forgets that the Kashmiri brand of Islam is heavily tilted towards Sufism-mysticism. While *burka* is widely worn by Pakistani women, that is not so amongst Kashmiri women who mostly go about unveiled. The Deobandi and Talibanized Islamists took exception to this and threw acid on a number of Kashmiri women badly disfiguring them. Most Kashmiris dislike Islamist radicals for whose presence in Kashmir they hold Pakistan responsible. The *fatwa* against Sania Mirza, the world famous tennis-star is a case in point.

India's disenchantment with the multinational fora like the United Nations came as a shock when the Security Council placed the victim and the aggressor on the same footing. Notwithstanding Nehru's high reputation in international field, when it came to brass tacks, Indian diplomacy failed to make a mark in diplomatic field. In fact, Pakistan gained an upper hand while Indian leadership proved rather naïve.

Notes

1. Mansergh Nocholas: ed. in chief, Constitutional Relations between Great Britain and India — *Transfer of Power*, Vol. 9; p. 71.
2. Schofield Victoria: *Kashmir in Conflict ; India, Pakistan and the Unfinished Conflict* , I.B. Taurus, London, 2000; p. 51.

3. Based on *Slender was the Thread* by Lieut. Gen. L.P. Sen, DSO, the then Brigade Commander of 161 Infantry Brigade under whose command, and his ingenious planning, this significant Battle was fought.
4. Akbar Khan: *Raiders in Kashmir*, Pakistan Publishers, Karachi; 1970, p. 70.
5. Korbel: *Danger in Kashmir*, p. 109.

SECTION-II

9

HYDERABAD POLICE ACTION

Operation 'Polo' : 1948

NIZAM STATE OF HYDERABAD

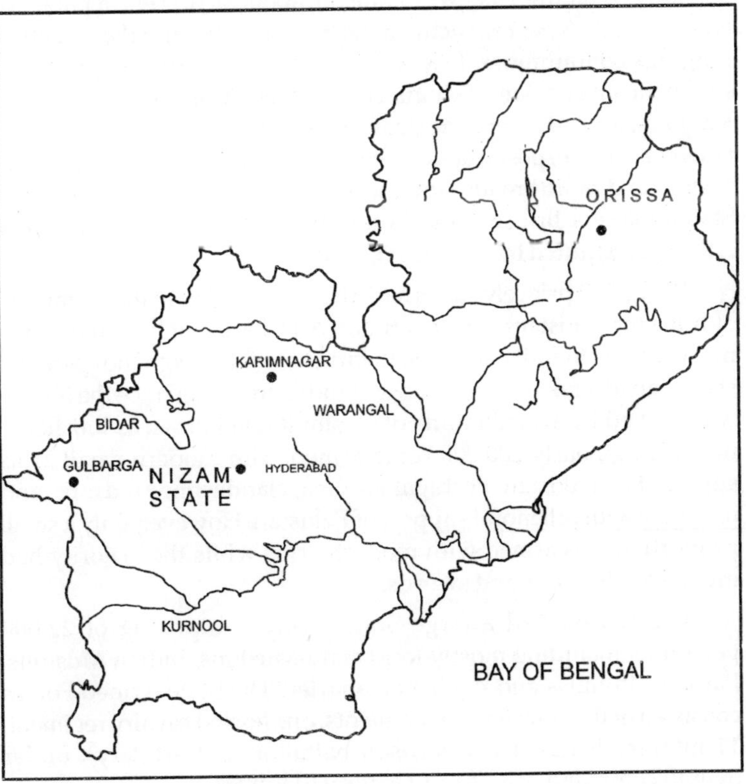

British paramountcy over the Princely States numbering nearly 565 lapsed on August 15, 1947 when India achieved Independence. According to British Parliamentary Act the princely states could accede to either of the new Dominions, or choose independence. That is the British way of graceful exit! Under the circumstances the latter course was not a practical proposition except for a couple of odd ones like Hyderabad, Kashmir etc., by virtue of their geographical location, size and resources. Practically all of them acceded to either Dominion barring major exceptions of Nizam State of Hyderabad and Jammu and Kashmir.[1] Hyderabad State in Deccan Plateau in Southern India came into being in 1724 under control of Nizam-ul-Mulk Asif Jha after the fall of Mughal Indian Empire. It was the largest and most prosperous princely state with the Nizam as the richest man in the world[2]. It covered an area of 214,190 sq km with a population of roughly 16.34 million[3], totally surrounded by Indian Territory. While the ruler was a Muslim about 85 per cent of populace were Hindus, 8 per cent actively hostile Muslims and the rest other religious communities. It was a multi-lingual state comprising of 48.2 per cent speaking Telugu, 26.4 per cent Marathi, 12.3 per cent Kannada and 10.3 per cent Urdu. The State had its own army, rail network, airline, postal system, currency (*halli*), telecommunication system and radio broadcasting service. It was the first Indian Royal State to accept British protection under the scheme of Subsidiary Alliance instituted by Arthur Wellesley.

While 562 princely states had already acceded to the Dominion of India (or Pakistan), Nizam Osman Ali Khan, Asif Jha VII decided not to accede to India or Pakistan but chose Sovereign Independent status, an ulcer deep in the midst of India. In his defiance the Nizam was backed by armed militia of Qasim Razvi known as Razakars[4] numbering nearly 200,000 some armed with modern small arms supplied by Pakistan, Portugal via Goa, clandestine air drops, and of course with full moral support of Pakistan. However, only a small proportion was armed with modern arms while the majority had muzzleloader guns and swords.

The Nizam had a large State Army comprising of 22,000 personnel including mostly local state-Muslims, Indian Muslims, Pathans, Rohillas and Arab mercenaries. The State Armed Forces consisted of three armoured regiments, one horsed cavalry regiment, 11 infantry battalions, a garrison battalion and artillery[5], under overall command of an Arab, General El Edroos.

HYDERABAD OPERATIONS: 1948

Map: Sholapur-Hyderabad-Vijayawada

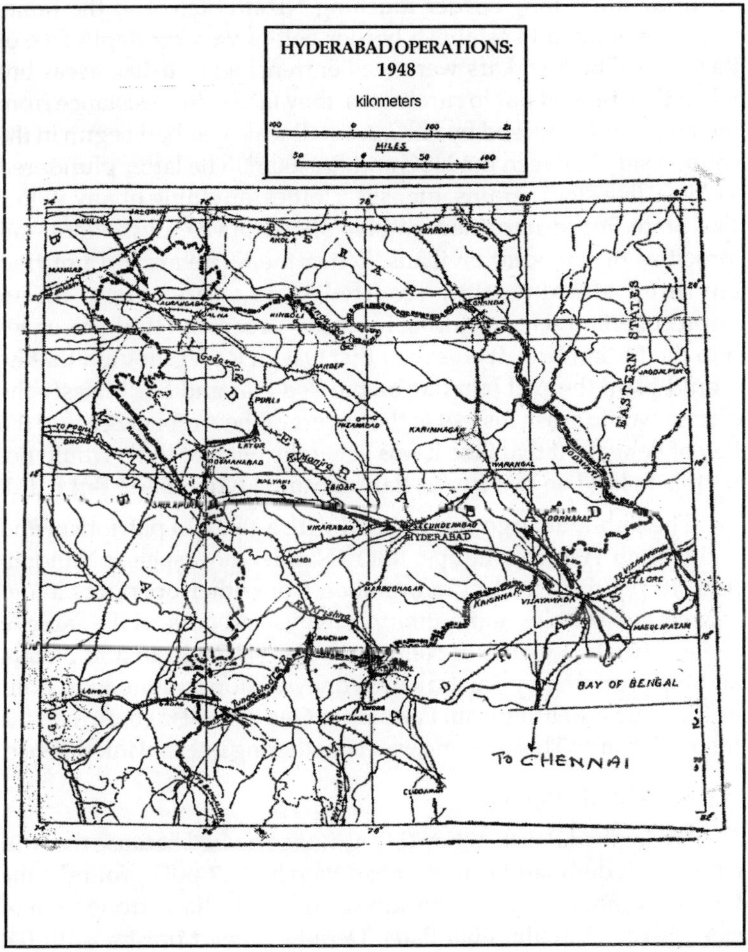

Civil Unrest

Soon after Indian Independence, Hyderabad State Congress (HSC) launched a flag *Satyagraha* to force integration of the State with India. Small scale raids by armed enlisted home guards were launched all over the border areas, prominent of which was by the men of the Angola district (then Central India) SP, Khusro Faramurz Rustomji, a distinguished Parsi IPS officer. Angola in Berar had about 52 miles long border touching Nizam State and the home guards managed to establish border belt of varying depth free of Razakars. The Razakars were well entrenched in urban areas but when they fanned out to rural areas, they faced stiff resistance from the village folks backed by HSC. A small scale war had begun in the countryside between the HSC and Razakars. The latter plundered *ad lib* – live stock, grains, utensils, clothes, anything of any value. The State Police remained passive spectators to all the loot and atrocities on innocent civilians. When the Razakars did not find anything of value, they resorted to rape and arson on an unprecedented scale resulting in steady stream of Hindu refugees into the Indian side. It was then that Qasim Razvi shouted that he would plant the Asif Jahi flag on the Red Fort and His Majesty the Nizam would wash his feet in the waters of the Arabian Sea and the Bay of Bengal. At that time it was generally felt that India would not be able to hold on two fronts, Pakistan and Hyderabad.[6] But it did!

The public at large was imbued with a sense of patriotism and enthusiasm. A telephone operator in Nander (now spelt as Nanded) used to regularly collect information from other operators about movement of trains and military convoys and pass on the same to India officials. Reports of collusion between Pakistan and Nizam and gun-running by Australian Sydney Cotton continued to pour in. Shipments of arms from Pakistan to Goa were also confirmed via the same route. This was one way of gathering internal intelligence.

"OPERATION POLO"

Hyderabad Police Action (HPA) was so named because the twin cities of Hyderabad-Secunderabad then had 17 polo grounds, the largest number in the Indian sub-continent. India's strong man of steel, Sardar Vallabh Bhai Patel, Deputy Prime Minister of India, was the moving spirit behind integrating the princely states that were states and estates into the Dominion of India to form one homogenous nation. Tortuously frustrating negotiations for a peaceful settlement of the problem were carried on between Mr. K.M. Munshi, India's Envoy and Agent General to Hyderabad and Nizam's envoys, his Prime Minister Laiq Ali and Sir Walter Monckton.

OPERATION POLO

Map: Advance by 1 Armoured Division

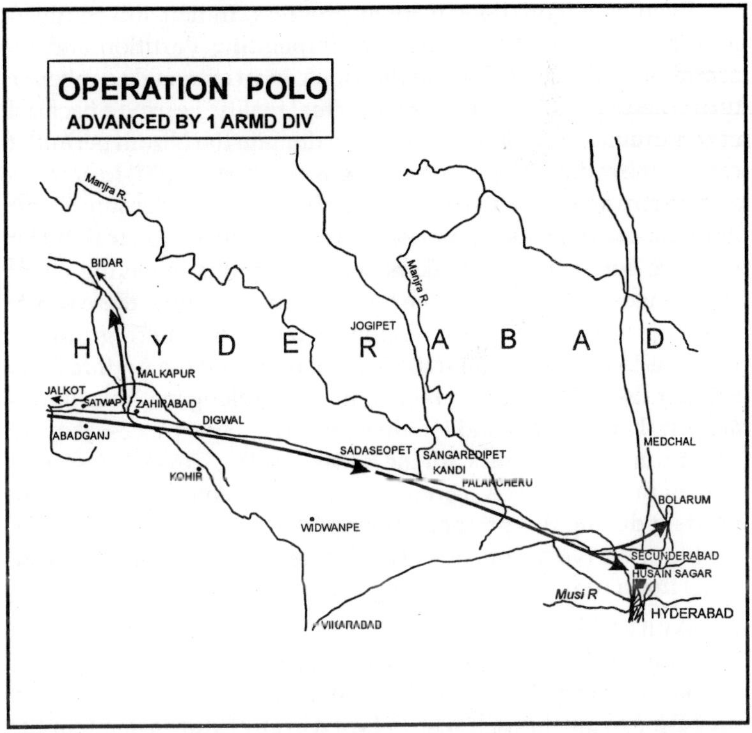

Lord Mountbatten used to preside over these negotiations, which went on and on, tiresome and frustrating, but the Nizam rejected every single proposal including a very generous one put forward by the Governor General, Lord Mountbatten. But the Nizam rejected them all. He was adamant on nothing short of a Sovereign Independent State directly as part of the Commonwealth of Nations. In fact, he had already declared the State as an independent nation on 15th August 47 and was not prepared to go back on that declaration at any cost, more so since then he had built up a formidable force of arms, besides a squadron of bombers stationed there by Pakistan for a consideration of Rs. 200 million. In order to realize his dream of complete independence the Nizam went to the extent of even seeking arbitration by the US President Harry S.

Truman besides approaching the United Nations. It is a pity that he was not tried for his acts of omission and commission and awarded a severe sentence, if not executed. But that is India and Indianess.

Even as negotiations were in progress, Indian sub-continent was in a chaotic state because of impending Partition and the communal holocaust. The situation took on an extremely dangerous turn when the Partition became an actual reality. Fearing a backlash of communal disturbances in his own domain the Nizam permitted chief of the radical Majlis-e-Ittehadul-Muslimeen (MIM) to organize a voluntary armed militia of Muslims, the Razakars, to ensure Islamic domination in the Deccan plateau. This in turn led to escalation of violence between the Razakars and the Hindus involving nearly 150 villages on both side of the borders. Concurrently, there was an uprising in the Telengana region of the state where groups of peasants led by the Communist Party of India and the Andhra Maha Sabha raised their flag of rebellion—The Telengana Rebellion — against their Muslim and Hindu landlords. In the process they got into a conflict situation with the Razakars also. Nevertheless, non-violent protests by HSC continued unabated. Another noteworthy incident during this pre-operations period was a failed attempt on the life of the Nizam outside his Palace on December 04, 1947 made by a Hindu nationalist belonging to the Arya Samaj.

With breakdown of negotiations by the middle of 1948 vigorous preparations for a war were underway, both in the Nizam State and in the Southern Command of Indian Army. The Nizam was preparing to ally himself with Pakistan in any future armed conflict with India for which Pakistan was ever so willing. It was all hush-hush as far as India was concerned. No inkling was given to outsiders as to what was cooking. Even senior civil officials at the highest level in South India had no idea of what was going to happen and when.

The spark for 'Operation Polo' came on September 06, 1948 when an Indian police post near village Chillakallu came under heavy fire from a raiding party of Razakars. The Indian army reaction was swift and effective. A squadron of Poona Horse and a company of 2/5 Gurkha Rifles under overall command of Major Abhey Singh was dispatched to investigate and deal with the problem for which further reinforcements were in readiness. However, it was a brief and quick action. When Abhey Singh's party was also fired upon, tanks of Poona Horse chased the Razakars to Kodar village in

Hyderabad territory. Armoured cars of 1 Hyderabad Lancers opposed the tanks in which one armoured car was destroyed and the state garrison at Kodar promptly surrendered.

Plan for Operation Polo was the brain child of Lieutenant General E.N. Goddard, General Officer Commanding-in-Chief Southern Command. Two main thrusts were planned: one from Vijayawada from the East and the other from Sholapur in the West. Lieutenant General Rajendrasinghji, DSO was in overall command. D-Day was fixed for September 13, 1948.

Day-One, 13 September 1948: On the western front the attack force from Sholapur was under command of Major General Chaudhari. It was divided into four task forces:

- STRIKE FORCE – Fast moving force comprising of motorized infantry, cavalry and light artillery;
- SMASH FORCE – Predominantly armour and artillery units;
- KILL FORCE – Composed of infantry and Sappers;
- VIR FORCE - Units of Infantry, anti-tank and Sappers.

The attack on Nizam State of Hyderabad commenced on the western front from Sholapur side. The advance was led by 7 Infantry Brigade astride Sholapur-Secunderabad Highway. Naldurg Fort was the first defensive position, the advancing force met in early hours of the morning. The position was occupied by 1st Hyderabad Infantry. Making use of speed and surprise the Brigade managed to occupy the vital bridge on River Bori intact en-route to the Fort. 2nd Sikh Infantry captured the Fort in a swift attack paving the way for an armoured column of 1st Armoured Brigade, part of the "Smash Force", to move ahead to the town of Jalkot, about 8 km away. Jalkot was captured around 09:00 am.

Lieutenant Colonel Ram Singh Commanding 9 Dogra, a motorized battalion, a Strike Force unit passed through while the armoured column quickly overcame resistance by Razakars and secured the town of Umarge, about 61 km away, by the afternoon of the first day. While advance on the main axis was in progress, another column comprising of the following besides ancillary units:

- One Squadron 3rd Cavalry,
- One troop 18th King Edwards Own Cavalry,

- One troop of 9 Para Field Regiment,
- 10 Field Company Engineers (Madras Sappers),
- 3/2 Punjab Regiment,
- 2/1 Gurkha Rifles.
- 1 Mewar Infantry,

This diversionary force reached the outskirts Tuljapur, an important town about 34 km north-west of Naldurg around dawn the next day. Surprise was complete. Tuljapur was defended by 1st Hyderabad Infantry and about 200 Razakars. They fought valiantly against a far superior force. The battle lasted about two hours after which the defenders surrendered. Further advance to Lahora had to be halted since the river had been in flood, heavily swollen. That was the end of Day-One on the western front during which Nizam State Forces suffered heavy casualties besides losing a big chunk of their territory. An interesting side incident was the capture of a British mercenary whose task was to blow up the bridge near Naldurg which he failed to accomplish.

Now reverting to the eastern front—the advancing force from Vijayawada was led by Major General A.A. Rudra. Its composition:

- One squadron 17th Poona Horse;
- One troop 19th Field Battery;
- Four infantry battalions for protection and security of L of C;
- Sappers and ancillary units.
- Two squadrons of Hawker Tempest aircraft based in Poona in direct support.

Hyderabad Forces had deployed two units of armoured cars, Humber and Staghound armoured cars to check the advance of Indian forces from Vijayawada. They offered fierce resistance to Indian advance. It took some time and casualties to overcome the defence put up by the Hyderabad forces. However, the advancing column secured Kodar by 08:30 am. They pressed home the attack and captured the town of Mungala by the afternoon. There were further important gains in this sector. 5/5 Gurkha attacked and secured a vital bridge at Tungabhadra while 1st Mysore Infantry secured a sugar factory at Hosepet under occupation by units of Pathans and Razakars who offered fierce resistance.

Jinnah had died two days earlier. "The wounds of communal violence that he and the Muslim League had inflicted would make millions of Muslims in India suffer for years to come. Jinnah had lived to be the Governor General; these others had lived merely to be killed, on the altar of communalism and hatred."[7]

Berar Sector too had a fair share of fighting on Day One. In Konergaon, Colonel Ajit Singh[8] was in command. At four o'clock in the morning everything that he had was thrown across the river at Konergaon and shortly thereafter the attack was launched. Fighting there was comparatively easy, resistance negligible since the post was defended only by Razakars and customs police. One Pathan,

Map: OP POLO; The Eastern Thrust

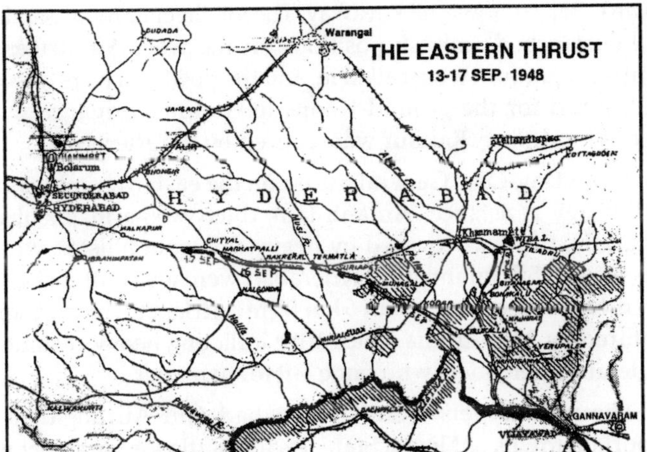

all by himself, had entrenched himself in a mosque and continued incessant vicious firing till a grenade knocked him out. The action was over by about 1300 hrs. The defending force had suffered heavy casualties, and so had the innocent civilians who came in the cross fire. However, a company of Pathans on high ground a few miles from Hingoli put up a stiff resistance which halted the advance for a few hours. There were several gory sights. Some Razakars were captured and were brought in to bury their dead comrades. Thus, by the end of the first day of fighting, Indian troops had penetrated deep into Nizam Territory and secured their objectives.

Day-Two, 14 September 1948: We shall start this day with Barmer Sector because of a rather peculiar development. Late at night some women of Kanergaon, knowing well that Indian troops, their saviours, had not committed any atrocities, against them, decided to escape from the horrors of Day-One by crawling up to the barbed wire fence. The sentries heard suspicious noises and fired resulting in death of some innocent women. But that was not all; more was to come later. Prisoners were being taken. And there were signs of revival in the village. A stream of refugees poured in for shelter on India side.

On the western front early morning aerial reconnaissance was carried out on the road leading out of village Umarge where ground troops had camped overnight before commencing advance eastwards towards Rajasur town, 48 km away. The intelligence reports indicated well entrenched ambush positions on the way. Air strikes from Tempest squadron were called in, and the positions were effectively neutralized for the ground troops to continue advance without serious hindrance. Rajasur was secured by the afternoon.

As on Day-One, General Rudra on the eastern front was faced with heavy resistance. An anti-tank ditch was a major obstacle. Naturally, this was covered by heavy fire from hillside where 1st Lancers and 5th Infantry of Hyderabad were well entrenched. This defensive position was about 6 km from Surriapet. The position was captured by 2/5 Gurkha Rifles after inflicting heavy casualties on Hyderabad defenders who came out to surrender.

The next targets were Osmanabad and Aurangabad, two important towns of Nizam State. As the battle for Surriapet was in progress, a squadron of 8th Cavalry and 3/11 Gurkha Rifles assaulted Osmanabad. The town was defended by determined Razakars in large numbers. They put up a stiff fight resulting in heavy street fighting. Ultimately, the Razakars surrendered having suffered heavy casualties.

Aurangabad was the prized target and the honour of capturing the city went to Major General D.S. Brar. The General planned to overrun the city with six columns of infantry and Cavalry. The civil administration was so overawed by the scale and possible intensity of attack that they decided to come out to surrender to the General.

Jalna was another town simmering with neglect! 3 Sikh, a company of Jodhpur Infantry supported by some tanks of 18 Cavalry resolved the issue. The civil officials, at least many of them thought at that point of time, that the entire operation would come to an end within a month. But events moved much faster and proved them wrong.

Day-Three, 15 September: Yet another interesting development on the subsidiary front in Berar Sector was a request by Colonel Ajit Singh to Mr. Rustomji, SP Angola, to send two companies of the State Armed Force (SAF) to Malhivira in Hyderabad State Territory for deployment as flank protection for his further advance into Nizam Territory. The SP promptly led the convoy to Malhivira. The road was infested with Razakars who took pot shots at the people on the road. After a risky drive of eleven miles which then felt like a very long distance, they reached the destination. The Colonel was then leading his advance guard to Hingoli. The SAF was deployed by Mr. Rustomji according to the Colonel's directions. Meanwhile the army was concentrating for an attack on Hingoli. The unfortunate part of the episode was that a very senior police officer of the rank of IGP in Nagpur called Mr. Rustomji on telephone and rebuked him taking serious exception to deployment of SAF on the grounds that what if one man was killed in the process! How short sighted and immature, as if it was a war only of the Army where death is of no consequence while one man of SAF is a precious life to be preserved as a specimen of cowardice. No, it was the IGP who was a coward and I wonder why the Government of Central Provinces did not sack him for this irresponsible attitude to the national cause and which in any case was called "Hyderabad Police Action"![9]

On the western front a company of 3/11 Gurkha Rifles provided the firm base and rest of the column advanced to Nominabad. The town was nominally defended by 3 Golcanda Lancers who surrendered after putting up token resistance.

On the eastern front General Rudra continued to face severe resistance. Although air strikes had cleared most of the defenses of Hyderabad Forces, the Razakars were a determined lot and continued to offer stiff resistance till the Purchas bayoneted out of their hideouts. Nevertheless, while retreating they managed to destroy the bridge at Music but failed to cover it by fire, a standard army procedure, with the result that the bridge was quickly repaired by the Sappers. In another incident a Razakar post was decimated by the advancing army at Narkatpalli.

Day-Four, 16 September: The development on the western front was not too encouraging in that advance by the motorized battalion under Lieutenant Colonel Ram Singh was slowed down by a minefield. This was the first regular minefield that Indian troops had encountered in Nizam Territory. It had to be cleared before advance could be resumed. The Sappers were deployed for the task and a clear passage for the armoured personnel carriers (APCs) and armoured cars was soon ready to take on restricted traffic. Soon after the advance was resumed the force encountered heavy gunfire from prepared ambush positions. Speed and surprise were the pass words for this operation. The ambush position was bypassed to be tackled by a holding force, and the advance continued to a point about 15 km beyond Zahirabad. By then it was nightfall. The menace caused by frequent ambushes by Razakars who were familiar with the lie of the ground and used it to utmost advantage, and consequent delay, was not acceptable to General Chaudhari. He ordered 75 mm guns forward to tackle all such points of resistance by pulverizing the ambush positions. By this time Indian troops were threatening the important town of Bidar.

The situation in Berar sector was no better. It was rather gloomy. The advance had been brought to a halt. "... some tactical genius on the other side had drawn the Sikhs into a neat little trap. Under cover of three hills, an incessant rain of bullets was poured into them for the whole day ..." maximum damage was done by snipers hiding on treetops causing casualties and demoralization. Later that night IGP from Nagpur ordered immediately withdrawal of SAF. Nothing could be more stupid than that—a poor reflection on our civil hierarchy who sometimes follow the book blindly in an idiotic manner without giving a thought to the prevailing situation. Of course, Colonel Ajit Singh was a practical soldier and did not care whose orders they were; he bluntly refused to let go SAF who had been integrated into this offensive-defensive battles.

Day-Five, 17 September: The Indian army entered Bidar in the early hours of 17th September. Meanwhile forces led by 1st Armoured Regiment had reached about 60 km from the State Capital, Hyderabad. General Chaudhari's motorized units which had entered the State from Osmanabad side had crashed through the poor defences and were well on their way to Hyderabad. An intercept from the Hyderabad State Army to all units read: "Give three months' pay to all ranks and standby for further orders."[10] Meanwhile another column secured the town of Hingoli. By the morning of that day it was writing on the wall that Hyderabad forces had been decisively defeated with high casualties and material losses. Around 4 o'clock in the evening a ceasefire had been declared although sporadic resistance from the die-hards amongst the Razakars continued here and there.

Faced with imminent defeat the Nizam-ul-Mulk had sought the resignation of the Prime Minister and his cabinet sometime late in the evening of 16 September. The resignations were delivered the next morning. The Nizam sent a personal note to Mr. K.M. Munshi, India's Agent General to the State summoning him to the Palace at 1600 hrs September 17. The Nizam informed Mr. Munshi that since the Cabinet had resigned he didn't know what to do. Mr. Munshi advised the Nizam to secure the safety of citizens of the state by issuing appropriate orders to Commander of The Hyderabad State Army, Major General El Edroos. The Nizam complied immediately. He further advised the Nizam to make radio broadcast welcoming the Police Action besides withdrawing his complaint to the UN Security Council. Munshi offered also to help draft the speech for his radio broadcast.

The speech was duly broadcast in English. There was no red carpet treatment, nor any ceremonials. No guard of honour or State Anthem either! In fact, it was Nizam's first ever visit to his Radio Station after which he drove straight back to King Kothi.

The Asif Jahi[11] dynasty had come to an inglorious end. The Deccan had ceased to be the stronghold of Islamic fundamentalists.

The Surrender Ceremony

It was a very simple ceremony, a necessary formality, without any fuss or fanfare. Major General J.N. Chaudhari sat on one side of the table and Major General El Edroos on the other. The ceremony was scheduled for 4:00 pm IST. General Chaudhari spoke first, rather somewhat gravely:

"I have been ordered by Lieutenant General Maharaj Rajendrasinhji, General Officer Commanding-in-Chief, Southern Command, to take the surrender of your army".

"You have it".

"You understand that this is unconditional".

"Yes, I understand".[12]

That was it! The two Generals shook hands. Chaudhari opened his cigarette case and offered him a cigarette. Edroos proffered a lighter. Chaudhari's team joined them and the party cheerfully drove to the residence of India's Agent General. A jubilant crowd had collected en-route. They vigorously cheered the hero of Hyderabad. He waved in return and then sat down to discuss the details with Munshi, Edroos and others.

The Aftermath

It may be recalled that Mr. Rustomji had become the youngest SP in IPS as well the youngest DIG at age thirty-two when he was appointed DIG eleven years after joining the service at a "princely salary of Rs. 1,950 plus all the perks and allowances" besides an American car and a very dignified driver. He certainly deserved all this and a lot more He was appointed DIG Hyderabad.[13]

He recalls: "Over the whole of Hyderabad state towered the personality of Gen. J.N. Chaudhari, the new Military Governor—a generous soldier, amiable, sociable, non-communal, clever, diplomat, and a good leader" He was extremely generous, generous to a fault in as much as he allowed the ex Prime Minister of the State, Laiq Ali to be detained in his sprawling bungalow with all the paraphernalia of a retinue of servants and assistants who had full liberty of coming and going in at their will. There was hardly any security check. And Laiq just disappeared. A bad case of excessive generosity to an enemy VVIP who would have been put on trial!

Mr. D.S. Bakhale was appointed Chief Civil Administrator. "He was a quiet publicity shunning administrator, a student of men and affairs, extremely diligent, firm and capable." In the midst of looting, murders and communal troubles, Chaudhari and Bakhale confidently and quietly worked together to restore the situation back to normal. They were an ideal team for this purpose.

While the Nizam was the primary accused of waging war against the Indian Dominion, he had to be appointed the 'Rajpramukh' of the integrated city of Hyderabad. However, when HPA commenced six Muslim Rohillas took out seven Hindus and shot them. Kasim Razvi and the six Rohillas were tried under orders of the the SP Aurangabad. But Rustomji recommended that there was no evidence against Kasim Razvi in this case. The recommendation was accepted; only the six Rohillas were prosecuted in the case. However, Kasim Razvi was convicted by the High Court in the much weaker Bibi Nagar case while in the Shoebullah Khan (editor of a nationalist Daily Imroze) murder case, Razvi got away lightly.[13]

Now back to Op Polo: Casualties for Indian forces were 32 killed and 97 wounded while the Hyderabad Forces and the irregulars suffered 1863 killed, 122 wounded and 3,558 captured.

Notes

1. Brines Russell: *The Indo-Pak Conflict*; Pall Mall. London, 1968; pp. 203-13. The opening ceremony of this two-lane Highway was performed in October 1971 by General Hamid, Chief of Pakistan Army.
2. The Nizam and his Muslim nobles held 40% of the total land area of the State.
3. 1941 Census.
4. Razakar is a Persian word. It means a volunteer who protects a king or the government. The fundamentalist militia organized by Qasim Razvi to support the Nizam'a rule called themselves Razakars. Their aim was to resist the integration of the State with the Dominion of India.
5. Gleaned from Autobiography of Major General Joyanto Nath Chaudhari.
6. Rajgopal, P.V. (Ed.): *The British, the Bandits and the Bordermen*; New Delhi, 2009; p. 124.
7. P.V. Rajgopal: *op.cit.* quoting K.F. Rustomji; p. 129.
8. Later Major General: He became Inspector General of Assam Rifles at Shillong.
9. Rajgopal: *op. cit.* From the *Diaries of Mr. Rustomji*; p. 130.
10. *Ibid.*, p. 133.
11. The system of ranks, grades and titles of honour was instituted by Akbar and it came to an end with the Nizam of Hyderabad in 1948.
12. Autobiography of General J.N. Chaudhar.
13. Firdunji Rustomji was then the Commissioner of Police.

10

ANNEXATION OF PORTUGUESE TERRITORIES OPERATION VIJAY: 1961

Map: GOA

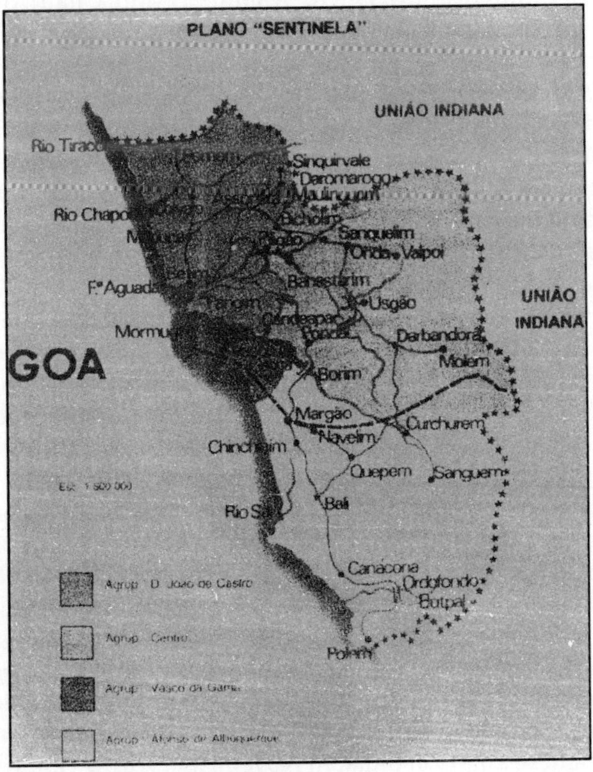

The armed action initiated by the Government of India to evict the intransigent Portuguese from their enclaves on the soil of India involved air, sea and land strikes for over 36 hours. The fighting was brief. It resulted in 34 Indians being killed and 35 wounded. The Portuguese suffered 31 killed in action, many wounded and 877 captured as POWs by the Indian Forces. It was a decisive victory for India ending 451-years of Portuguese colonial rule in India.

Historical Background

The Cape Route from Europe to Asia was discovered by the famous Portuguese sailor Vasco da Gama when he reached the famous port of Calicut on May 17, 1498. Vasco da Gama told the first Indian he met on the Malabar Coast that he came to seek 'Christians and spices'. The Portuguese soon monopolized the lucrative spice trade between the Indian Ocean and the Red Sea. They dominated the sea route between Egypt and the important Western Indian sea-ports of Cambay (now called Khambat) and Chaul thereby completely monopolizing the spice trade. The situation was further aggravated by yet another sea-venture by the Portuguese when a fleet of thirteen vessels under Pedro Alvarez Cabral arrived in middle of A.D. 1500. Instead of confining to trade they became over-ambitious and started interfering in internal affairs of Indian states and resorted to political intrigues, particularly against their Calicut host in favour of his rival the King of Cochin. This foreign naval domination and political interference severely affected trading interests of Muslims in India and the Middle East. Sultan Mahmûd Begarha, King of Gujarat in alliance with Sultan Ghauri of Egypt decided to restore status quo ante. The Egyptian fleet under command of Kurdish Governor of Jeddah, Amir Hussain, in consort with the Indian fleet under Malik Ayâz, a Turk, defeated the Portuguese commanded by Dom Lourenço near Chaul, south of Bombay in 1508. However, in 1509 the Portuguese fleet inflicted a crushing defeat on the Indo-Egyptian fleet near Diu. The Portuguese were back to square one, the top position, and Sultan Mahmûd granted them a site near Diu to set up a factory there. Similarly, in 1510 Krishnadeva Râya granted permission to the Portuguese to build a fort at Bhatkal since the former was using Portuguese Governor Alfonso de Albuquerque's (Captain General 1509-15) good offices to import quality horses from Europe. In fact it was Albuquerque who laid the foundations of Portuguese power in India after he was appointed as the Governor of Portuguese affairs in India. In November 1510, he captured the strategically located rich port of Goa[57] from Bijâpur Sultânate and developed its fortifications to make it impregnable. He encouraged his countrymen to marry non-Muslim Indian women to secure loyalty of their progeny - a race long known as *Luso-Indians* and now as Goans – for Portugal. By the time Albuquerque died in 1515, Portugal was the strongest naval power on the west coast of India. Soon Portuguese further spread themselves to include settlements of Diu, Daman, Salsette, Bassein, Chaul Bombay besides San Thomas near Madras and Hugli in Bengal. The Portuguese called their colonies of Goa, Daman and Diu as their empire along the Indian Ocean, *Estado Portuguese da India.*

The Portuguese were all out to control the maritime trade of Indian Ocean, by hook or crook, besides perfidy. Their methods were extremely cruel and were "based on the doctrine that no faith need be kept with infidels, unusual even in the turbulent north of the day, made them generally detested."

On regaining his Kingdom Sultan Bahadur had sought the assistance of the Portuguese in his wars against Humâyûn which was declined. After the war against the Moguls he requested the Portuguese Governor Nunho da Cunha to come over to meet him. But he did not. So in February 1537 the Sultan decided to go himself to meet him on board his ship. But he was treacherously drowned by the Portuguese, and his entire entourage was murdered. His successors were weak and, taking advantage of the situation, Akbar annexed Gujarat in Mogul Empire in A.D. 1572. However, the Sultan soon recovered his lost Kingdom (Gujarat) from the Moguls. Notwithstanding the conquests of Akbar the Mogul supremacy over Hindustan was far from complete. Kashmir in the north Kashmir was under a local Muslim dynasty while other Himalayan states were independent. In the north-west Akbar's half brother governed Kabul almost independently while Sind and Multan had become free of Imperial control after death of Sher Shah Sûri so had Orissa and Malwa while south of Vindhyas lay the powerful vast empire of Vijayanagar. The Muslim Sultanates of Khândesh, Berar, Bidar, Ahmadnagar and Golkunda were their own bosses while the Portuguese were in control of Goa and Diu. Akbar's legacy was indeed precarious. Nevertheless, the second battle of Pânîpat between Afghâns and Moguls proved decisive in favour of the Moguls soon after which their sovereignty over Hindustan became almost complete.

Annexation of Gujarat was followed by capture of Surât in February 1573 bringing Akbar in contact with the Portuguese. Since the Moguls' had no experience or expertise on the seas, they took no interest in building sea-power and the Portuguese continued their expansionist activities on the west coast of India. Further, their domination of Red Sea trade continued unabated right up to Qandahâr, an important trade center. The Portuguese had also established themselves above Sâtgoân in Bengal and strengthened their positions around Hugli. They levied heavy duties, excise duties on tobacco, indulged in evil practices of slave trade, captured many Hindu and Muslim girls to convert them to Christianity besides capturing two slave girls of Mumtaz Mahal. Emperor Shâh Jahân ordered the Governor of Bengal, Qâsim Ali Khan to punish the Portuguese. Hugli was captured in September 1632 after a siege lasting three months during which heavy casualties were inflicted on the Portuguese. A large number were taken prisoners, taken to Agra where they suffered terribly. The Portuguese (pirates) were humbled once again when their island stronghold of Sondîp in the Bay of Bengal was annexed by the Moguls and Chittagong was captured in 1666 from their ally, King of Arâkân. However, the Portuguese domination was enhanced with their occupation of additional settlements of Damân, Salsette, Bassein and Chaul. However, they lost Salsette and Bassein to the Marathas in 1739.

Although Portugal was the earliest European power to take a foothold on Indian shores, their decline came about due to the following causes:

- Religious intolerance against the so called infidels so much so that no Hindu temple was allowed to be built in Goa! They stooped so low as to harass the Syrian Christians of Malabar to secure their submission to Roman supremacy;
- Clandestine trade practices;
- Discovery of Brazil diverted their colonizing zeal towards the West;
- Failure to compete with other European trading companies.

No wonder therefore that the Portuguese were a detested lot in the Indian sub-continent. The Portuguese mingled their blood with the Indian but still remained 'alien and sterile'. "The legacy of

Portugal and sixteenth-century Europe to India was the Goans, the Catholic community in India with its missions begun by the enthusiastic St Francis Xavier, a *lingua franca* of which traces still linger in the ports, and a faint odour of intolerance. The first western cultural assault on India had failed."

Nationalist Movement

In 1928, a French educated Goan engineer Tristao Braganza da Cunha founded the Goa Congress Committee. He published two pamphlets, "Denationalization of Goa' and 'Four hundred years of Foreign Rule'. Dr. Rajendra Prasad, Pandit Nehru and Subhash Chandra Bose, amongst many others sent messages of support. On the advice of the then Congress President, Subhash Chandra Bose, da Cunha set up a branch office of his Goan Congress at 21 Dalal Street Bombay. It was affiliated to Indian National Congress. During the visit of Ram Manohar Lohia to Goa in June 1946 while he was advocating Gandhian non-violence, the Portuguese disrupted the meeting at Panjim, arrested Lohia, da Cunha, and others and put them behind bars. Portuguese action led to further protests, violence and disruption of services in the territory besides giving rise to "The Free Goa Party" and 'United Front of Goans" who actively participated in mass protests, perhaps with the connivance if Indian authorities.

At the time of Indian Independence, the Portuguese possessions on Indian soil were:

- **Goa** extending for about 100 km along the western coast of India for about 400 km south of Bombay for a breadth of about 64 km making a crescent shaped territory with an area of 3635 km^2, capital Panjim;
- **Daman** on the western coast of India at the entrance to the Gulf of Cambay about 160 km north of Bombay having a detached settlement of Pargana Nagar Haveli to the east isolated from it by a narrow strip of Indian Territory, and a tiny settlement of Dadra, altogether 213 km^2;
- **Diu** consisted of some territories on the main land, the island of Diu and another island 19 km to the east, Panikota making a total of less than 39 sq km. Diu has a small but excellent harbour.

Sketch: DAMAN, DIU & NAGAR HAVELI

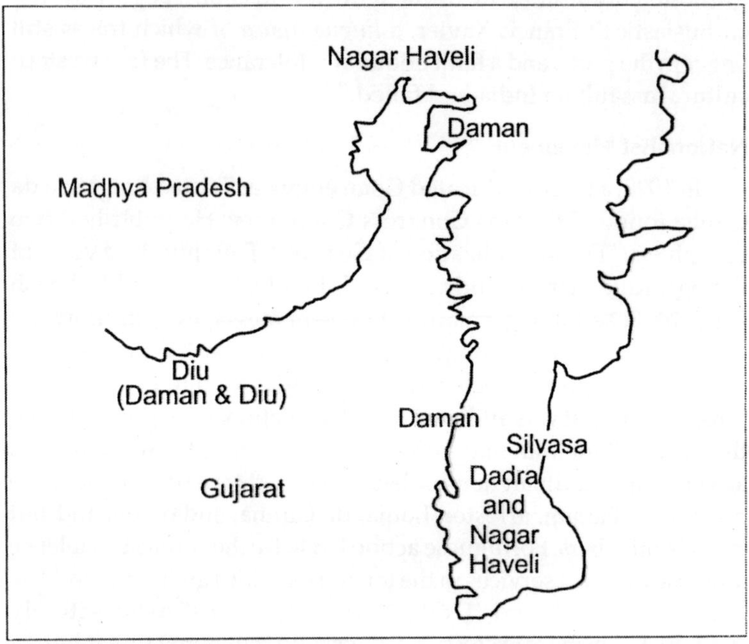

When the Indian Government approached Portugal for a diplomatic solution to the imbroglio, the latter responded that their territory in India was not a colony; it was a part of metropolitan Portugal, and hence its status was not subject to negotiations. Consequently, India withdrew its diplomatic mission from Lisbon on June 11, 1953 and also instituted visa restrictions between Goa and India. Consequently, Portuguese enclaves of Daman, Diu, Dadra and Nagar Haveli were cut off from the Portuguese main base at Goa. This encouraged the Goan nationalists to liberate the detached Portuguese pocket of Dadra, about 160 km north of Bombay on July 21, 1954. This historic event in turn led to another tiny pocket of Portuguese "Eastern Empire", Nagar Haveli, lying east of their enclave of Daman and separated from it by a narrow strip of Indian territory, eleven days later. The liberation of these two otherwise insignificant places was the beginning of the end of Portuguese colonial rule on Indian soil.

The climax to the nationalist movement came on 15th August 1955 when about three to four thousand Indian nationals tried to enter Goa at six locations. Portuguese police used indiscriminate firing to repulse them resulting in heavy casualties, may be nearly thirty or so killed and many wounded. Consequently, India closed down its consulate office on September 01, 1955. However, all through 1956-60 efforts at Indian national and highest International levels including the US President and UN Security Council continued to be made to arrive at a peaceful settlement of the problem, but all in vain. Eventually, it was the Portuguese who provided the spark to ignite the looming war clouds when on 17 November 1961 their garrison in Angediv Island fired upon the Indian passenger steamship Sabarmati, passing in the 1.6 km wide water-channel between the mainland port of Kochi and the Portuguese held island of Angediv, resulting in death of one passenger and injuries to some others including the Chief Engineer of the vessel. Taking the provocation a step further, on night 24/25 November, the same garrison fired on a group of Indian fishermen in about twenty boats killing one person and injuring many more. That was the proverbial last straw that rocked the Portuguese boat. Consequently, on November 27, Indian Navy ordered INS Kirpan and INS Rajput to patrol in the general area of Karwar. Active hostilities appeared imminent.

The Hostilities

Resolution of Angadiv Island incidents could not be considered as the final solution of the festering problem of foreign powers holding on to their colonies on Indian soil. It was not a solitary incident either. The Government of India, therefore, issued instructions to the Army Chief to capture all Portuguese occupied territories for India. The task was assigned to Lieutenant General J.N. Chaudhari (of HPA Fame) General Officer Commanding-in-Chief Southern Army who selected Major General K.P. Candeth, General Officer Commanding the 17 Infantry Division for this mission. Following additional troops were placed under his command:

- 50 Para Brigade;
- 1st Maratha Light Infantry for assault on Daman;
- 20 Rajput and 4 Madras for capture of Diu.

Air Officer Commanding-in-Chief Western Air Command, Air Vice Marshal Eric Pinto was specially assigned the task of commanding all air resources earmarked for operations against the

Portuguese. These were concentrated at the bases in Poona and Sambra while Rear-Admiral B.S. Soman was appointed Theatre Naval Commander.

In the first place, the Indian Naval Task Force comprised of two warships: a destroyer INS *Rajput*, and an anti-submarine frigate INS *Kirpan* were deployed off the coast of Goa. Four Task Groups were assigned for actual assault on Goa:

- Surface Action Group comprising of INSs *Mysore, Trishul, Betwa, Beas* and *Cauvery*;
- Carrier Group based on INSs *Delhi, Kuthar, Kirpan, Khukhri* and *Rajput* centered around the light aircraft carrier INSVikrant;
- Mine Sweeping Group comprising of INSs *Karwar, Kakinada, Cannonore* and *Bimilipatan*;
- The naval contingent had the support of *Dharini*

Indian economic blockade of Goa began in 1954. When Indian invasion took place, the Portuguese had one Navy sloop NRP *Alfonso de Albuquerque* armed with four 120mm guns, four rapid firing guns, five merchant navy ships, three light patrol boats each armed with a 20 mm Oerlikon gun. Portuguese ground forces consisted of 3995 men including 810 native soldiers who were more of a paramilitary security force than an army contingent. The police force consisted of 1040 personnel besides 400 border guards—the latter were divided amongst the three enclaves. Mines, ammunition and communication equipment were woefully short in quantity and quality. The defence strategy was centered around *Plano Sentinela* that naturally divided Goa into four sectors—quite a formidable force to resist the Indian might!

The situation of Portuguese air force and air defences was in pathetic state. There were two transport aircrafts, both belonging to one or the other airlines; Air defence was limited to some obsolete anti-aircraft guns manned by gunners who had been smuggled into Goa disguised as soccer teams. Deceit was a dominant characteristic of Portuguese.

During mid December the Lisbon Government ordered that relics of patron saint of Goa, St Francis Xavier, be transferred to home country for preservation for posterity lest the same be damaged during the hostilities. Of course they knew very well what was in store for them. To cap it all orders were also issued to destroy all buildings of non-military heritage. However, the Governor, Vassalo e Silva did not comply regarding the Administrative Headquarters housed in Idalcao Palace in Panjim on the grounds that the evidence of Portuguese greatness in the Orient must be preserved.

In the face of all the foregoing evidence, and much against the sane advice of many senior defence services officers including the Defence Minister General Moniz Salazar, on 14 December 1961 the Prime Minister ordered the Governor General Vassalo e Silva ordered the Portuguese forces in Goa to fight till the last man, and not to surrender at any cost—a mission of self-inflicted suicide indeed, if ever there was any! He did so in the hope that the Goan forces would be able to hold out for at least eight days during which the Prime Minister would be able to garner international support against the Indian Invasion of Portuguese metropolitan sovereign territory.

The concept of 'Op Vijay'

- Initial objective: Mapuca-Bicholim-Sanquelin-Ponda-Margoa. Final Objectives: Velha Goa-Panjim-Mormugoa;
- Air Force to achieve air superiority, Dabolim airfield to be made unusable through air action;
- Destruction of wireless station at Bambolim—Goa's only direct link to Lisbon;
- Indian Navy to neutralize enemy's coastal batteries, blockade ports of Mormugoa, Panjim and Daman to ensure that no Portuguese ships, naval or merchant, entered or escaped from these ports;
- 1 Maratha Battalion Group to enter Daman via Vapi, capture airfield and the town (limited air support provided);
- 20 Rajput to enter Diu by crossing the narrow tidal creek separating Diu from the mainland at night on improvised rafts, capture airfield, the fort and the town (limited air support provided). For this part of the operation INS Delhi to provide close naval support during day light hours besides one company of 4 Madras to provide fire support from Gogla by capturing it one hour before assault crossing by 20 Rajput;
- Capture of Angediv Island entrusted exclusively to the Navy;
- Belgaum to be railhead, airhead and site of Tac HQ Southern

Command where Lieutenant General J.N. Chaudhuri and Air Vice Marshal Eric Pinto were located, besides the Civil Affairs Officer Shri Noronha and DIG Nagoo.

Before going on with the account of multi-pronged Indian advance into Goa and capture of its capital Panjim, I shall first deal with the spark that ignited the fireworks.

Map: ANGEDIV ISLAND

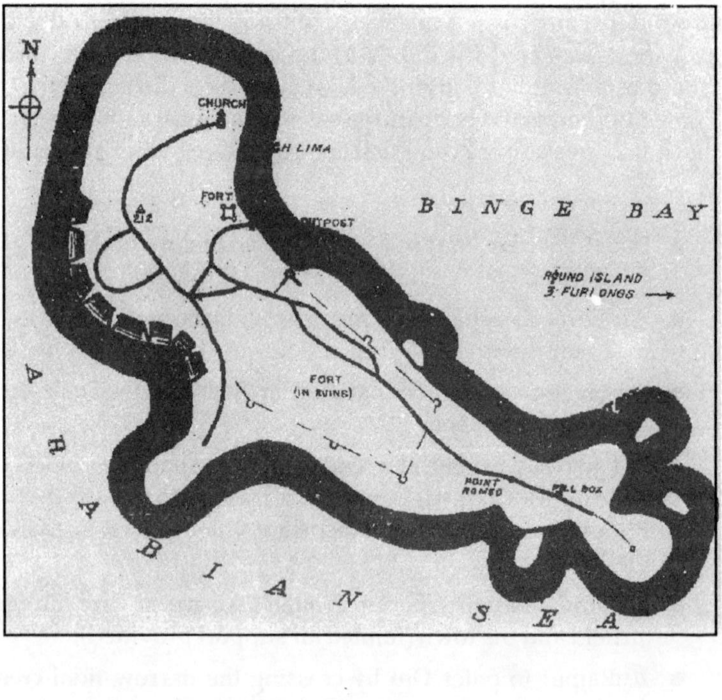

Angediv is a small island barely 1.6 km in length and 0.3 km from east to west situated south-west of Karwar on the west coast of India. Vasco de Gama visited the island in AD 1498 and again in 1502-03 when he made it into a base of operations. A fortress was built during the period of Vice-Rei D. Francisco de Almeida, it was the first fort built by the Portuguese on Indian soil.

Capture of the Island was entrusted to a Naval Task Force initially organized into 'Surface Action Group' consisting of one cruiser (*Mysore*) three frigates (*Betwa, Beas* and *Trishul*) and 'Carrier Task Group' (*Vikrant, frigates Khukri, Kuthar* and *Kirpan,* and destroyer *Rajput*) under command of Rear Admiral B.S. Soman. A minesweeping force comprising of INSs *Karwar, Cannanore* and Bimlipattam was on call. Cruiser INS *Delhi* initially allotted to 'Carrier Task Group' was taken off and reallocated to support ground attack on Dui at H- Hour on D-Day. It will thus be seen that ships of Indian fleet were required to participate in operations against all the three different places – Angadiv, Goa, and Diu. In other words, major part of Op Vijay was entrusted to the Army (attack on Goa) while Air Force was to play a deciding role in Daman and Diu. Angediv was Navy's exclusive baby, a hard nut to crack as it turned out to be.

The task assigned to INSs *Mysore* and *Trishul*: Physical occupation of Angediv Island as early as possible. *Trishul* rounded the North Point and was in position on the west side. It was noticed that no flags were flying on either of the two flagstaffs on the Island. At about 0700 hrs she lowered her boats in which two sections of the assault party were embarked. Meanwhile *Mysore* was in position on the east of the Island and fired her Bofors guns around 0700 hrs November 18 on suspected pillboxes at a range of nearly 2.7 km. *Trishul* also fired her Bofors at close range while the first assault wave was on its way to the beach. The second wave left soon thereafter but *Trishul* could not give it covering fire since the first wave was already on the beach and was moving ahead. When the second wave was about 150 yards from the beach, the Portuguese hoisted a white flag in front of a church. However, within minutes one of the gun positions on hilltop opened fire on the second wave causing casualties. Nonetheless, the assault boats though holed and damaged pressed on while *Trishul* fired her Bofors on some white soldiers taking position near the white flag. Firing after raising white flag was a treacherous act for which the Portuguese soldiers had no compunction, albeit it was bitter experience for our sailors. Our Marines stormed the island, the defenders raised white flags, The marines were lured by this deceitful mean activity and suffered – seven marines killed and 19 wounded including two officers. *Mysore* did not give covering fire at this crucial moment since the Captain refused permission for direct firing reasoning that only indirect firing was permitted as per orders from higher ups. At this some young officers, notwithstanding the threat of court martial, barged into the Bofors gun area and gave covering fire to the beleaguered second wave thereby saving many precious lives. The casualties were evacuated to Mysore. The Systemic Failures of the senior officer(s) were neutralized by the zeal and initiative of the younger officers!

The southern slopes of the hill had been cleared of enemy but the assault on northern portion was held at bay by strong opposition. *Trishul* therefore fired some more salvos at north point and plastered the northern hill as well as another nearby hillock taking care not to hit any church or any place of worship. Since no further progress could be made in the face of strong enemy opposition, both landing parties were withdrawn. The next day, November 19, *Mysore* bombarded the hillocks from the southwest while *Trishul* brought down heavy fire from the southeast. Soon nine white Portuguese were spotted under the white flag hoisted on the flagstaff. They had their hands raised over their heads and one of them was waving a white flag also. The first landing party was therefore ordered to take charge of these prisoners and those on the nearby beaches and bring them over to *Mysore*. Subsequently, the entire area was thoroughly searched and national flag hoisted on Angediv Island in the afternoon of November 19, 1961.

Indian casualties in this particular operation were:

- Killed: 7 Sailors;
- Wounded: Officers 2, Sailors 17; Total: 26.

Portuguese casualties:

- Killed: 1 officer, 6 soldiers;
- Wounded: 4 soldiers; Total 11.

Air War

According to usual military procedures the Indian action commenced on December 01 with active patrolling-reconnaissance in force of the coast line by frigates INS Betwa and INS Beas while aircraft carrier INS Vikrant was deployed as a precautionary measure. This naval activity was followed a week later by IAF to assess Portuguese air defence system. There was none! However, a vampire night fighter flying over Dabolim airport was met with five rounds of anti-aircraft guns which were soon put out of action.

The mandate to Air Vice Marshal Eric Pinto:

- Destruction of runway of Goa's only airfield Dabolim, but without damaging the terminal building and allied facilities;

- Destruction of wireless station at Bambolin;
- Denial of airfields at Daman and Diu (but not to be attacked);
- Support advancing ground troops.

Using small and light Canberra bombers, IAF dropped 63,000 pounds bombs on Dabolim runway putting it out of action on December 18. A second raid caused further damage to the runway, However, patch repairs by local labour cleared about 700 meters of the runway at night and the only two passenger aircraft which constituted the Portuguese 'air force' managed to evacuate families of some senior civil and military officials to Pakistan. They had to jettison a lot of non-essentials and suffer damage to the fuselage besides a burst tire on way to Karachi. The IAF refrained from firing at the civil passenger aircraft. Meanwhile, the wireless station was put out of action by Hawker Hunters. There was no interference by enemy action while the IAF was acting in support of advancing ground troops. However, in one case of friendly fire, two Sikh soldiers were wounded while another friendly fire caused nominal damage to one de Havilland Vampire. Score equaled!

Map: DIU OPERATIONS

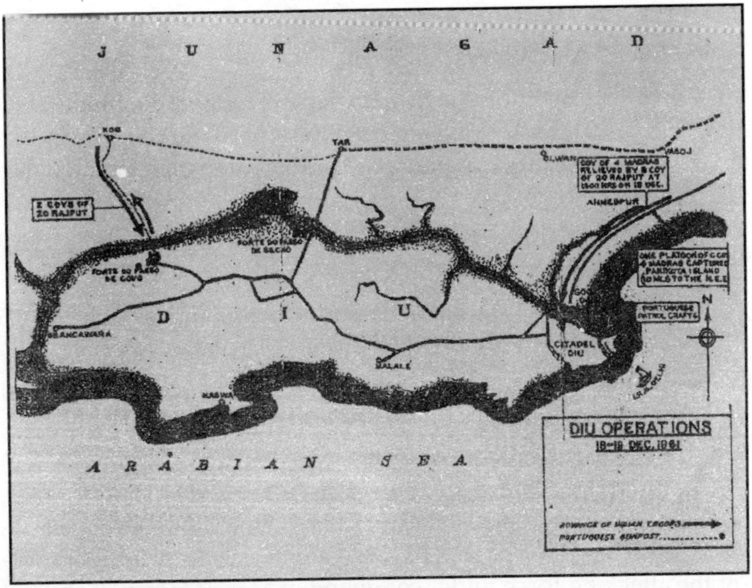

18th December was indeed the D-Day for all Portuguese settlements. Daman's artillery positions were continuously harassed by Mysteres while Diu had more than its fare share of air action. ATC of Diu airfield and Diu Fort were destroyed in the morning. Its fortifications facing the mainland were destroyed and throughout the D-one at least two aircrafts were all the time in the air over Diu in close support of the assaulting infantry. Anti-aircraft units were soon silenced and before noon the people were seen waving white flags. Further air action was called off.

Ground Forces

Troops to Tasks:

- **Goa:**
  - 17 Infantry Division less one brigade;
  - 50 Independent Para Brigade less one battalion under command 17 Infantry Division;
  - 2 Sikh LI under 50 Para Brigade;
  - 7 Cavalry less one squadron under 50 Para Brigade; (in addition to Division's own Armor Regiment)
  - 24 Medium Artillery Regiment;
  - 74 Mountain Battery;
  - 3 Air Observation Flight;
  - In addition to Division's own Engineer Regiment, HQ 20 Infantry Division Engineers, two field companies, one field park company, two bridge companies maintenance platoon;
  - And other assorted Army Troops, Signals, and service units.
- **Daman:** 1 Maratha with under command an ad hoc 25 pounder battery ex Artillery School, Deolali.
- **Diu:** 20 Rajput and one company of 4 Madras under command of a brigadier.

It had been decided that all the three Portuguese enclaves will be captured simultaneously. Therefore D-Day and H-Hour for Goa, Daman and Diu was exactly the same – First light December 18, 1961 (05:15 hrs). The capital of Goa, Panjim was the prime objective of the attacking force under command of Major General Candeth,

GOC 17 Infantry Division. Three thrusts were undertaken for entry into Goa:

- Major thrust was made by the main force of the Division less one brigade from the east along route Anmod-Molem-Ponda, an all weather macadam surfaced road running through the countryside provided fast easy access to both armour and wheeled vehicles. The ground was suitable for armour operations even though the first few kilometers were somewhat hilly. Moreover, the two river crossings on this axis of advance were comparatively easier.
- A subsidiary entry was made from the north along Dodamarg-Assonora-Bicholim by troops of 50 Independent Para Brigade. The plan of advance included the possibility of diversion westward towards Mapuca and thence onwards to Betim in the south. This route like the eastern one was capable of taking a brigade group worth of troops.
- Since strategic surprise was not at all possible, deception measure included a feint entry by an infantry company, nicknamed 20 Infantry Brigade, from the south along route Karwar-Majali-Canacona – the intention being to make the enemy believe that another brigade worth of troops was entering from the south so as to draw some forces away from the eastern and northern routes of entry. This decoy force was to operate directly under HQ Southern Command.
- Speed was the essence of this operation. The possibility of Portuguese destroying the civil infrastructure facilities, massacre of Indian and Goan nationals could not be ruled out, besides a reference to UN Security Council which might lead to a premature ceasefire order.

On the northern axis a company level patrol was sent out on night 17/18 December to ascertain if the RCC Bridge down the road was intact. The Portuguese had demolished the bridge at 05:00 am just in the nick of time. The Portuguese got the information about the impending border-crossing by Indian troops from a night broadcast over the All India Radio! The demolition of the RCC and steel bridge beside it considerably delayed the advance on the northern route. Unfortunate, but there it is ... Another patrol on the same axis was assigned the task of occupying three villages to facilitate move forward of advance guard. While the first two villages were captured without any resistance, the third was a well prepared defensive position held by an infantry platoon supported by a troop of Portuguese armoured cars. One armoured car and a few trucks were knocked out. The Portuguese suffered : 3 killed, 2 wounded and 24 captured while we lost one NCO. Advance on this axis started at H-Hour by 2 Sikh and 1 Para (Punjab) on different routes. Both Battalions raced forward to have the honour of entering Panjim first. That was the spirit and morale of Indian troops liberating part of their motherland!

The leading troops (A Squadron 7 Cavalry) reached Bantam early in the evening around 5 pm from where the capital Panjim was barely 5-600 meters away across River Mandavi. Squadron commander of 7 Cavalry fired a few shots. The Portuguese lowered their flag in front of the Governor-General's Secretariat and hoisted a white flag instead. So it was the subsidiary thrust that reached the vicinity of the objective first! But the armour could not cross the river on its own steam and went into night harbour. Around 08:00 pm a priest from Panjim came in a boat to the Squadron's night harbour with a letter of surrender written in Portuguese. Meanwhile 2 Sikh LI column reached Bentim around 06:00 pm, just an hour behind the armor. The Squadron Commander Major Sidhu took the letter to Lieutenant Colonel Cherian Commanding 2 Sikh LI. However, although the Colonel wanted to cross the Mandvi and grab the honour of being the first to reach Panjim, as luck would have it, he did not have the orders to do so, all efforts to contact the Brigade Commander having failed. So he declined to order crossing to accept the surrender of Panjim. Perhaps, a Colonel was considered too low a rank to accept surrender of a colonial power!

It is beyond my comprehension why such protocol should come in the way of successful completion of a fast moving operation where speed is the essence, and has been officially so stated. Every opportunity to confront the enemy must be grabbed immediately. But it did not make any substantial difference in the present case. Fortunately, General Chaudhury had passed direct order to 50 Para Brigade that the leading battalions should get into Panjim as quickly as possible. 2 Sikh LI was all set to do the honours. Armor, Artillery guns and mortars were deployed to cover the crossing and two companies of Sikh LI went across to Panjim around 07:30 am, their objectives being Police HQs, Customs House, Governor General's Palace, Secretariat and the Military Camp. There was practically no resistance from the Portuguese side who had no will to fight a doomed battle in any case. Portuguese General Manuel Antonio Vassalo e Silva, C-in-C of Armed Forces of "Portuguese State of India" unconditionally surrendered to Brigadier KS Dhillon, Commander 63 Infantry Brigade at 08:30 pm on December 19, 1961.

Daman and Diu had already surrendered during early part of the day. It was all over within 40 hours!!

Casualties

The Portuguese casualties were:

- **Killed:** 2 officers, 16 soldiers;
- **Wounded:** 11 soldiers; total 29,
- **Prisoners:**

❖ Officers:	24
❖ Soldiers	568
❖ Police	9
❖ Local Police	268
❖ Portuguese civilians:	8
Total :	**906**

Indian Casualties:

- **Killed:** 2 officers, 1 JCO, 3 OR and 7 Sailors
- **Wounded:** 2 officers, 1 JCO, 15 OR and 17 Sailors;

Total 48

(Portuguese and Indian casualties in other sectors have not been reflected here.)

Aftermath

Consequent on the capitulation of Portugal on issue of their Indian enclaves, the India External Affairs Minister Mr. Y.B. Chavan and the Portuguese Minister of External Affairs, Dr. Mario Soares, signed at New Delhi on December 31, 1974 a Treaty on "recognition of India's sovereignty over Goa, Daman, Diu, Dadra and Nagar Haveli" and related matters. Diplomatic relations between the two countries which had been broken off in 1955 were re-established. Both parties believed that the Treaty buried twenty-years of conflict and established a basis for friendly relations and cooperation by the exchange of delegations in economic, technical and cultural spheres.

SECTION-III

11

THE ENCHANTING NORTHEAST

NORTHEAST INDIA AND BANGLADESH
BHUTAN AND ARUNACHAL PRADESH

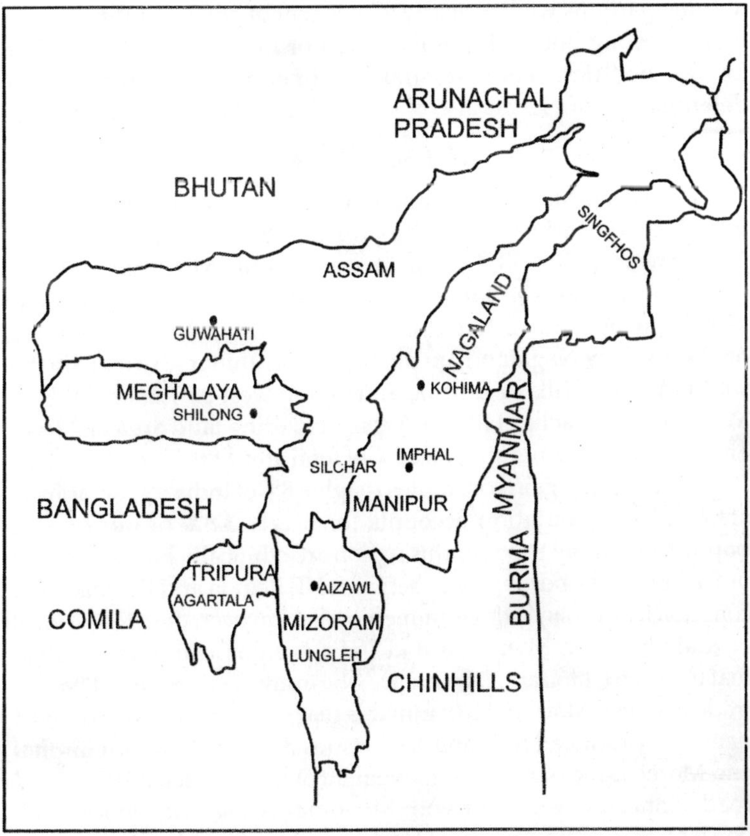

Having spent nearly two decades of my early youth in the Northeastern region of India, I can safely vouch for its fascinating natural beauty, rich cultural heritage, ethnic and linguistic diversity, richness in natural mineral resources awaiting to be tapped for economic advancement of the tribal communities that go to form the eight distinct states of the region. The colourful people of the region, particularly their womenfolk, charming and always smiling, willingly and voluntarily saying a sort of hello in the American style, has been a pleasure par excellence. Their colourful enchanting dances in equally varied and colourful dresses, different in every one of the eight states, are a treat to watch. Indeed, we in the rest of India should be proud of being blessed with such populace in our midst, notwithstanding the past and somewhat still active insurgency in some parts, as well as nearly 98 per cent of border of this unique region resting not with the mainland of India but with different foreign countries. Therefore, strategic importance of the region from defense point of view is also of special interest to a military man.

11-1 MANIPUR

The name 'Manipur' ('Land of Gems') is of recent origin, first introduced in early 18th Century during the reign of Hindu King Garibniwaz (1709-48)[1] when it was called 'Meetteileipak' or 'Kangleipak'. But the kingdom is indeed far more ancient. It is situated in the southeastern corner of Northeastern India – bounded on the north by Nagaland, on the east by Myanmar (Burma), on the south by Chin Hills of Burma, and on the west by Lushai Hills of Mizoram and Cachar Hills of Assam, covering land area of 22,327 km^2 which represents about 8.52% of total area of the North Eastern Region. The NE region constitutes roughly 8% of India's geographical area and its population accounts for nearly 3.8% of our overall population. Many tribes of this region are ethnically linked to those of Burma. Cross-border trade between NE Region and Burma was a common feature since times immemorial. However, the present level of trade between Myanmar and India is significantly lower than that between China and Myanmar.[2] The irony of this so called border trade between Manipur-Myanmar is that none of the Indian export items are produced in Manipur, besides the road between Imphal and Moreh is too narrow for movement of heavy truck traffic. Good road connecting Manipur with Myanmar is *sine qua non* for cross border trade for prosperity of land-locked ancient Manipur State.

The valley of Manipur, a plain area is at the center stage of the state while the remainder 90% of the land mass is the thickly forested hills surrounding the valley. It is a strategically located sensitive frontier state having 352 km long international border with Burma. Foreigners required special permission to enter the State and that too only by air to Imphal, and restricted to the capital only for a maximum of mere ten days. It is of interest to note that the four NE regions provide India with a 'unique access' towards Southeast Asia and Indo-China. It has a common border with Bangladesh, Bhutan, Burma, China and Nepal for a length of 1500 km leaving barely 20 km with the mainland of the home country. A paradoxical situation indeed! The NE states of Manipur, Mizoram, Arunachal Pradesh and Nagaland share 1463 km long border with Burma leaving a mere 2% with the rest of Indian land mass! In addition, Arunachal Pradesh also has a long border with Burma. Is there any justification for this 2% physical connection to tie it down with the socio-cultural-economic-political ethos of rest of 98% land mass for mere theoretical satisfaction? – I certainly don't mean to advocate separation or disintegration; but I do mean a pragmatic approach to emotional integration. After all, relationships between the Burma, Meitei and Ahom Kingdoms were determined primarily by this geographical configuration. The transformation came about only after the British Indian Empire emphasized its geo-strategic concerns in the frontier region and promulgated colonial restrictions for movements across these frontiers.[3]

Manipur is divided into nine districts with its capital at Imphal having an airport named Tulihal. The valley is divided into five districts while the hills constitute remaining four. The population is predominantly Mongoloid. They speak Tibeto-Burman languages. However, the *lingua franca* of the State is the mother tongue of the Valley people, the Meitei's. According to 2001 Census the State population was 22, 93,896 with low density of 107 per sq km against national average of 324 and constituted about 6% of North-East population. The state is multi-ethnic having three tribes: Meitei in the valley, Nagas, Kuki and Chin tribes in the hills, the latter two tribes speak different languages/dialects (Tibeto-Burman) while the Meitei' language, Meiteilon is Sanskritized.

Land Reforms are another sore point with the masses. Political manipulations and vote-bank-politics have ensured that bulk of the land ownership remains concentrated in the hands of rich landlords depriving the poor tillers of the land of their rights of ownership. They continue to work for the rich on subsistence levels of wages. For instance: Small and marginal farmers own barely 24%of the arable land even though they constitute over 70% of landowners. On the other hand, their rich masters, 30% of the populace, own 76% land. Absentee landlordism is the order of the day. And our National Congress with a socialist agenda claims high success rate in land reforms Height of injustice indeed! And how do they manage this? You know it as well as I do ... Corruption and manipulation at the higher or the highest levels is the crux of the problem. But that is not all. The poor farmers are perpetually under debt, under tight clutches of money-squeezing clever money-lenders forcing many debt ridden farmers to resort to suicide to escape harassment. Indeed very fertile ground for insurgency and violent Naxalite movements.

Historical Background

The ancient history of Manipur goes as far back as the Tang Dynasty of "Qi" tribe of Central China. However, after 18 BC the story is totally blank when for about 700 years there was no ruler as such, and the region came to be called "Tai-Pang-Pan". The history of Manipur thereafter takes shape in AD 33 when a ruling dynasty came into being. It was a period of stability. In the text of Treaty between East India Company and King Jai Singh the name of the Kingdom is stated as 'Meckley' but the coins issued by Jai Singh and his successors mention the name as 'Manipureshwar'= "Lord of Manipur". In other words during the 18th Century the Kingdom was known by three different names: Mekhala, Meckley and Manipur.

Manipur remained a totally independent Sovereign State in its own right except for the period of seven years during 1819-26 when it was under occupation of Burmese forces. The same Dynasty continued to rule till as late as 1891 when the sovereign State came under British rule consequent of Anglo-Manipur War of 1891. It is noteworthy that the Manipur King signed the first Anglo-Manipur Treaty with the British in 1762 primarily to guard against the growing Burmese menace. Jai Singh became the king after a series of conspiracies hatched by the members of the royal family including one to murder King Garibniwaz by his own son Ajit Singh. Subsequently, British attempted to neutralize the Burmese threat in the North-East by launching a military expedition which failed completely[4].

While Manipur was under British hegemony, the Maharaja continued to rule unhindered. It was a peaceful state where rule of law prevailed equally for one and all, with some exceptions borne out of idiosyncrasies of the Maharaja and his personal ego-problems, but otherwise there were hardly any aberrations. The Meitei were a highly religious community, they still are. Vaishnava precepts were strictly observed in the valley. Cow slaughter was strictly prohibited, so was liquor for the Hindu Meitei. The ban on cow slaughter was strict that when the Viceroy's request personally conveyed through the then Governor of Assam, Sir Andrew Clow, in 1942 to permit cow slaughter towards war effort during Second World War, Maharaja Bodhchandra Singh flatly refused permission.[5] The British were far more pragmatic than our political leaders and did not bulldoze their way through.

The Meitei are essentially a very religious and orthodox community. They would not eat food cooked by outsiders and school boys used to take bath before having lunch. The women were required to cover their heads in the presence of the Maharaja. By virtue of its unique historical past the people of Manipur used to follow several faiths. During pre-historic period the early Manipuris were devotees of a Supreme deity "Lainingthou Soralel". This form of religion focused on animism and ancestor-worship, as used to be the practice amongst many other tribes of the North East. A number of local gods (*Lais*) were so worshipped. This phase gave way to Manipur's ancient indigenous religion that was known as Sanamahi. It was rich in mythology and colourful rituals. This religion believed in one God, Sidaba Mapu worshipped by one and all. Copper plates dating back to AD 763-773 issued during the rule of King Khomtekcha bear testimony to worship of Sidaba Mapu.[6] Hinduism came next. It has a long tradition in Manipur. With the passage of time and development, a qualitative change took place during the reigns of Kings Kyamba and Khgemba in the 15th Century when Vaishnavism penetrated Manipur. A strong wave of Gaudiya Vaishnavism from Bengal swept the valley in the 18th Century which transformed the socio-religious life besides accentuating the ethnic divide. Since the rest of the tribal population continued to follow their traditional religious beliefs and practices. In the process, Meitei were no longer a tribal community, Hinduism thus took roots in the spiritual soil of Manipur.

Treaty of Yandabod[7]

Sometime during early 1820's Burmese incursions in Cachar region of Assam led to worsening of relations between British India and Burma. In 1824 the Burmese even raised their flag on Shahpur Island. They also demanded withdrawal of Company of troops from the Island. This provided the impetus for the British to raise a local armed levy of Manipuris with a view to establishing an independent state of Manipur to act as an effective buffer between Burma and British Indian possessions. The 500-strong native force was to be under command of Gambhir Singh, a Prince of Manipur.

The worsening situation with Burma led to the first Anglo-Burmese War of 1825 that ended with signing of Treaty of Yandabod on February 24, 1826. Article 2 of the Treaty provided: "should Gambhir Singh desire to return to that country (Manipur) he shall be recognized by the King of Ava as the Raja thereof." Consequently, Manipur became an independent State, to act as a buffer-screen between the Burmese and the British Northeastern territories, more so since Burma and Manipur were already hard core enemies. On the face of it, this Treaty appeared to be harbinger of peace between British India and Burma. But that was not to be. Yandabod was followed by two more Anglo-Burma wars that ended the constant turmoil in 1886 with the annexation of Burma in British-Indian Empire. Interesting and unexpected fallout of Yandabod was the Jiri Treaty of 1833 that represented an instrument for exchange of territory, besides multi-benefits of trade and defense-alliance between Manipur and the Government of East India Company, as well as demarcation of the boundary between Cachar and Manipur. Since then River Jiri and the western bend of Barak River have come to be accepted as the inter-state boundary.

In the same vein I might as well cover here the vexed question (1834) of status of Kabo Valley which, after defeat of Burmese forces became part of Manipur State by virtue of conquest when Raja Gambhir Singh pushed the Burmese forces beyond Ningthee River (Chindwin) in 1826. The Burmese Government nursed a deep long standing grievances on account of this loss of a strategic territory. Consequently, Burmese continued their pursuit operations but without success. Concurrently, the British were keen on making their ports at Pegu and Shahpuree safe from Burmese hostile incursions. Towards this end in view, the Governor General-in-Council decided to hand over Kabo Valley to Burma as a mark of 'expediency and gratification'. Consequently, Kabo Valley was transferred to Burma effective January 09, 1834 for which the Government of Manipur was to be paid a compensation of 500 Sicca Rupees, not by the beneficiary (Burma) but by the British![8] That is all part of diplomatic-political manipulations!

Turmoil in Manipur Palace

The question of succession to the throne of Manipur during the seven years period, 1844-51 gave rise to a number of complications. The British Government did not interfere in the internal feuds of various claimants, nor did the British declare Manipur as a British Protectorate despite a specific request from the Maharaja of the State. To cap it all, Maharaja Chandrakirti died in 1886. He had eight sons, the eldest of them Suchandra Singh succeeded his father to the throne. With eight claimants to the throne serious trouble was waiting in the wings. The eight princes got into a fight, four on each side, resulting in a palace revolution. The ruling Maharaja made a pretence of abdicating in favour of the next eldest brother Kullachandra Singh who was head of the opposite group. Accordingly, the new Maharaja ascended the throne and appointed the former Senapati, the head of the revolt, as the new Yuvraj.

On reaching Calcutta Suchandra Singh complained to the Government of India that he had been forcibly removed from the throne by his younger brothers, and sought help of the British to restore him to the Kingship. Accordingly, a report was called for from the Political Agent from which it was concluded that Suchandra Singh was unfit to be restored to the throne, and therefore Kullachandra Singh be recognized as the ruling King of Manipur. It was also decided that the leader of the revolt should be deported. The British Government instructed Mr. Quinton, the Chief Commissioner of Assam to implement these decisions. He reached Imphal with a force in March 1891. On the refusal of the Raja to surrender to Tikenderjit Singh, the force launched a night attack on the palace. The Manipur forces were defeated and the British took over the administration of the state on April 27, 1891. However, the Viceroy Lord Lansdowne decided not to annex the state and issued a *Sanad* recognizing Churachand Singh, a minor from the royal family as the Raja. Nonetheless for all practical purposes Manipur lost its independence in 1891. The sovereignty of the Monarchy was no longer in vogue. The transfer of power to the natives was only nominal, which remained centralized in the hands of the Chief Commissioner and his British officers without any accountability to the people or the Maharaja of the state – a negative political change from the peoples' government to a bureaucratic government. The first set of reforms affected by them was replacement of system of *lallup* (forced labour) in April 1892 by house tax @ Rs. 2 per annum in the valley and Rs. 3/- in the hills. Payment of land tax in kind was replaced by a uniform land tax of Rs. 5 per *pari* (2.5 acres). Raja Churachand Singh attained majority in 1907 but he had no authority in administration of the state. However, the Maharaja continued to exercise considerable influence in religious affairs. He was head of the Brahma Sabha and collected unlawful levy from the people of the valley, mostly Hindus. Since the Brahmins were supreme in socio-religious matters they misused their position to exploit the people at large. All religious rites and ceremonies—birth, death, marriage, laying foundation stones, construction, *et al,* could be performed only through the medium of the Brahmins. The Maharaja was on the side of the Brahmins and that made him unpopular with the educated elite. [9]

The period 1891-1947 is replete with anti-British movements some of which were also anti-feudal at the same time:

- Women's War 1904;
- Kuki Rebellion 1917-20;
- Zadonang Movement 1905-31;
- Women's War II 1939, popularly known as Nupi Lal.

India became independent in 1947, so did Manipur when Manipur Constitution Act 1947 was promulgated. Manipur Assembly was formed representing the valley and the hill districts. Constitutional Monarchy was thus established with Maharaja Kumar Priyobarta as the Chief Minister. This process of democratic reforms came to a sudden halt when the Maharaja was called to Shillong by the Governor of Assam for consultations. He was forced to sign the agreement for merger of Manipur State in the Dominion of India on September 21, 1949 and the State was relegated to the status of a Part 'C' state under the Constitution of India. (The State had already been forcefully merged in the Dominion of India on October 15 1949) Needless to say that the people of the State had never been consulted before the merger agreement was signed at Shillong. Manipur was conferred the status of a Union territory of

India in 1956 and became a full-fledged State on January 21, 1972. By then ethnic conflicts and insurgency were rampant in the State. A case of too little too late—the usual failing of Indian Polity, a legacy of Nehru-Gandhi Dynasty!

In 1991, a radical new element was introduced in India's foreign policy by the then Prime Minister, late P.V. Narasimha Rao. It was designated as "Look East Policy" (LEP). It took some time for the new doctrine, which involved much closer interaction with our neighbours in East Asia and South East Asia in economic, diplomatic and developmental fields besides building communication infrastructures like rail-road communications facilities, to take roots. The third Indo-ASEAN summit was scheduled in Laos to push forward in that direction. The first Indo-ASEAN Car Rally flagged off at Guwahati on 22nd November 2004 by our Prime Minister Manmohan Singh added a new dimension to LEP. The rally passed through Manipur on 24th November 2004 bringing some ray of hope to the people of this far off frontier state for better economic prospects by way of trade, tourism, economic development. But that was just a passing phase only. While there is talk about Manipur being integrated with 1,360 km Trans-Asian Highway Project linking India-Myanmar-Thailand in Phase I. The next phase will link with Indo-China. Inclusion integration of Manipur in the rail map of India is well on the cards and hopefully will not remain a pipe dream. It is not clear how and when these dreams are going to materialize. Despondency and consequent insurgency, particularly in respect of 'Nagalim' continue unabated.[10]

Shortage of electric power has been a constant bane of Manipur ever since it lost its independence in the wake of expansion of British Empire. No worthwhile projects were initiated under the Colonial regime with the result that Manipur has remained a non-industrialized region with agrarian economy as the basis for its sustenance. The New Industrial Policy announced in 2003 envisaged construction of Tipaimulh Hydro-Electric Project, Loktak Downstream Hydro-Electric Project, and the Irang HE Project. Unfortunately, these projects either remain partially complete or totally incomplete. Either way, benefits of these projects have not reached the villages while large areas of their arable lands have been submerged. The poor farmers are neither here nor there! And Naga insurgency continues to take a heavy toll. The burden of economic deprivation continues to exact its heavy toll.

GENESIS OF INSURGENCY

The root cause of the insurgency in the first place was a simple request by a citizen of Manipur, a Naga separatist leader, General Secretary of National Socialist Council[11] of Nagalim (Isak-Muivah) [NSCN-IM], **Thuingaleng Muivah** to visit his native village, Somdal in Manipur. Under the constitution of India he had every right to visit his home and people. But permission was denied by Chief Minister Ibobo Singh who headed the Secular Progressive Front (SPF) Government in Manipur state on grounds of security. This was in the first week of May 2010. It is understandable that the proposed visit was politically motivated. However, notwithstanding the political considerations of Naga demand for a separate independent the state, that consideration by itself cannot be accepted as the reason to deny a citizen legitimate right to visit his home village. And as for Manipur, the situation had not taken a turn for the worst at that point of time. All said and done, the visit could have been allowed to go through with necessary security guards of Manipur in attendance, besides other precautionary measures.

As it was, the blockade of National Highway 53 connecting Imphal with the plains of Assam via Kohima had been started on April 11, 2010. It was initially organized by some students and other organizations as a protest against proposed elections to Manipur Hill Areas Autonomous District Councils (ADC) under the aegis of Ibobo Singh Government. But Mr. Muivah was not connected to that blockade. That is all the more reason why there was no justification for denial of permission to him to visit his birth place. But within hours of denial of permission the NSCN-IM also joined the blockade thereby further worsening the overall situation. Had Chief Minister Ibobo Singh been more discreet and pragmatic, it is well on the cards that insurgency in Manipur may not have taken the intensity and ferocity that it did. This was a major failing of Indian Polity in handling a sensitive issue in an equally sensitive frontier strategic State. Even if the State Chief Minister was not amenable to the visit, why did the Governor of Assam and the Central Government not have the foresight to gauge the consequences! A serious blunder on the part of all concerned!

Perhaps, the simplest course would have been for the Governor or the center to place a helicopter at the disposal of Mr. Muivah and accord him a suitable welcome on arrival at his village, a lost brother back home at last! Political immaturity of the highest order, to say the least! In this unfortunate imbroglio Ibobi and Muivah have emerged as powerful leaders of Meitei and Naga nationalism so much so that they openly and uninterruptedly run parallel governments in their respective regions of influence. The Indian Polity continued to be mute spectator to extortion and other illegal activities by these leading lights of the North East. Just to quote one instance: Notwithstanding the presence of army and paramilitary forces in the region controlled by Muivah, 780 Kukis were killed in the ethnic violence that erupted in 1992-93, and Muivah is believed to be the master mind behind this massacre.

A large number of Naga political outfits subscribe to secessionist ideology. They have been demanding a separate independent sovereign state of Nagaland, NAGALIM to be more precise. The proposed State would include all tribes of Naga ethnicity in Nagaland, Arunachal Pradesh, Manipur, Burma, Mizoram, and the adjoining areas into one composite Naga State—on the same lines as the Khalistani movement did in Punjab. Here it is noteworthy that NSCN-IM is much smaller and weaker organization, mostly restricted to geographical area of Manipur Hills; NSCN (Khaplang) and NSCN (Unification) are much stronger outfits operating for the same cause besides some other smaller groups. However, Naga Hoho is the apex body of Naga Tribal Organizations.[12] Some foreign based organizations, generally supported by Christian Church leaders provide moral and financial support besides armaments and safe passage-sanctuaries. Unfortunately, the Central Government has not been able to take Naga Hoho into confidence—yet another example of failure of Indian Polity.

Indo Naga Ceasefire

An equally serious contributory factor that fanned the fires of insurgency in Manipur was the extension of territorial limits of Indo-Naga Ceasefire to Manipur under orders of the Central Government. The people of Manipur took exception to this uncalled for step. Large scale protests and violent demonstrations led to police firing resulting in death of 18 persons on June 18, 2001. The Government of Manipur declared June 18 as the "Manipur Integrity Day". A memorial was built at the site, Kekrupat, in honour of the martyrs. The prolonged agitations and demonstrations provided a pretext to United Naga Council (UNC) to resort to non-cooperation and civil disobedience movement thereby creating a serious law and problem for the Ibobi Government. UNC withdrew all private schools in Naga areas of Manipur Hills from the Board of Secondary Education Manipur (BSEM), publicly burnt text books of BSEM. UNC went a step further and launched a "No Tax Campaign" and handed over the house tax of 98,894 Naga households for the year 2006 to the Prime Minister's Office (PMO)[13]. All this and lot more was done to further the movement for Naga integration.

The foregoing chain of events was not limited to territorial limits of Manipur State; in fact it was in the context of integration of all ethnic Nagas under one flag. However, the irony of the situation was public statements by some officials of the State government that there were no Nagas in Manipur, and therefore the insurgency in Manipur was an internal matter of Manipur State Government. It was indeed exasperating! Complete breakdown of law and order, frequent protests and demonstrations etc., disrupted daily life to such an extent that public disenchantment with the civil administration had reached the point of no return.

Economic Blockade of Manipur

Manipur is a completely landlocked state. It is connected to the rest of India via three National Highways:

- NH 39 starts from Numaligarh in Assam and ends at Indo-Myanmar border covering a distance of 436 km of which 115 km lies in Assam, 100 km in Nagaland and 211 km is in Manipur State. It is Manipur's economic life line. About 400 trucks used to ply on this road daily bringing in essential commodities. In the wake of Muivah episode, Naga organizations blocked all traffic to Manipur effective April 12, 2010[14]. In order to lift the blockade the Union Government deployed 16 companies of paramilitary forces in Manipur and six in Nagaland. The Chief Secretaries of Nagaland and Manipur were summoned to Delhi for a meeting with Home Secretary G.K. Pillai. With 68 days into the blockade the condition of the valley-people suffering crippling deficiencies and sky-high prices of essential commodities needs hardly any elaboration. Unfortunately, the blockade was nominally lifted since bus-truck drivers of Manipur insisted on an assurance from the Government of Nagaland and the State Police that effective steps are taken by them to stop extortion by militant groups operating along Highway 39 passing through Nagaland. While some relief convoys under security provided by the paramilitary forces did manage to get through, the impasse continued, and so did the suffering of Manipur.

- NH 53 starts from the junction of NH 44 at Badarpur in Assam. It connects Silchar (Assam) with Imphal. It is an alternative economic life-line for Manipur bypassing Nagaland but is far more hazardous in as much as it passes through Naga dominated trouble-prone hill districts of Manipur where the situation has taken a turn for the worse since the Muivah episode, a creation of Okram Ibobi Singh Government at Imphal, which ordered the 'farcical elections' to Autonomous District Councils (ADCs) at the most inopportune time even though the elections were going to be held after a gap of 20 years, literally buying trouble for the state population. If the elections could not be held for 20 years, heavens would not have fallen if the same were not held for another couple of years! Just think about it, Mr. Ibobi Singh and the worthy Congress Party! – Many Congress candidates were elected unopposed while some booths did not record any turnout.[15]

Although NH 53 covers a distance of 320 km only of which 220 km lie in an area which is nominally under Manipur State. The road alignment for a distance of about 95 km passing through Tamenglong district is highly prone to frequent landslides, mud and slush. Unless it is realigned with suitable drainage and protective works like retaining walls etc., on the hill-valley sides, and Naga menace is eliminated, this alternative route is not a practical proposition. Albeit it is often being used as such with large gangs of migrant labour clearing the debris. Moreover, HW 53 has 12 suspension bridges which are not suitable for sustained heavy truck traffic. At present, this road link too requires as much security arrangements as HW 39 and the journey may take anything from 6-8 days!

Incidentally, HW 53 was opened on July 18 as an alternative route after large scale deployment of security forces. But it had to be closed to traffic within 24 hours as the insurgents damaged a vital bridge on River Irang.

There is no plausible-rational reason why all four hill districts of Manipur – Chandel, Tamenglong, Senapati and Ukhrul – be ceded to the so called Nagalim. That would mean depriving the original

Manipur State of 90% of its territory leaving merely the Imphal Valley to constitute the erstwhile glorious State of Manipur. It stands to reason that one of the solutions is to detach a certain part of Tamenglong district to Nagalim, evacuate the remaining Nagas to 'Nagalim sector' thereby secure the economic life-line of the State. Give and take philosophy has to be accepted, but from the political stand point it is easier said than done.

A long term solution is extension of rail link from Jiribam to Imphal which would certainly be costly and time consuming. But if China cou d build a rail link to Lhasa through a far more difficult terrain, I see no reason why the Indian engineers cannot do the same in much easier terrain.

I need hardly state that the simplest solution is to resolve the imbroglio of Naga insurgency in Nagaland through political means rather than as a law and order problem. But do we have the political will-wisdom and leadership of that caliber on either side? I doubt very much, at least for the present. In this direction a viable solution is to seek the good offices of Naga Baptist Church Council which has considerable influence in the region. This has to be done in coordination with the Manipur Church that has some influence amongst the hill Nagas of Manipur. Their joint effort would go some way in defusing the ugly situation.

There is no one single solution to the imbroglio. It has to be a coordinated effort of various alternatives contributing towards a lasting solution. Meanwhile, in order to alleviate the economic crunch of the Meitei why has the Government of India not subsidized the sale of essential commodities in Imphal Valley? They did that in Kashmir Valley from day-one under the patronage of Mr. Jawaharlal Nehru. Was that so because the Kashmir Valley population was Muslims whom the Congress wanted to woo as their 'vote bank', and the Imphal Valleys is populated by Hindus who, willy-nilly, are going to vote for the Congress in any case? As usual, it is the Congress Minority Card that decides the issues!

NH 150 passes through three different states of NE India—Mizoram, Manipur and Nagaland. This National Highway links Seling in Mizoram at junction with NH 54 with Kohima at the junction of NH 53 covering a distance of 700 km. The section of NH 150 that passes through Manipur is known as Tipaimukh Road. Unless some understanding can be reached with Myanmar towards utilizing this route to supply Manipur, this NH is not a practical proposition, besides being much too long a route.

Conclusion

The British were a mature lot with vast experience of handling other nationalities and their administration besides expanding their Empire through diplomacy combined with military force. In spite of provocation by Manipur they did not annex Manipur in British Indian Empire. They kept it as a buffer state. On the other hand, Indian political leadership was totally inexperienced in administration at the national level and annexed Manipur without much thought about its strategic importance. Various steps taken by the Government of Assam and the Central Government alienated the people completely. Extension of Naga Ceasefire without territorial limit was the last straw that kindled the conflagration of insurgency and sharpened ethnic divide.

Paucity of road communications has been a severe bottle neck. Road density in Manipur is woefully low - as low as 48.19 km per 100 sq km of land area against 100.99 km per 100 sq km for the rest of India. The road density in the hill districts is barely 10% of that in the valley! How can economic development take place under such poor infrastructural conditions?[16] Other statistics when compared with all India data are equally dismal, if not more. It is therefore pointless to flog the statistical dead horse anymore!

The people of Manipur are justified on being bottled up in a landlocked state barring the tenuous link with Myanmar, the same does not hold good for the rest of North East region, at least not as landlocked as is often claimed. Not that the region does not require more opening up towards the neighbouring countries; it certainly does. But the fact is that fairly brisk cross border trade continues despite the limitations of good road communications. The prosperous underground economy of the North Eastern states is solid evidence of this. I have personally observed that most modern consumer goods are available in large quantities in almost every town in the region. And they are all smuggled across the porous borders of Burma, Thailand and China. Trans-border insurgencies could not have possibly survived but for these common bonds of under-ground trade and age old ethnic affinities. You walk into Guwahati, Tinsukhia, Imphal and the neighbouring towns to see a variety of consumer goods of latest design and quality at fairly cheap prices. It will thus be seen that, as it is, underground economies of North Eastern states are already fairly globalized than what is conceptualized under the LEP.

Insurgency in Manipur, and for that matter in the entire North Eastern region, is not a law and order problem. It cannot be resolved by taking recourse to draconian laws enacted in Delhi or Shillong. These are purely economic-developmental issues requiring political wisdom and sagacity. Industrialization of economically backward areas is urgent need of the hour in which peoples' involvement and participation is essential for successful implementation of planning process. Unfortunately, Indian Polity has not learnt the futility of pursuing military solutions to basically political, religious or ethnic conflicts. They are mutually exclusive in nature and each requires a different political approach by seasoned leaders, and not dynastic youngsters.

The malady of regionalism encouraged by self seeking vote-bank political leaders of repute is bound to give rise to conflict of interests. Emotional integration rather than territorial integration has to be the rule. Freedom and regional autonomy are *sine qua non* for curbing the forces of disintegration. Indian polity has to rise above squabbling over 'vote bank', party-politics, rigging of elections, *et al*. Above all, rampant corruption at all levels of the government, particularly at the higher ministerial levels as well as at the highest level, has to be brought under control. Last, but not the least, bureaucracy and judicial system needs to be overhauled.

A tall order indeed! But it is high time Indian polity faces the uphill task lest insurgency and disintegration destroy the very fabric of our democratic institutions.

Last but not the least: Parliamentary Democracy has become fashionable alright; but is it indeed suitable for our social and economic ethos? More so in the light of our totally corrupt, mostly immoral, self seeking polity who are by their very nature manipulative both of bureaucracy and constitutional authorities in order to satisfy their personal whims and interests. They openly tell white lies thereby murdering the truth, and get away with them scot free in public and private. How long are we going to live with unfulfilled dreams of our revered leaders like Gandhi and Nehru?

The question therefore arises: What is the alternative? – That has to be the subject of a separate thesis.

To summarize: The insurgency in Manipur and NE India is a litany of faults of Indian polity, one after another, without exception, and our polity alone with its systemic failures are to blame. Insurgency in various parts of the country is our own creation, and not of the people of the regions concerned. Introspection and political maturity is the need of the hour, and not draconian laws which further alienate the people. These are not law and order problems alone; the aspirations of the people, satisfaction of their socio-economic needs through development and industrialization with a mix of matured judgment are the right approach to resolve these problems, and not the persistent obsession of New Delhi and Shillong with security concerns alone.

Lest I forget: Revival, modernization and marketing products of Manipur's age old art of handloom-weaving and indigenous methods of dying as part of cottage industry development and household industry must be given high priority to eradicate rural unemployment, thereby improve economic conditions of rural areas where, of late, agricultural production has seen a steep downward trend due to various reasons.

PS: I have deliberately not touched upon the Kuki insurgency since I believe that once the 'Nagalim' issue is resolved in so far as Manipur is concerned as suggested earlier, the Kukis of Manipur Hills are likely to fall in line. I say this on the strength of personal experience of having walked through the entire length of what used to be known as Lushai Hills. Kukis' psyche is far more different from that of the Nagas who too are gradually appearing to fall in line.

11-2 UNITED LIBERATION FRONT OF ASSAM (ULFA)

Paresh Baruah, belonging to Jaraigaon village in Dibrugarh district of eastern Assam, along with four others founded ULFA on April 7, 1979, at Rangghar in Sibsagar district in an amphitheatre of the erstwhile royal family of Ahom kingdom with the avowed objective of creating a "Sovereign Assam". His modus operandi: Brutal mindless killing of Hindi speaking migrant workers, illegal immigrants from Bangladesh, some Bengalis and even some business people too, *et al* – in short, his illegal outfit went all out to intimidate people from other parts of India to leave Assam to Assamese alone. In some instances Hindi speaking people living in the same locality as the Assamese were separated from the latter and shot at point blank range. Terror tactics were the rule of operation clean-up resorted to in 2000-2003, and thereafter in later years.

Baruah proclaimed himself as the "Commander-in-Chief" of ULFA. His personal worth exceeds Rs. 500 crores and he leads a lavish life style in Dhaka's posh areas like Dhanmondi, Mirpur, and New Eskara Road (which I used to visit while in Dhaka in 1972) and abroad. He often uses his alias Kamruj Zaman Khan, or Zaman Bhai.[17] After more than three decades of savage strife and brutal killings, recent media reports indicate a thaw in as much as ULFA is now inclined to engage in a peaceful dialogue. When, where and how: That is the million dollar question not withstanding some sort of vertical split in the higher echelon of leadership of the movement.

The movement to drive out illegal Bangladeshi immigrants started in 1979. Later, when ULFA became dependent on Pakistan, ISI and Bangladesh for money, training, arms etc. They became soft n those elements, and instead started celebrating the brutal killings in Assam to arm-twist New Delhi to accept their conditions. Bihari workers have been the target of ULFA for many years. They have shifted their families back home besides large numbers have fled from Assam. In 2006 ULFA alleged that outsiders had set up 'Mini Bihar", "Mini Bengal" and "Mini Rajasthan" in different districts of Assam and that these must be dismantled.

Noted Assamese writer Goswami took the initiative to start dialogue to bring peace to the troubled state and its populace after three decades of insurgency. But ULFA pulled out of peace parleys after three rounds of talks out of sheer rigidity of approach to the vexed issues involved, particularly regarding their demand for jailed executive committee vice chairman Pradip Gogoi, publicity secretary Mithinga Daimari, cultural secretary Pranati Deka and Adviser Buragohain. An ULFA delegation headed by Anup Chetia was flown into Delhi to meet the then Prime Minister Narashima Rao 1992; but the attempt did not make any headway since ULFA was not serious about peace negotiations. Unfortunately, GOI is not in a position to halt foreign assistance that ULFA continues to receive in large measure.

During the last couple of years the people of Assam are tired of disturbed conditions and violence in their midst. ULFA appears to have been isolated in the process. They are coming round to their senses and have apologized for massacre of 13 school children in a bomb blast in 2004 which they now accept as a mistake. That indeed had led to their serious isolation from the Assamese public.

During 1992 and 2001, ULFA is reported to have killed 642 civilians and 269 security personnel. Now they have apologized for their brutalities and announced unconditional peace talks with the GOI. However, the two main factions are not of one mind on the subject of negotiations. The outlawed organization is now vertically split. While the Chairman Arbinda Rajkhowa is positive on the subject, the ever elusive self styled "Commander-in-Chief" Paresh Baruah has rejected the proposal. May, be his luxurious life style, his wife Bobby better known as Sufia Begum and two sons, Tashim Khan and Akash Khan, are instrumental in this refusal to come to peace-terms for personal reasons. But the fact remains that the decision to open negotiations was taken by the general council of ULFA attended by amongst others by vice chairman Pradip Gogoi, deputy commander-in-chief Raju Baruah, self styled foreign secretary Sasha Choudhury, finance secretary Chitraban Hazarika, cultural secretary Pranti Deka and octogenarian political ideologue Bhimkanta Burgohain. All these eight senior leaders are out on bail now. The government facilitated their release with a view to resume peace talks. All this background came to naught because intransigence on the part of the "Commander-in-Chief" and his cohorts.[18]

ULFA cadres were not restricted to Bangladesh alone for shelter, training and arm. Myanmar was also actively helping them ae well as some other insurgent outfits. If India wanted to defeat insurgency in the Northeastern region, rebel bases in neighbouring countries had to be dismantled. India shares 1640 km unfenced border with Myanmar. There are about twenty thousand foreign guerilla fighters belonging to various insurgent groups, mainly ULFA and UNLF, in Myanmar. India's foreign policy towards Myanmar was therefore re-crafted by the then Prime Minister P.V. Narashima Rao to:

- Evict Indian separatist-insurgent groups from its territory;
- Balance increasing engagement between China and Myanmar;

- Use Myanmar as a gateway to Southeast Asia region;
- Harness hydrocarbon resources of Myanmar for mutual advantage;
- Provide Myanmar with an alternative for economic development and defence assistance.

Myanmar's ruling military Chief General Than Shwe had asked India for helicopters, helicopter gun-ships, heavy rockets, GPS devices etc. India was prepared to supply these and other military hardware but was skeptical if Myanmar forces could effectively use such sophisticated equipment. India therefore suggested joint military operations to achieve the common objective. Counter-insurgency cooperation between the two countries has thus produced good results. During his visit to Delhi in 2004, the General assured India that his country would not permit anti-India activities from its soil. A list of insurgent camps in Northern Myanmar was also sent for dismantling the same, In a reciprocal gesture of goodwill India transferred arms including 105mm light artillery guns, T-55 tanks, etc, besides two Islander Surveillance aircrafts to Myanmar Army.

Trade between the two countries has expanded from about $88 million in 1990-91 to $569 in 2005-06. India has also announced plans to invest nearly Rs. 850 crores for development of infrastructure for growth of regional trade. India is also engaged in exploring and transporting part of Myanmar's 300 billion cubic meters of gas reserves to its Northeastern region. Since India does not have transit rights through Bangladesh, alternative routes by inland waterways and road are being developed to Mizoram and onwards to rest of Northeast region. India is also developing Myanmar's road network, setting up hydroelectric power stations, communication and IT projects as part of its efforts to balance the Chinese influence. India's Border Roads Organization (BRO) had completeed Tamu-Kalewa-Kalemyo Road in 1997 and carried out repairs and resurfacing of the same in 2006. A highway from Moreh in Manipur Mae Sot in Thailand through Bagan in Myanmar is well on the cards, besides a hydroelectric project on River Chindwin in Myanmar's northwest, parallel to Nagaland and Manipur.[19] In this connection it should be noted that tribal population in Nagaland, Manipur and Mizoram have close ethnic similarities with those in Myanmar, and hence the need for India to show greater sensitivity to that country.

After the foregoing digression now back to ULFA:

Notwithstanding the aforesaid setback, and in order to bring ULFA into political process, the State Government released a number of top leaders of the banned outfit. The last one to be released on bail is ULFA Chairman Rahkhowa. talks within the framework of Indian constitution for a "just and honourable solution" did resume on February 10, 2011 more in the nature of an ice breaker than substantive in content. The eight-member ULFA delegation was led by its chairman Rajkhowa. India's Home Secretary Pillai chaired the meeting. Meanwhile, it was agreed by both sides to set up a seven member Committee comprising of three members from ULFA, two each from the Central and Assam State governments to look into some basic issues:

- ULFA camps, their locations, strengths;
- Status of the cadres and arms;
- Surrender policy and detailed modalities for discussions before substantive round of talks begin in May after the Assembly elections.
- ULFA will take no part in the election process.

However, they assured that they would not come in the way of "desire and aspiration of the people of Assam". It was termed as a "confidence-building round" of talks in which ULFA did not raise any demands which they would take up later during the substantive round. Just a day or so before the preliminary talks commenced, Bangladesh evicted three leaders of the outfit across the Dawki border in Meghalaya. They were identified as 'captain' Antu Chaudang, 2nd Lieut. Pradeep Chetia and one Saurav Chaudang , a close associate of Paresh Baruah. An Assam Police team took them into custody and whisked them away to Guwahati.

Before the Ulfa delegation went in for the first formal talks, Home Minister P. Chidambaram met them and assured them that "the Government of India and the Government of Assam will engage them in sincere and meaningful talks and I am confident that we will find a just and honourable solution." Spokesman for the ULFA delegation stated: "We have noted the recent statement of Prime Minister Manmohan Singh that the Indian Constitution is flexible enough to accommodate the desire and aspirations of all people. Through the talks, therefore, we propose to evaluate various facets of the Constitution and to explore the viability of protection and enrichment of the sovereignty of the people of Assam in all its dimensions - political, social and cultural within the flexibility as mentioned by the prime minister." While the initiative for the ceasefire has to come from the government, ULFA has not indulged in any violence for the past one year. Nevertheless, "ULFA is still a banned group" although they have dropped their demand for sovereignty in order to start peace talks.

ULFA delegation is reported to have made a courtesy call on the Prime Minister who, incidentally, also represents Assam. The Prime Minister reiterated that ULFA Chairman had assured him that there would be no untoward incidents or disturbances during the Assembly polls due in May.

11-3 GARO HILLS

Garo Hills with a population of approximately three lakhs and a total area of 8084 sq km occupies the western part of the state of Meghalaya. It separates the Assam valley from the plains of Mymensing and Sylhet district of Bangladesh. It occupies a commanding position at the entrance of Assam. These undulating hills of varying heights covered with lush green forests form a remarkable range acting as a sentinel against any incursions from the erstwhile neighbouring Burma. All Garos belong to one matrilineal tribe and have common cultural traditions, dialect, and family-kinship structure. Since the tribe is matrilineal, means land can be inherited through the female line only and women have a high status having commanding power over the household. The youngest daughter is the heiress and her husband is the only son-in-law in residence; all other daughters have to move out after marriage and set up their own household—exactly the same as amongst the Khasis of Meghalaya. The Garos are a matrilineal tribe and call themselves as A'chik or Mande. They live in small villages, about 10 to 60 households each, a sort of settlements called Akhings, each under the control of the *machong*, a sort of informal village council, held under custody of Akhing chief known as Nokma. At "pan-community level the Garos were divided into different sub tribes like Atong, Awe, Abeng, Chibok, Chisak, Kochu, Matgangch, et al. They had certain marginal differences, nonetheless the basic kinship and socio-cultural organizations remained the same, thereby maintaining tribal solidarity. Several popular unverified folktales recall migration of Garos from Tibet along the banks of the Brahmaputra perhaps through tracts of Bhutan, Dhubri etc. But the institution of matriliny crept in after they entered Goalpara and Garo Hills.[20]

In the distant past Garos are believed to have indulged in head-hunting, more like the Nagas used to. Possession of skull was a symbol of Garo chivalry that used to bring honour and social prestige to the hunter. Skulls so possessed had considerable market value. During 1807 and 1816, 116 persons were killed and 157 villages[21] burnt by the Garos in the course of their depredations. It is such acts of frequent raids, loot, arson and headhunting that raised the British eyebrows ultimately leading to subjugation of the Garos. However, internecine quarrels within the *akhing* which were frequent occurrences were amicably settled by the village elders under leadership of the Nokma.

In the past agriculture was based on slash-and-burn technique called *jhuming*. However, at present they are slowly taking to settled cultivation. Cotton, chilli, peppers and ginger are the cash crops.

Garos first came in limelight during frontier disturbances in 1788-89 when the then Governor General Lord Cornwallis instructed the then Commissioner of Dacca to undertake an inspection tour of the area. The latter has given vivid description of the hills and its people, particularly of the womenfolk wearing a reddish cloth about sixteen inches long, having blue or white stripes, tied at the upper corner on the right.[22]

Depredations by the Garos continued off and on. The prevalence of malaria in endemic form and heavy rains precluded mounting of successful military expeditions to subdue the warring tribesmen. They were finally subjugated by 1872-73 after permanent administrative headquarters were established in 1867 at TURA, the then district HQ. It is now the seat of the Autonomous District Council administration. In 1976 the district was divided into two: East and West Garo Hills with Tura and Williamnagar as their respective headquarters. Since then a number of urbanized areas have developed with a college at Tura.[23]

ULFA is just one of the facets of insurgency in the North-East, albeit a significant one. Recently there were ethnic clashes on Assam-Meghalaya border between Rabha and Garo in Hatigaon area of East Garo Hills district. Incidents of arson were reported on both sides despite a curfew. Several houses were set ablaze. Fortunately, there were no casualties although a large number of houses were burnt down and many families rendered homeless. In order to prevent any escalation of violence, the army staged flag march in the two districts along the interstate border as a confidence building measure.

11-4 NAGALAND

The five-decades-old insurgency in Nagaland is the longest running insurgency in Asia, first led by its charismatic elusive leader Phizo under the banner of Naga National Council (NNC) demanding "Sovereign Naga Nation". It was not, and is still not, confined to the geographical boundaries of present day Nagaland; it engulfed, and still continues to do so, all along the ethnic Naga belt spreading its tentacles far and wide in neighbouring Indian states besides Myanmar too. With the formation of a separate state of Nagaland within the purview of Indian Constitution, relatively peaceful conditions now generally prevail in the region since 1997. However, sporadic severe violent disturbing incidents in neighbouring areas do continue to cause to arise from time to time. The cause célèbre: ambitious demand for Nagalim – merger of all ethnic Naga elements into one homogeneous entity irrespective of geographical constraints, foreign or otherwise. This vociferous persistent demand is spear-headed by National Socialist Council of Nagalim Founder Chisi Swu and General Secretary Thuingaleng Muivah. After the ban on the organization was lifted, both visited India after a lapse of 36 years in 2003 and held talks with top Indian leadership. The two leaders held many rounds of talks at foreign locations and again arrived in New Delhi in December 2004 to consult cross-sections of Nagas to arrive at a consensus for an honourable solution. The NSCN arrived at an accord with GOI and signed the same at Shillong. It came to be called the "Shillong Accord".

Thuingaleng Muivah and S.S. Khaplang both opposed the "Shillong Accord" signed by NSCN. Consequently, NSCN split into two factions on April 30, 1988; NSCN (K, for Khaplang) and NSCN (I-M), 'M' for Muivah, an equally charismatic leader, who was clever enough to retain the link with the founder, Isak Chisi Swu by having prefix 'I' for his faction. Muivah is a Tangkhul Naga, which are in a majority in parts of Nagaland. He originally belongs to a village in Manipur state of the Union of India.

Both NSCN (I-M) and NSCN (K) are claiming as the sole

representative to establish Nagalim ('Greater Nagaland') – "Peoples' Republic of Nagaland." There is bitter violent blood thirsty rivalry between the two factions resulting in loss of many lives. In so far the severity of violence is concerned, NSCN (I-M) appears to have an upper hand. This has been evident all the more so since NSCN (K) signed a ceasefire agreement with Delhi in 2001. The former accuses the latter of compromising on the fundamental demand of a cohesive all inclusive Naga entity. However, it is noteworthy that negotiations on the long sanding demand of NSCN (I-M) were also initiated at political level on the 30-point demand of the rebel group. Seven rounds of substantive talks have since been held and only NSCN (K) has since signed the ceasefire agreement. I-M faction therefore accuses the K faction of forsaking the Naga cause. In the process level of fratricidal violence has substantially come down despite the paper-agreement for non-violent agitation between the two towards an honourable solution to the imbroglio. Incidentally, their manifesto is based on economic development based on the principles of Socialism with a spiritual bias – "Nagalnd for Christ". By far the vast majority of Nagas are Christians by kind courtesy of the British and other Presbyterians. While on the subject of Manipur, Assam or Arunchal Pradesh where Nagas have been living since times immemorial, Muivah says: "We are mot claiming any territory which is not ours. First the British divided us and then the Central government. It is our right to stay under one administrative unit."[24] About eight thousand delegates attending the 4th Naga Peoples' Consultative meeting held at NSCN (I-M) Hebron Camp near Dimapur in 2005 pledged support to the ongoing peace process. Isak Swu also attended the meeting which adopted a four-point Declaration calling for an honourable solution to the Naga imbroglio.

Notwithstanding their constant rhetoric for a peaceful honourable settlement, both Muivah and Isak are based in Thailand and Holland. They have established a government -in-exile called the Government of the Peoples' Republic of Nagaland (GPRN) with the usual departments-ministries with a budget of INR 200-250 million. Naga Hoho is the apex body of all the numerous Naga tribes-clans and a prominent Naga leader, S.C. Jamir, till lately, was the Governor of Maharashtra and Goa.

11-5 BODOS

Bodos are of Indo-Mongoloid racial stock. Their original home lies north of Himalayas and west of China. The word 'Bod' means 'homeland'. In India the Bodos are scattered all over the Northeast region. In upper Assam they are known as Sonwal and Thengal Kachari while in western Assam they are identified as Boro Kacharis. In Cachar they are called Barman while in North Cachar they are Dimasa. In Bengal and lower plains of Nepal they are designated as Meches. Small pockets of this tribal community are scattered in Bhutan and Myanmar also. Bodos are Hindus by religion and their supreme God is Shiva.

Living so dispersed over such wide areas amongst different tribal-ethnic groups is bound to lead to ethnic-social tensions from timer to time. In order to present some sort of united front to confront their opponents as well as the civil administration they formed a terror group called Bodo Liberation Tigers and the National Democratic Front of Bodoland. After some clashes and timely action by the authorities, a ceasefire came into effect. At present both these groups are more or less defunct, and generally peaceful conditions prevail in various Bodo habitats.

However, the fire of insurgency may lie dormant for some time but it does not die a natural death. Perhaps it was the deployment of SSG that seemed to have lulled the authorities to believe that they had succeeded in crushing the Bodo insurgency. As soon as the smouldering ambers get an opportunity, the conflagration is not far away. Of late, the Bodo-insurgency has once again raised its head. In March 2011 anti-talks faction of NDFB rebels ambushed a CRPF convoy killing eight Jawans and injuring ten others.The Bodo-embers thus got a spark and during first week of April 2011 when, besides killing a number of innocent civilians on Assam-Bodo border, a party of SSG was ambushed at Lalveti in Assam Kokrajhar district just a few days before Kokrajhar was to go in the second phase of polls. *Times of India* dated April 06, 2011 reported that the attack took place near Bhutan border when a contingent of SSG was out on patrolling duty. Two Jawans were killed in the ambush and some are reported missing. This sudden rise of Bodo-insurgency was a prelude to recently concluded elections in Assam which otherwise were more or less peaceful.

The foregoing episodes reinforce the conviction that insurgency shall remain active till the socio-economic disparities and injustices are resolved.[25]

11-6 MIZORAM

During 1953 and thereafter when I visited this small strategic stretch of land, it was known as Lushai Hills district of Assam. Its eastern limit forms part of Indo-Myanmar border while on the western side is the Indo-Bangladesh border. It is bounded on north by Sylhet (Bangladesh) and Cachar (Assam), on the west by Chittagong Hill Tracts, on the south by Northern Arakán and Chin Hills (Burma) on the east. For its obvious strategic importance, the British administration declared the district as a completely excluded area under Chin Hills regulations, barring entry of all non-Lushais without a permit from the Government of Assam.

MAP : LUSHAI HILLS DISTRICT OF ASSAM

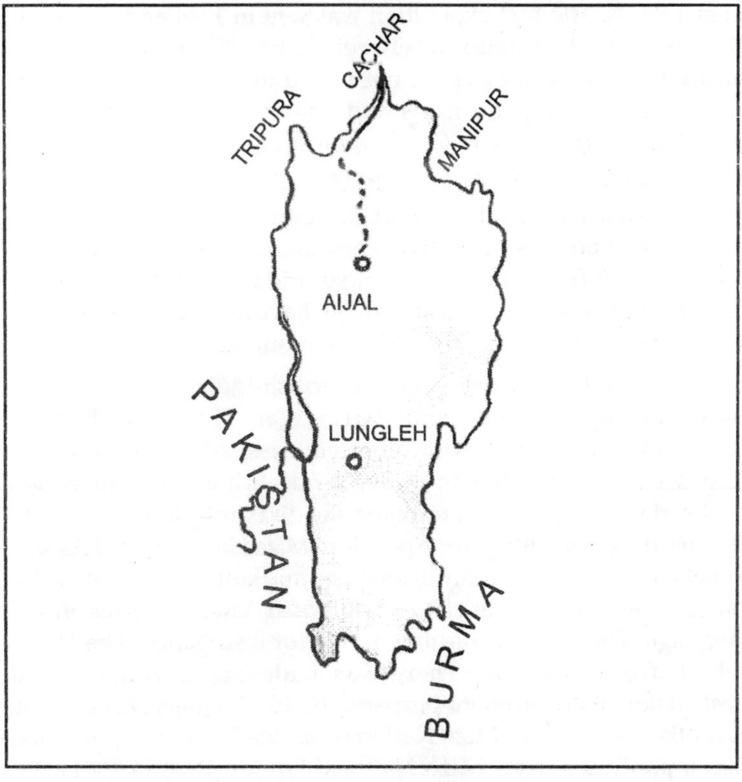

Mizoram comprises of a series of low altitude hill ranges, 3300 to 5000 ft AMSL, running almost due north-south covering an area of 21,087 sq.km. These hills are densely covered with bamboo and cane which grow in abundance. The Tropic of Cancer passes through the middle of the district now called the State of Mizoram with Aizal as the capital. Though it used to be one of the largest district in pre-partition India, it was sparsely populated, barely two lakhs plus population. An all weather highway is under development to provide direct route between Mizoram to Assam and the rest of Northest India.

We hear of the Lushai people for the first time in Indian history in 1777, during the time of Warren Hastings, when the Chief of Chittagong appealed to the British for protection against raids by the Vinkis, the name by which they were then known to the Chief. Their raids on the plains of Cachar and Chittagong were a serious nuisance. A number of expeditions were mounted against the then Lushai Hills. The first expedition was sent in 1844 and the last in 1895-96 with a few others in between, but most were unsuccessful primarily because they could not penetrate through the difficult terrain, thick bamboo forests and heavy undergrowth. Heavy monsoons during May to October, mosquito-menace and leeches made life unbearable for British and Indian troops.

The Mizos are a sturdy short statured Mongoloid race whose original habitat was in Burma. They are divided into numerous clans, about fifty of them but all take pride in calling themselves 'Mizos'(highlanders). The women folk have masculine features by virtue of generations of hard labour in mountains and jungles.

Mizo youths were recruited in British-Indian Army in large numbers during the Second World War. This gave them an opportunity to interact with other cultures. After the War they returned to their rather primitive land with a new and varied civilisational experience. However, the disastrous famine of 1959-60 caused great hardship to the people of Mizo Hills district of Assam. Relief measures were totally inadequate and suffering was great. To cap it all, the Government of Assam imposed Assamese as the official language. The ground was now fertile for insurgency. The Mizos rebelled in a big way. There was widespread violence and destruction of government property, besides killings of Assamese and other non-Mizos. Mizo National Famine Front was converted into a political party - Mizo National Front (MNF) in 1961 with

Laldenga as its president with the object of carving out an Independent Sovereign State of Mizoram. Armed struggle towards that end lasted for two decades from 1966 to 1986 with loss of many lives and property. The district was accorded the status of Union Territory in 1972 and finally full statehood in February 1987 after the peace accord was signed on June 30, 1986. Laldenga took over as the first Chief Minister. The Union Government released INR 3 crores for rebuilding the churches destroyed during the insurgency and more than two crores as compensation for those killed during that period. Under Laldenga's leadership the State has emerged as one of the most stable states of the Union with high level of developmental activities.

Mizoram has the distinction of having the highest literacy rate in the country.

11-7 "LOOK EAST POLICY"

The Northeast is an epitome of unity in diversity—ethnic, cultural, linguistic, and what have you. The region is a conglomeration of eight states, each one of them unique in its own right. The scenic beauty of the region, its pristine waters, clean air, and of course its beautiful charming colourful people, all combine to win one's heart and mind. I have spent nearly two decades in the area and the desire to visit again and again is indeed overpowering.

Till the recent past the region was a hot bed of violence and insurgency. However, of late things have cooled down considerably and generally peace prevails in the area. Development works and public welfare measures, agricultural inputs, easy loans at low interesr rates, banking and allied facilities, etc. have instilled a new sense of confidence amongst the people who no longer consider themselves as apart from the rest of Indians. It is the neighbouring foreign agencies like China, ISA, Bangladesh, *et al.*, which have instigated, and still continue to instigate ethnic and economic disturbances from time to time. But now that India has adopted "Look East Policy", 1991 has marked a strategic shift in India's overall perspective of the world in general, and the eastern theatre in particular. India's basic tool of interaction with Southeast Asian countries, trade, communications and economic development are getting a big boost, besides increased employment opportunities to the tribal people. In fact, Verrier Elwin-Nehru era policy of keeping the tribals isolated as museum pieces has been completely reversed since that bygone era.

Although rather late in the day, common sense has prevailed amongst the bureaucracy and political leadership that the answer to extremism and insurgency is not the use of police-paramilitary forces; instead economic development and patience is the panacea. The creation of the Union Ministry of Development of North Eastern Region has gone a long way in eradicating insurgency in that region. The states in the region receive special treatment for approval of Plan-funds in that they receive 90 per cent of Plan assistance as a grant and only 10% is treated as loan as opposed to other states of Union where the percentage is 70 and 30 respectively. It is sincerely hoped that that similar approach gains an upper hand in tackling the Naxal-Maoist insurgency in the so called "Red Zone". Since states in the "Red Zone" are rich in mineral resources, similar favoured treatment of sharing Central tax revenue would be adopted towards tribal belts of this Zone also.

The Union Government has also realized that the Northeast is very remote from the main centers of economic activity in the mainland India. It is much closer to Dhaka, Yangoon and Bangkok than to Kolkatta-Delhi-Mumbai or Chennai. The Union Government has also come to appreciate that insurgency in the North-east is not a law and order problem; it is more to do with ethnic and political inconsistencies. Similarly, insurgencies in the Red Zone are also not a law and order problem. The latter stems from economic deprivation, and haves versus have-nots syndrome.

Notes

1. Aribam Indubala Devi (Ed.): *Amazing North East – Manipur*; Vij Books, 2010; p. 38. During the same period it was also called 'Mekhala'.
2. According to Business daily during 2007-08 Myanmar's border trade with China was about $977 M while with India it was a mere $15 million.
3. Paper by Sanjeev Thingnam in LEP ed. By Thingnam Kishan Singh; pp. 93-94. When Alaung-Paya King of Ava Invaded Manipur, the latter were forced to seek British military assistance.
4. *Ibid.*, p. 43.
5. Jiten Nongthombam Dr.: Civil War like Situation in Manipur; Maxford Books, New Delhi, 2011, p. 91.
6. Aribam Indubala Devi, *op. cit.* p. 20.
7. *Ibid.*, p. 45.
8. *Ibid.*, p. 47.

9. Jiten Nongthombam Dr., *op. cit.*, p. 194.
10. Thingnam Kishan Singh, *op. cit.* Paper contributed by Hanjabam Iswworchandra Sharma; pp. 132-34. According to Sanjeev Thingnam, economic opening of the landlocked Northeast to its neighbours might be one way of resolving the insurgency problem in the region —*Ibid.*, p. 109.
11. Das Kanti Rajat, *Manipur Tribal Scene*; New Delhi 1942, pp. 18-19. NSCN is a political group mostly comprised of Tangkhul Nagas generally living in the hill regions of Manipur.
12. Jiten, *op. cit.*, pp. 11, 9.
13. *Ibid.*, pp. 3-4.
14. A similar economic blockade in 2005 lasted 52 days causing untold misery to the people of Manipur valley.
15. Jiten, *op. cit.*, p. 54.
16. Hanjabam Isworchandra Sharmas Paper in *Look East Policy & India's North East* ed. by Thingnam Kishan Singh; New Delhi, 2009; p. 123 read with p. 135.
17. Chaudhury Roy Dipanjan, *Northeast Diverse Complexity*; Har-Anand, New Delhi, 2008; p. 30.
18. TOI NNT datelines-Guwahati February 07 and 09, 2011.
19. Chaudhury Roy Dipanjan, *op. cit.* p. 63.
20. Kar Chandra Parimal, *Garos in Transition*; Cosmo Publications, New Delhi, 192; pp; 22, 46-47, 53.
21. Kar, *op.cit.*, quoting Mackenzie, 1884; p. 50.
22. Rizvi S.H.M. & Shibani Roy, *Garo (Achik) Tribe of Meghalaya*; B.R. Publishing, Delhi, 2006; p. 3.
23. Kar Chandra Parimal, *Garos in Transition*; Cosmo Publications, New Delhi, 1982; p. xiii.
24. Quoted in *Northeast Diverse Complexity*; p. 36.
25. *ToI*, April 26, 2011.

9. [illegible]

10. [illegible] ... the problem ... [illegible]

11. [illegible]

12. [illegible]

13. [illegible]

14. [illegible]

15. [illegible]

16. [illegible]

17. [illegible]

18. [illegible]

19. [illegible]

20. [illegible]

21. [illegible]

22. [illegible]

23. [illegible]

24. [illegible]

25. [illegible]

12

NAXALBARI-MAOIST MOVEMENT

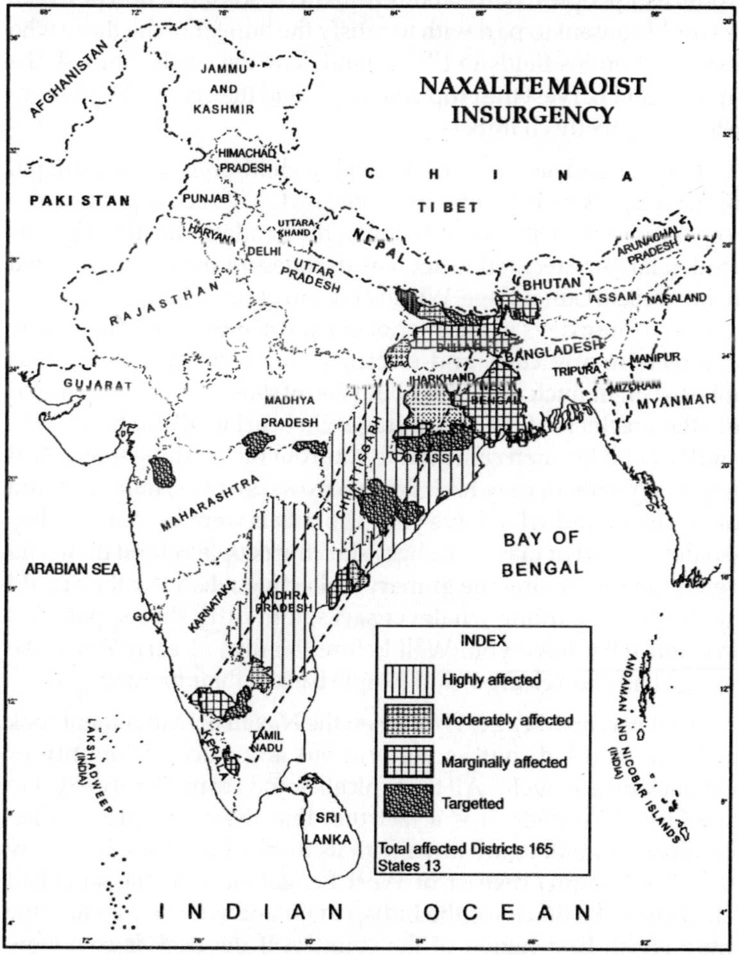

The name is neither fictional nor notional. Indeed, Naxalbari actually and physically does exist as an extremely poor, wretched, dirty and filthy conglomeration of mud huts on the tri-junction of India, Nepal and Bangladesh. No paved streets, drains, sewerage or toilets. Just the shacks where people lived like as if God did not exist for them; God was only for the rich landlords. Hunger, starvation, hardly any clothing, cold in winter, extreme heat in summer, dust and muck pervaded all over. The populace had no grains to fill their, or their children's bellies while the landlord had more than a few hundred quintals of rice and *daal* stored in his godown – the produce of peoples' hard labour from his fields a fraction of which he would consent to part with to satisfy the hunger of the those who had toiled on his fields to till his land, sow the seeds, nourish the saplings and harvest the crop when ripe, and then carry the produce to his ever greedy chambers.

Hunger and sight of one's starving children is a powerful jolt for the people towards action of some sort. After some perfunctory preparations the tribal population of the hamlets, mostly migrants bonded labour, decided to act. The darkness of the night provided them excellent camouflage. Whoever heard of street lights, or security guards in those days in the interior of rural countryside. There were no streets in any case, and electricity for security lighting was unheard of. In pitch darkness about 200 of those Adivasis ventured into the precincts of the rich storage. On hearing all the hoo-ha the landlord and his men came out to confront the seething mass. And they let go with all they had. Bows, arrows, swords, hammers and tongs, stones and what have you. The tribals were in control. They had the support of mass of hungry starving people behind them and were soon ransacking the granary, collecting whatever they could lay their hands, filling whatever sacks, torn dirty sheets, pots and tins, and what have you. Well before the rays of early dawn the storage had been cleared, and people back in their hamlets.

That was on May 24, 1967 when the Naxalbari Movement took birth, unheralded, but as yet without any trace of identity or nomenclature as such.[1] All these niceties and cosmetics were yet to take form. However, it is a fact that that there is a place called Naxalbari, a small dusty town with its own decrepit small railway station, in Siliguri district of West Bengal close to the so called "chicken neck" that joins the Indian mainland with Assam and the entire North-East region of the country. If the neck is somehow squeezed, there would be no means of surface communications between the two parts of the country – A consequence of partition of India as well as subsequent birth of independent sovereign Bangladesh.

Leaving aside the digression – besides having its own rail station, Naxalbari has its state highway too, straddling the route that links northern Bihar to northern Bengal, passing through thick forests and rich farmlands, and of course the tea estates, a reminder of the colonial era. However, the Naxalbari we are talking of now is not a town as such; that was no place for birth of a monstrosity, a revolutionary movement that spread its tentacles far and wide. As usual, the colonial-style administration headed by the communists (CPI-Marxists) sent in a police contingent to restore law and order. However, the fact is that it was not a law and order problem, but a genuine struggle of the exploited peasants, the deprived tribal and urban proletariat for social and economic survival. The initial squad of police was not aware of the enormity of what had hit the landlords. They too suffered the ire of the desperate starving tribals. Reinforcements were sent in. By that time the hungry masses had vanished into heavy air of nearby thick forests, dispersed in small groups and raised some sort of shanty shelters, cooked and eaten well. They hid the remaining stock in caves and some sort of holes, covering them with leaves and dirt. However, soon some of them were caught, put in jails, tortured into confession and the case went up before the judge who refused to believe the prosecution story that a few frail human beings, suffering malnutrition over a period of time, could possibly remove and physically carry away a few tons of food grains in a matter of 3-4 hours in the thick of darkness.

Naxalbari was not the first peasant uprising in modern India. It may be recalled that even as early as 1946 there was a *Tebhaga* (three parts) movement in undivided Bengal which demanded that share of landlords be reduced from one-half of crop to one-third. The movement petered out when the landlords resorted to cruel repression with the aid of provincial police force.

The unfortunate fact is that Parliamentary Democracy as enshrined in our Constitution has failed to deliver over the last half century. The Indian Polity has failed to solve the problems of hunger, poverty and homelessness. In turn these are accentuated by illiteracy and unemployment-underemployment. Prevailing socio-economic and political conditions are conducive to violent activities by the left extremist elements. On the other hand extreme right elements in the society continue to incite violent reaction to leftist demands with religious fanaticism adding fuel to the fire. No wonder therefore that news of police firing in Naxalbari area, killing dozens, spread like a wild fire giving rise to what has come to be known as "Naxal Violence" in official parlance. In fact, all revolutionary activities are dubbed extremists and the participants are clubbed together as Naxalites or Maoists[2], and in vernacular press as *Naxali* or *Maovadi*. However, it must be appreciated that what the authorities consider as a problem (the violence), the Maoists consider the so called extremism as a solution to socio-economic-political problems of the deprived exploited classes. The gulf between the 'haves' and 'have-nots' has created a wide range of disturbed zones of violence. Armed revolutionary guerilla squads called *dalam* have taken over the countryside, lock stock and barrel. They are armed with a wide variety of armaments: bows and arrows, choppers, knives, country made hand-guns besides of course the sophisticated weaponry supplied through ISI, LTTE, China, Nepal, *et al.* The extremists have enough money to buy what they want—the money comes from extortion, protection money, and ever so rampant corruption in official circles. As for the ISI, Jammu and Kashmir was its first base for destabilizing India; North-East India is the second in coordination with such outfits as United Liberation Front of Assam (ULFA), and its third target against India is now the Naxal dominated areas.

The Maoists are growing in strength and violence day by day. Now they have become more active in UP and Bihar, besides the southern slices of the Red Corridor, which is no longer a corridor but has become a Red Zone. Last year the Maoists killed 1169 persons including 277 security personnel while their cadres lost only 275. Their cadre strength has increased from 4,000 in 2008 to 15,000. Maoist leadership organized 93 intensive training camps in 2010 while the CRPF personnel fire a mere twenty rounds each in every training year. At this rate it would take 8-10 years for CRPF to take on the Maoists by which time the later might become still more powerful. It is estimated that continued deployment of at least three lakh personnel for twenty years is required to contain the Maoist threat. In Chhattisgarh alone 146 battalions (1.2 lakh personnel) are required to achieve optimal deployment against the present 26 battalions (22,000 personnel). A negative factor in the rise of Maoist-violence is the expertise in Improvised Explosive Devices (IED) acquired by the Maoist.

According to Major General (Retd) G.D. Bakshi: "If the CRPF is required to perform the lead role in Counter-Insurgency, it will have to be radically restructured and transformed by reducing the age profile, changing its operating ethos, to function as a battalion and large intake of former short service commissioned officers and former army personnel from the BSF and infantry battalions." "Grey Hounds" of Andhra Pradesh are a success story worth emulating by all other affected states.[3]

The Orissa-episode of kidnapping and subsequent halt in anti-Naxal operations in order to obtain release of kidnapped officials has caused demoralization amongst the security personnel engaged in CI operations in Southern districts of the State. "The Government's soft approach towards Maoists may spoil our hardwork put in for anti-Maoist operations." On the other end of the spectrum,

Gorkha Jan Mukti Morcha (GJM), which has been in the forefront of a low-level insurgency to carve out a separate State of Gorkhaland, has openly expressed satisfaction with the proposed package announced by the Rail Minister for Darjeeling Hills. "This is the first time that any Railway Minister has thought of Gorkhas ... She is a dynamic person capable of achieving what she has proposed."[4]

The Naxal Zone in UP extends over districts of Chandoli, Sonbhadra and the area along the Bihar border. UP has decided to use helicopters to keep an eye on densely forested inaccessible areas. The Indian authorities have now decided to acquire the Belgian shepherd special breed canines, *Malinois*, the dogs that helped the US "Seals" to locate Osama bin Laden. The breed that is being trained for the Indian forces is the litter of an Israeli male Malinois with an American bitch.[5] In Bihar itself the Naxals issued a 'pharman' for candidates for Panchyat elections in the districts under their domination to withdraw their nominations for fear of their lives. All 15 candidates complied without exception! Such is the strength of their hold.

The Government is helpless in the face of non-governance, for which only the Government itself is entirely responsible. The authorities have reacted with Development versus Maoism – the former in name only, or with kind courtesy of the latter, but otherwise the only people who have access to the revolutionary zones are the revolutionaries themselves. They dictate the law. They run the day to day administration. They dispense justice through *'lok adalats'* (peoples' courts) where justice is swift and often cruel without the accused being given a chance to defend. In fact, the mere fact that a person has been accused of anti-people activities is by itself proof enough of his guilt. The absence of governance by the government is the primary cause of Naxalism-Maoism gaining ground from Nepal in the north to Andhra Pradesh in the south – from Pashupati to Tirupati as succinctly described by the BJP stalwart L.K. Advani. It boils down to simple truth that if you do not govern the area, it is no longer yours. May be it is yours on the map, but that is only a piece of paper and not real estate. For the leftists it is a question of life and death while for the government it is merely a bureaucratic job.

The official strategy is the deployment of *Salwa Judum* – a state enterprise of locally recruited cadres under their own Special Police Officers (SPOs), armed, trained and paid for by the State. Their modus operandi is to forcibly evacuate the local tribal indigenous population from their homes and hearths and resettle them in make shift slums at a nominal compensation of Rs. 12,000 per household, to build their own houses in the resettlement colonies, slums most degrading, without any hygienic or sanitary facilities, and clean drinking water. In fact, no water is the rule. You dig your own wells. And if the State installs hand pumps, more often than not, the same do not work since the Naxals make sure that the people do not use such facilities provided by the State. The people are prohibited by the *dalams* from using state facilities for their day to day living. The atrocities wrought by the Maoists gangs have scared the hell out of the peoples' minds so much so that they sometimes voluntarily seek shelter in the Salwa Judum camps, leaving behind their personal belongings, homes, farms and cattle. "Rather than being a 'peace mission', the Salwa Judum has created a situation where violence has escalated." It is noteworthy that Salwa Judum has the support of both the Congress and the BJP.[6]

Rightist vigilant groups like Ranvir Sena, Nagrik Suraksha Samitis, Jan Jagran Abhiyans, *et al.*, have added the plethora of organizations that have been working to counter the extremist violence, loot, arson, random killings, killing of so called police-informers – all this and a lot more have pitched tribals against tribals, peasants against peasants. However, it is significant that the Naxals-Maoists are not criminals. They are driven by ideology and their ranks have often been swelled by highly educated elite from the universities, students and well to do families, who again are goaded by their conscience to work for the deprived poor. Students from Delhi University are the prime example of this do-good-types. On the other hand, government recruits in enterprise like Salwa Judum are like mercenaries who are paid to do what the authorities want them to do. NGOs are yet another set-up, mushrooming all over, some honest to the core out to do good for the poor deprived victimized landless peasants, while a few black sheep are out to make a quick buck in the garb of charitable-social work.

The attitude and behaviour of the powers that wield the authority, is more often than not, totally callous and irresponsible towards the have-nots oppressed classes. This provides the Maoists-Naxals a powerful weapon to resort to violent methods to achieve their ideological objectives. Just to quote one instance to illustrate the point: Tea estates in Bengal-Assam and other parts of North-East India are owned and run as private enterprise. They make good money in international and domestic markets. When the going is good, the estate is looked after; the labour force gets paid more or less regularly; medical and other facilities are made available. However, when the markets are down, prices touch the bottom, the estates are totally neglected. The Tea Gardens just walk out, abjuring their responsibility towards the plants and the labour as if it is none of their business hereafter. The tens and thousands of poor labour is left destitute. They have nothing to fall back upon. In some cases, the workers are denied subsidized rations, health benefits and are paid half wages to effect savings. This is fertile ground for the Maoists to pursue their tactics while the government continues to look away completely ignoring the situation as if it is none of their business. The end result has been Gorkha National Liberation Front (GNLF). And that is a full fledged story by itself in which ethnicity, unemployment, and emotional rhetoric played a major role in bringing Darjeeling Gorkha Hills Council into being as a devolutionary form of governance by Subhash Geising as the leading light of the prime tourist destination in the east. Be that as it may, the regulation dress for the tea estates labour continues to be a *lungi* and a vest!

The international vested interests have a significant role in the rise of Maoist-Naxal revolutionary violence in the Red Corridor spreading across the entire length and breadth of India. Introduction of genetically modified seeds wrote another chapter in the chequered history of Green Revolution in India. No doubt, India benefitted from the GM technology in as much as our agricultural output witnessed a steep rise. The farmers, particularly in the peninsular India's cotton growing belt as well as northern fertile land mass were indeed happy with rising prosperity. But then dawned the realization that GM seeds made India dependent on foreign technology of once-at-a-time. The GM seeds had to be imported again and again from the foreign corporations since seeds could not be gathered from the harvested crop. And seeds were not the only bone of contention ... herbicides and pesticides of foreign corporations came along with the GM seeds. So did a propaganda-handle for the Maoists-Naxalites to further their revolutionary goals of spreading peoples' liberation army and all that goes with it as per Chairman Mao's Red Book!

Bricks are the basic building blocks of construction industry fed by brick kilns located away from urban centers, the main consumers of the product. Since most kilns are manually operated, they are labour intensive which in turn leads to exodus from villages to labour camps abutting the kilns. Landless rural population ridden by unemployment and caste-divide have no option but to acquiesce to diktats of the Sardars who recruit both men and women alike and make sure that the labour is retained as bonded-labour, in one way or the other. However, young girls are preferred as bonded labour for the pleasure of all those connected with the brick trade. Shanties abutting the brick kilns owned and operated by rich urban elite provide both privacy and protection for all the cruelties and sexual harassment inflicted on the illiterate bonded work force.

Caste brutalities are a matter of routine in India's rural hinterland. So is callous attitude of local authorities and the mafia rules the roost. The landless suffer atrocities all because they do not own any land. Poverty is pervasive in the countryside. All this adds up to fertile ground for spreading Maoist-Naxals revolutionary ideology. The irony of the situation is that even in the leftist ruled states landless remain landless and persecuted notwithstanding the legal framework for land reforms and eqitable distribution of excess land held by the landlords.

Political and social courage are contagious. "History teaches us genuine grievances which drive revolutionary change are seldom addressed by revolution, that those who foment change are seldom those who seize power that follows the collapse of the old order, and that often one form of tyranny replaces another."[7]

After the ouster of the King, Maoist Government was formed in Nepal in 2008. A special committee was formed for merger of the PLA in the Sate Army to form a strong natonal security force. This process started after the UN's exit from Nepal's process. The opposition Maoist Party started handing over the second division of its PLA to the Government on January 22, 2011, in a symbolic gesture indicating that nearly 20,000 combatants had disassociated themselves from the mother party to start a new life at the national government level. The ceremony marked taking down of the PLA flag – two AK-47's crossed before the poster of the Himalayas with a red star in ascendence - and the national flag was hoisted in its place. The Government of Nepal and the Maoist Chief Pushpa Kamal Dahal, who had also been the supreme commander during the ten years long "Peoples' War" from 1996 onwards, signed an agreement on that day under which the PLA came under the Special Committee for the Supervision, Integration and Rehabiltation of the Maoist cadres.[8]

The land issue is the main plank of the Naxalbari-Maoist Movements. It is not a terrorist movement *per se* and its leadership is ideologically motivated. Its socal base is the welfare and resolving genuine grievances of the tribals in remote backward areas, besides the untouchables all over the country. It is indeed very unfortunate that the Central and various State Governments lack the political will and commitment to equitably distribute the surplus or wasteland to the landless peasants. Moreover, the bureaucracy and law and order agencies do not function in a people-friendly manner thereby alienating the people at large. "Fake encounters", moneylenders, contractors and the mafia further pile up the grievances against the State machinery which treats the symptoms as mere law and order problems, rather than social and economic issues. In the process the State generates insurgency from which, at times, the bureaucracy-security forces derive illegal financial benefits. Corruption thus becomes rampant.

Land is indeed the primary concern of tribal communities. Industrialization and high scale development-projects cannot by themselves resolve the lop-sided socio-economic conditions. Recent high profile killing of General Manager of Reliance Power and wounding of his eight team-members in Chhatra district, about 100 km from the Jharkhand State capital in first week of April 2011 is an outstanding example of Maoist strong hold in the area, "RED ZONE".

The *Times of India* dated April 08, 2011 reported that a high powered team headed by Manoj Kumat Ojha, General Manager of Reliance Power including the Company's Vice President Hiren Bhuj and six other top officials went out on inspection tour of proposed site for the Rupees twenty thousand crores mega power plant in Telalya. After visiting several villages in Chatra the team was on its way back to Raipur, the State capital, when two teenagers suddenly appeared out of the surrounding jungles and blocked the road. They started firing indiscriminately and disappeared back to their hideouts. Ojha died on the spot while Bhuj got a bullet in his hip. Five other officials in the team were seriously wounded – This episode goes to emphasise the vital importance for the bureaucracy and NGOs to adequately enlighten the tribals of the benefits of development, and the compensation-bonanza that would accrue to them, not only immediately but in the long term too. Advance payment of part compensation, handing over of legal papers for subsequent benefits etc. should be distributed to avoid such tragic incidents.

Notes

1. When the CPI (M)-led United Front Government took office in West Bengal on 2 March 1967, the extremist faction of the Party organized revolts by landless peasants at Naxalbari, Kharbari and Phansidewa in Darjeeling district. All three places are in a compact geographical zone and were suffering similar conditions of extreme poverty. They joined hands together and later formed a separate party under the name and style of Communist Party of India (Marxist-Leninist) – CPI (ML) – under the leadership of Charu Majumdar and Kanu Sanyal. CPI (M) tried hard to accommodate the extremist separatist

faction but the latter refused to relent. Consequently, the CPI (M) Government ruthlessly suppressed the CPI (ML) in West Bengal.

2. There are at least 28 Maoist insurgent groups operating on Indian soil while another seven are in in our peripheral neighbours - 4 in Bangladesh, one each in Bhutan, Nepal and Sri Lanka - making a total of at least 35 such groups in the Indian sub-continent. There is close nexus between the Indian and Nepalese Maoist groups. They have formed what is termed as the "revolutionary corridor" while CPI (Maoist) continues to be the most lethal Naxal group in India.
3. *India Today*, April 25, 2011; p. 56.
4. *ToI*, March 01, 2011.
5. *ToI*, dated May 10, 2011.
6. Chakravarti Sudeep, *Red Sun*; Penguin Viking, India, 2008; p. 47.
7. Gregory Shaun, Associate Professor, University of Bradford, in *Times of India*, January 30, 2011.
8. *Times of India*, dateline Kathmandu, January 14, 2011.

SECTION-IV

13

SINO-INDIAN WAR 1962
Stab in the Back

Kameng Frontier Division of NEFA

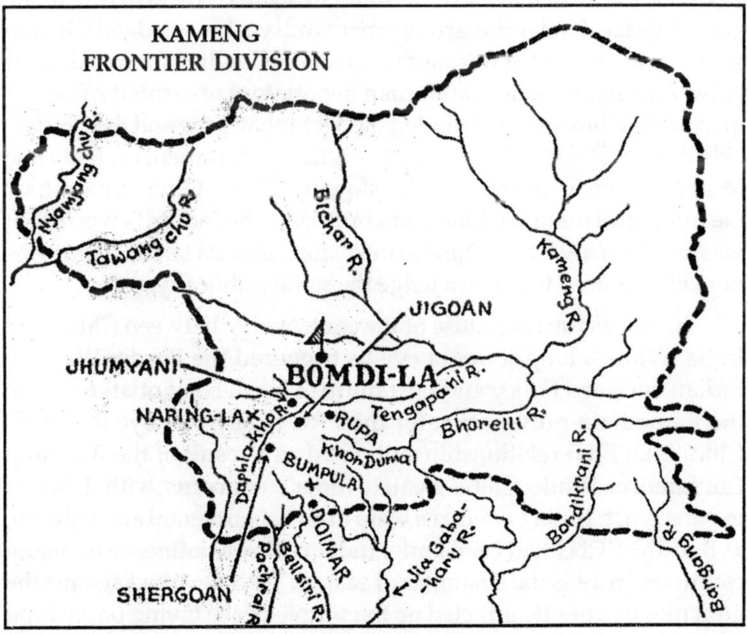

India and China had age old friendly relations, not so much in the economics-trade sphere but more in the spiritual field. When Peoples' Republic of China was formed in 1949 India was keen to revive the old relationship. However, after coming to power, the

PRC announced that its army would be occupying Tibet. India sent a letter of protest to China proposing negotiations on the Tibet issue. But PRC was more active in posting troops to the Aksai Chin border. In August 1950, China expressed its gratitude to Indian attempts to stabilize the India-China border. To clear any ambiguities, Prime Minister Nehru stated in Parliament in 1950: "Our maps show the McMohan Line as our boundary. We stand by that, and will not let anyone else come across that boundary."

The Chinese Army defeated the Tibetan army at Chamdo in 1950 and Lhasa recognized Chinese sovereignty over Tibet in 1951. By this time China had extended numerous posts within Indian Territory in Aksai Chin while the Indian Army asserted control of Tawang overcoming some armed resistance and expelling its Tibetan administrators. Notwithstanding the Chinese aggressions, in 1954 India concluded "Panch-sheel" – the Five Principles of Peaceful Coexistence, which in fact amounted to 'armed co-existence' in the garb of Peace. Under this arrangement India acknowledged Chinese sovereignty in Tibet. It was more of an understanding for co-existence between a tiger and a goat! Indian negotiators presented a frontier map to the Chinese that included the McMohan Line and the Chinese side did not object. At this time, the Indian government under Prime Minister Nehru promoted the slogan "Hindi-Chini Bhai-Bhai" meaning Indians and Chinese are brothers. The Indian Government was perhaps aware of Chinese intrusions into its territory but was not yet prepared to acknowledge the same publically.

Tibet was the root cause of the controversy between China and India. While a long series of events triggered the Border War, the Indian Forward Policy and the failure of border-negotiations were the immediate provocation for the PRC to say bye-bye to Hindi-Chini Bhai Bhai relationship cultivated as a result of the Bandung Conference. While China treated India's concerns with Tibet as expansionist, India's concerns were in fact sentimental and cultural, as Buddhist Tibet had been under Indian cultural influence for many centuries. In 1958 the Khampas of eastern Tibet revolted against the atrocities frequently inflicted on the simple peace loving population of their country. It was a serious uprising against the occupation forces. There was bitter fighting with heavy casualties on both sides. The Chinese crushed the rebellion with a heavy hand. Severe reprisals followed soon thereafter. There was deep resentment amongst the Tibetan population against Chinese atrocities and antireligious propaganda by the communists. In such vitiated hostile atmosphere the Chinese invited His Holiness to a cultural function in Peking. On the advice of his advisers he declined the invitation. The Chinese used threats to cajole him to come to Peking, but he steadfastly refused. When confirmation was received in Lhasa that Delhi had agreed to grant His Holiness political asylum in India, he fled Lhasa under cover of darkness accompanied by trusted bodyguards. Flank protection for the escape route was provided by Khampa warriors.

The Dalai Lama with his immediate entourage crossed the McMohan Line into the Republic of India on March 31, 1959. His Holiness received rousing welcome by throngs of cheering Indian masses all along his route in India. Top PRC leader Mao Zedong, the 'helmsman", felt humiliated by the reception the Dalai Lama received in India. The Tibet disagreements heightened in the Chinese media, which openly criticized Nehru for his Tibet policy. However, India continued negotiations about Tibet. Nevertheless, India wished to express goodwill to China and repeatedly denied the claims of it having a hostile design in Tibet.

In August 1959, the Chinese army took an Indian patrol prisoner at Longju, which India claimed to lie directly on the McMohan Line. There was another bloody clash in October at Kongka La in Aksai Chin in which nine Indian frontier policemen were killed. Consequently, Indian Army assumed responsibility for the border and pulled back patrols from disputed areas.

On October 2, Nikita Khrushchev defended Nehru in a meeting with Mao. The Soviet Union's siding with Nehru, as well as the United States' influence in the region, gave China the belief that it was surrounded by hostile forces. On 16 October, the Chinese Government received reports of Indian expansionism on the Thag La Ridge and approved PLA's plan of a "self-defensive counterattack" against Indian positions. However, Mao decided against further escalation because he feared that India would retaliate by permitting the U.S. to station U-2 surveillance aircraft on its territory allowing CIA to photograph China's nuclear test site. A few days after Kongka Pass incident, Chinese Prime Minister Zou Enlai proposed that each side withdraw 20 kilometers from a "Line of Actual Control". Nehru responded with a proposal to turn the disputed area into a "no man's land". However, China continued to maintain that India was planning to seize Tibet and turn it into a "Buffer Zone".

China's 1958 maps showed Aksai Chin, a 14,670 sq miles large chunk of land between Ladakh and Bhutan as Chinese territory. In 1960, Zhou Enlai proposed that India drop its claim to Aksai Chin and China would withdraw its claims from NEFA. This was a subtle move to deceive India, more so since Zhou had consistently refused to accept the legitimacy of India's territorial claims. He visited India four times in 1960 towards this end, but fortunately and for a change, Nehru did not agree. During April 1960, Zou stayed in Delhi for nearly a week during which he met Nehru every day. They spent nearly twenty hours in conversation. It is reported that hurt and hostility pervaded these discussions. Aksai Chin was strategically vital to China since the highway passing through this stretch of huge land-mass was essential to maintain an effective control over the Tibetan plateau. And Nehru wasn't ready to simply concede the territory. He remained firm that there would be no boundary negotiations until Chinese troops withdrew from Aksai Chin and areas south of the British McMohan Line. This was unacceptable to China, which never recognized the legal validity of the McMohan Line. Nehru stated "We will never compromise on our boundaries, but we are prepared to consider minor adjustments to them and to talk to the other side about them." Obviously, China reached the incorrect conclusion that Nehru was continuing his "grand plans in Tibet".

The Forward Policy

At the beginning of 1961, Nehru appointed his trusted officer Lieutenant General B.M. Kaul, a Kashmiri and a Supply Corps officer, as Chief of General Staff although he had no operational or General Staff experience, by superseding twelve officers senior to him, most of whom were far more competent than Kaul. This appointment caused a serious rift between the Defence Minister and the Army Chief, General K.S. Thimayya who resigned in protest. *Hindustan Times* wrote that "Krishna Menon Must Go" instead of Thimayya. The generally pro-government newspaper accused Krishna Menon of reducing the armed forces to a "near demoralization" by trying to create, at the higher level, a cell of officers who would be personally loyal to him and Nehru. But Kaul was a Kashmiri, so was Nehru. And that's all that mattered to Nehru. Unilaterally appointing senior military officers for active operational duties without taking into consideration the service background of the officer, without even the courtesy of consulting the Chief, was a strange new phenomenon in military matters, particularly when the choice was based on purely personal grounds without consulting the Army high command – a Systemic Failure of newly acquired political powers without the necessary background, leave alone any experience. By this decision alone, Nehru and Krishna Menon together sealed the fate of Indian Army and the impending Sino-Indian War of 1962.

In the summer of 1961, China began patrolling along the McMohan Line. They entered parts of Indian administered regions causing political unrest. In response the Indian Army was directed to establish posts right on the McMohan Line, at places facing far superior Chinese outposts. There were eventually 60 such outposts, including 43 north of the McMohan Line. General Kaul was confident through previous diplomacy of his superiors that the Chinese would not react with force. That was the political perception at the time, which General Kaul had imbibed and now put into practice which had no place in military thought and strategy. But Kaul was no military general either; he was a political general who was his masters' voice in so far as Nehru-Krishna Menon duo was concerned.

India and Chinese posts were separated by a narrow stretch of land. China had been steadily spreading into those lands and India reacted with the Forward Policy to demonstrate that those lands were not unoccupied. He, of course, did not believe he was intruding on Chinese territory. British author Neville Maxwell traces this confidence to Mullik, who was in regular contact with the CIA station chief in New Delhi. Mullik may therefore have been aware of Mao's sensitivity concerning U-2 flights.

The initial reaction of the Chinese forces was to withdraw when Indian outposts advanced towards them. However, this appeared to encourage the Indian forces to accelerate their Forward Policy even further. Thus, they came to perceive the Forward Policy as "creeping annexation of Tibet". In response, the Central Military Commission adopted a policy of "armed coexistence". In response to Indian outposts encircling Chinese positions, Chinese forces would build more outposts to counter-encircle these Indian positions. This pattern of encirclement and counter-encirclement resulted in an interlocking, chessboard-like deployment of Chinese and Indian forces. Despite the leapfrogging encirclements by both sides, no hostile fire occurred from either side as troops from both sides were under orders to fire only in self defence. In any case the Indian military was not ready for full-scale combat. It was already facing border disputes with Pakistan in Kashmir. Indian military leaders who proposed that India should prepare for a full scale attack were ignored or dismissed.

The motive for the Forward Policy was to cut off the supply routes for Chinese troops posted in NEFA and Aksai Chin. The Forward Policy was continued because of its apparent initial success. However, the Forward Policy rested on the assumption that Chinese forces "were not likely to use force against any of our posts, even if they were in a position to do so". No serious reappraisal of this policy took place even when Chinese forces ceased withdrawing. Nehru's confidence was probably justified given the difficulty for China to supply the area over the high altitude terrain over 5000 km from the more populated areas of China. Moreover, Nehru under-estimated the Chinese as a matter of intellectual habit based on his idealism and the high pedestal he thought he stood on as a statesman of international standing. He just could not think in military terms nor did he have much respect for the Indian military brass either, which came fairly low on his scale of precedence. His directive to General Kaul was based on the mistaken premise that China would not resort to force against India. This totally misplaced political misconception percolated down the military command structure – a very unfortunate Failure of Indian Polity.

Goa: Portugal refused to surrender the Goa to the Indian Union. In 1961, the Indian Army had been sent into Goa, a small region without any other international borders apart from the Indian one. Although this action met little to no international protest or opposition, China saw it as an example of India's expansionist nature, especially in light of heated rhetoric from Indian politicians. India's Home Minister declared, "If the Chinese will not vacate the areas occupied by it, India will have to repeat what she did in Goa. India will certainly drive out the Chinese forces" while another member of the Indian Congress Party pronounced, "India will take steps to end [Chinese] aggression on Indian soil just as she ended Portuguese aggression in Goa". Totally irresponsible rhetoric by ignorant politicians reflecting systematic failure of Indian Polity! They were not aware that Chinese Army strength was five times that of India's, and was equipped with the latest Soviet arms and military hardware. On the other hand Nehru-Krishna Menon duo had made sure that Indian army's archaic arms and equipment were more suitable as museum pieces rather than for fighting a modern war. They had a psychological revulsion against acquiring American-European arms besides being scared of possibility of a military coup if the Defence Services were strengthened in any way. Indeed a systematic failure if ever there was any.

By early 1962, the Chinese leadership began to fear that India's intentions were to launch a massive attack against Chinese troops, and that the Indian leadership wanted a war. By mid-1962, it was apparent to the Chinese leadership that negotiations had failed to make any progress. The Indian Forward Policy was increasingly perceived as a grave threat, more so since India continued to send probes deeper into border areas to cut off Chinese supply lines. Foreign Minister Marshal Chen Yi commented at one high-level meeting, "Nehru's forward policy is a knife. He wants to put it in our heart. We cannot close our eyes and await death." The Chinese leadership believed that their restraint on the issue was being perceived by India as weakness, leading to continued provocations, and that a major counterblow was needed to stop perceived Indian aggression.

The Chinese perceived Indian Forward Policy as an attempt at "creeping annexation" of Tibet. This misunderstanding of Indian motive was to become the leading cause of Chinese resorting to full scale war against India.

Early Incidents

Various border-incidents between Indian and Chinese troops flared up throughout the summer and fall of 1962. According to Chinese sources, in June 1962, a minor skirmish broke out between the two sides in which the Chinese military suffered dozens of casualties, both killed and wounded. While both sides maintained close contact throughout September 1962, hostile fire occurred only infrequently.

In May 1962 the Directorate of Military Operations in India had suggested that the air force should be readied for use in NEFA and

Ladakh. The Air Force was considered a feasible proposition to overcome the Chinese troops' numerical superiority. Indian Army in the war zone was a mere ten to twelve thousand while the PLA troop strength was about eighty thousand. The Chinese air force was assessed as only capable of limited strategic raids which could be countered by the Indian Air Force.

In June 1962, the Indian Intelligence Bureau received information about Chinese military buildup along the border that could result in a war in which Pakistan might attack simultaneously in the west. Chinese airfields in Tibet and Yunnan were addressed as a threat to Indian cities, as the PLAAF could conduct heavy bombings through their use of Soviet aircraft.

The Chinese initiated another diplomatic communication on July 8 to protest against an alleged Indian incursion into the Galwan valley of Ladakh. Press reports allegedly released by the Government of India claimed that India had gained 2,000 mi^2 of territory from the Chinese. However, in their diplomatic reply to the Chinese, India denied that any incident had taken place, or official press reports issued on the subject. The fact was that China was the aggressor both in India and Tibet, having illegally occupied a large chunk of Indian Territory in Aksai Chin. On 10 July 1962, 350 Chinese troops surrounded an Indian post at Chushul, in the Galwan Valley. They used loudspeakers to contact the Gurkha troops stationed there. The Chinese attempted to convince the Gurkhas that they should not be fighting for India, and to abandon the post. After heated arguments the Chinese withdrew from the area. Nonetheless, there were clashes in this sector in the third week of July 1962. At this stage India drastically revised its "Forward Policy" on July 22, 1962, in as much as it was now decided to push back the Chinese from posts they had occupied in Indian Territory. Whereas Indian troops were previously ordered to fire only in self-defence, all post commanders were now given discretion to open fire upon Chinese forces if threatened.

In August 1962 the Chinese improved their combat readiness all along the McMohan Line. New ammunition dumps, stockpiling of ammunition, weapons and gasoline etc., was accelerated. However, there were no indications of additional manpower buildup. China's preparedness for war strongly contrasted with India's, which had largely neglected its military throughout the 1950s. Nehru believed that the Himalayas were a large enough defence against China. However, the Korean War had provided China with ample experience in mountain warfare. This neglect on India's part would decide numerous pivotal battles where logistical inadequacy and lack of leadership led to defeat after strong starts.

Confrontation at Thag La

In June 1962, Assam Rifles had established an outpost at Dhola as part of the ongoing forward policy. It was located on the southern slopes of Thag La ridge overlooking the village of Le in Tibet. Dhola post lay about one mile north of the line drawn on paper by Mr. McMohan, but certainly south of top of the ridges. India's interpretation was that the McMohan Line was supposed to represent the top of the ridges all along. The line drawn by Henry McMohan was thick, and it was on a small scale map. The Indian Government maintained that the intention of the McMohan Line was to set the border along the highest ridges, and that the international border fell on the highest ridges of Thag La, about 3 to 4 miles north of the thick line drawn by Henry McMohan on the small scale treaty map. It is the thickness of the line and small scale of the map that was confusing the real issue of line of highest ridges being the real boundary. Nevertheless, in August, China issued diplomatic protests accusing India of violating even the McMohan Line, and Chinese soldiers began occupying positions at the top of Thag La, north of Indian positions. The Chinese started to believe that independent India's leadership was a "reincarnation of British imperialism". Peaceful coexistence soon turned into "armed coexistence".

In early September Dhola-Thag La ridge in the narrow valley of Namka Chu river, about sixty miles west of Tawang, became the center piece of contention. The borders of India, Tibet and Bhutan all meet in this region. The precise alignment of the McMohan Line here was in dispute. On September 8, 1962, a 60-strong PLA unit – which the Indian local commander is alleged to have reported as 600 – descended from the heights and occupied positions on the Thag La ridge which dominated one of our posts at Dhola. Neither side opened fire for 12 days. However, a decision was made on September 9 to evict the Chinese from the southern part of the Thag La Ridge, by force, if necessary. Nehru's protégé, General Kaul had meanwhile assumed command of a fictitious Corps, which was barely worth two divisions plus in infantry numbers, but without the full complement of supporting arms, particularly artillery fire support. Inputs for Mr. Nehru emanated from this HQ. Two days later all forward posts and patrols were given permission to fire on any armed Chinese who entered Indian Territory.

Mr. Nehru's directives to Defence Minister V.K. Krishna Menon were unclear. India's response, code named Operation Leghorn, got underway only slowly. As the Chinese numbers were exaggerated to 600 instead of about 50 or 60, the 9 Punjab battalion numbering 400 riflemen, was sent to Dhola. By the time the Punjabis reached Thag La Ridge in the Chedong region on September 16, north of the McMohan Line, Chinese controlled both banks of the Namka Chu River and had occupied a position that dominated one of the Indian posts at Dhola. The day after that our 'Corps Commander' ordered his men to re-take the Thag La ridge. According to the official Indian history, on September 20, Indian eastern command ordered all Indian posts and patrols to engage any Chinese patrols within range of their weapons. On September 20, at one of the bridges on the river a firefight developed, killing nine Chinese and Indian soldiers, triggering a long series of skirmishes for the rest of September. On 3rd October Zou Enlai visited Nehru in New Delhi promising there would be no war between the two nations and reiterating his wishes to solve the dispute diplomatically.The stalemate continued for almost three weeks. Finally, on October 03 Lieutenant General Umrao Singh who advocated prudence was replaced by Lieutenant General B.M. Kaul. On October 4, a special Border Command was created, under Lt. Gen. B.M. Kaul. Task: evicting the Chinese from Dhola-Thag La area. D-Day for "Op Leghorn" was fixed October 10. To dislodge the Chinese from Thag La he moved two battalions from the plains. These troops had only light clothing, no snow clothing, light weapons, no mortars or rocket launchers. After marching up the mountains through mud and rain, they reached the Namka Chu valley on the afternoon of 9th September. These troops were in no condition to fight. They needed a breather, heavy weapons and snow clothing, besides supplies and ammunition. But that was not to be. The Chinese attacked on the morning of September 10. They fought hard but they were already drained by the march up, were outnumbered and outgunned[1], and of course out-generaled too.

Because of the difficulties involved in directly assaulting and taking Thag La, Kaul decided instead to occupy nearby Yumtso La to the west, to position his troops behind and dominate the Chinese positions. This task was entrusted to Brigadier John Dalvi who informed the General that he lacked necessary supplies and resources to take the pass. On October 9, Kaul and Dalvi agreed to send a patrol of 50 soldiers to Tseng Zong, the approach to Yumtso La, to occupy the position to provide cover to the rest of the battalion's move forward for occupation of Yumtso La. On October 10 this patrol of 50 jawans encountered a Chinese strong position held by some 1,000 soldiers. Indian troops were in no position for battle, as Yumtso La was 16,000 feet (4,900 m) above sea level and Kaul did not plan on having artillery support for the troops. The troops did not have snow clothing either. The Chinese troops opened fire on the Indian patrol under the belief that they were north of the McMohan Line. The Indians were surrounded by Chinese positions which used mortar fire. However, the Patrol managed to hold off the first Chinese assault, inflicting casualties. At this point, Indian troops appeared to be in a position to push the Chinese back. However, Brigadier Dalvi opted not to fire, as it would mean decimating the Punjabis who were still in the area where the Chinese were regrouping. They helplessly watched the Chinese ready themselves for a second assault. The Indian Patrol began their retreat in the face of second Chinese assault, realising the situation was hopeless. The Indian patrol suffered 25 casualties. The Chinese too had some. This was the first instance of heavy fighting in the War.

Some Indian troops, including Brigadier Dalvi who commanded the Forces at Thag La, were also concerned that the territory they were fighting for was, strictly speaking, not Indian Territory. Indian troops marching to Haggle had suffered in the previously inexperienced conditions, since they did not have any 'snow clothing' at all. Two Gurkha soldiers had already died of pulmonary edema. This attack had grave implications for India. Nehru tried to solve the issue but it was too late. By October 18 it was clear that the Chinese were preparing for an attack on India, with massive troop buildups on the border. A long line of mules and porters had also been observed supporting the buildup and reinforcement of positions south of the Thag La ridge.

Chinese Offensive

Chinese Multi-pronged Attacks : Thagla Ridge-Namka Chu River

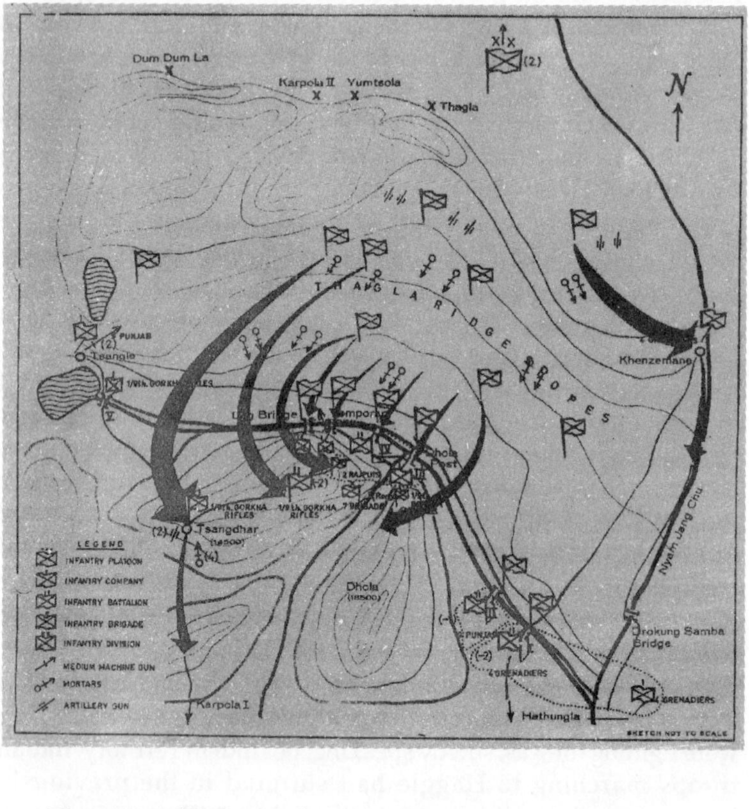

The inevitable had to happen. The three year old phony war finally became real on the night of 19/20 October 1962 when the PLA launched two simultaneous attacks, 1000 km apart, in Ladakh and across the McMohan Line. The *blitzkrieg* across the mighty Himalayas had begun. In the western sector, the PLA mission was to expel our forces from the Chip Chap valley in Aksai Chin while in the east the PLA objectives were both banks of Namka Chu River. Some skirmishes also took place at Nathu La in Sikkim, then an Indian Protectorate and now an Indian State. After four days of fierce fighting the PLA achieved its objectives — a substantial portion of the so-called disputed territory.

Our defences on the South bank were manned by one under strength battalion. On the other hand the PLA had three regiments, each almost equivalent to an Indian brigade, on the north side of the river. The Indians expected Chinese forces to cross via one of five bridges over the river, and sited their positions accordingly to defend those crossings. As our troops settled for the night, the PLA crossed over the shallow-October-river and made their way to the other side. They regrouped into battalions on the Indian-held south side of the river in the camouflage of the night, with each battalion assigned against a specific defended locality of Rajputs. At 5:14 am Chinese mortar fire began pounding the Indian positions. Simultaneously, the Chinese cut the Indian telephone lines. At about 6:30 am the Chinese infantry, who had been positioned behind the Indian defences, launched their surprise attack in conjunction with flank assaults. The Chinese troops overwhelmed the Indian defences and forced them to vacate their entrenched positions south of the McMohan Line. It was not a tactical withdrawal from Namka Chu; it turned into a disorganized route, more like a massacre, kind courtesy poor planning and poor generalship. Fearful of continued losses, Indian troops escaped into Bhutan on their way to safety in India. However, Chinese forces respected the border and ignored Tsang Le. Although by now the Chinese troops had occupied the area which was under dispute in the confrontations at Thag La they did not end their aggression at this time or place. Instead, they continued to advance deeper into the rest of NEFA. On 23 October, Chinese troops launched a three-pronged attack on Tawang, which our forces evacuated without any resistance. Thereafter the Chinese advance continued deeper into Kameng district. The PLA attacked our positions near Se La and Bomdi La on 17 November. These positions were defended by the 4 Infantry Division. Instead of attacking by road as expected, PLA forces approached via a mountain trail, and their attack cut off a main road and isolated 10,000 Indian troops. Se La was very high, and faced with this strategic problem, the Chinese captured Thembang, which was a supply route to Se La.

In the meantime the Chinese activated the eastern extremity of NEFA. On 22 October, at 12:15 am, the PLA launched a mortar attack on Walong, right on the McMohan line. A contingent of 400 troops brought heavy fire on the lightly held Indian post there. Lights fired by Indian troops on 23 October showed the presence of numerous Chinese milling around the valley. Our troops retaliated with their mortars against the Chinese but the PLA then lit a bushfire to create great confusion all round. The Chinese eventually captured Walong at the cost of more than 200 dead or wounded. Our casualties were of course very heavy.

By this time most of the disputed territory in the Aksai Chin region (So ıth Xinjiang), an area of the size of Switzerland, had come under Chi.ıese control. Remnants of Indian troops had been quickly eliminated. Operations launched by PLA on October 20 in the Chip Chap Valley, Galwan Valley, and Pangong Lake were equally successful. Most Indian troops positioned in these posts fought and were either killed or taken prisoner. Indian forces were significantly outnumbered in every action they fought against the PLA. They were thin on the ground and lacked combat readiness, suitable weaponry and snow clothing: It may be recalled that India did not support its encircled troops in these outposts. For instance: Galwan post had been surrounded by PLA in August but it did not receive any land support from India since then. After the 20th October attack, this post was not heard from again.

Late on 19 October, Chinese troops launched various attacks throughout the western sector. By 22 October, PLA succeeded in clearing all posts north of Chushul. This was followed by a battle on October 24 on the Rezang La Ridge for possession of the air strip located on this Ridge. The Chinese suffered 1,000 casualties, with 109 killed. After realizing the magnitude of the attack, Indian Western Command withdrew many of the isolated outposts to the south-east. Daulet Beg Oldi was also evacuated, but it was south of the Chinese claim Line and was not approached by Chinese forces. Indian troops were withdrawn so that they could regroup and be ready if China probed south of their claim line. Meanwhile PLA had wrested control of territory previously administered by India to strengthen PRC diplomatically. The majority of Chinese forces had advanced sixteen kilometers south of the border. By October 24, four days of fighting were followed by three weeks of lull. Zhou ordered PLA to stop further advance. By then Indian troops had retreated into more heavily fortified defences around Se La and Bombdi La which would be difficult to assault.

Map: Chinese Deep Penetrations in Kameng District

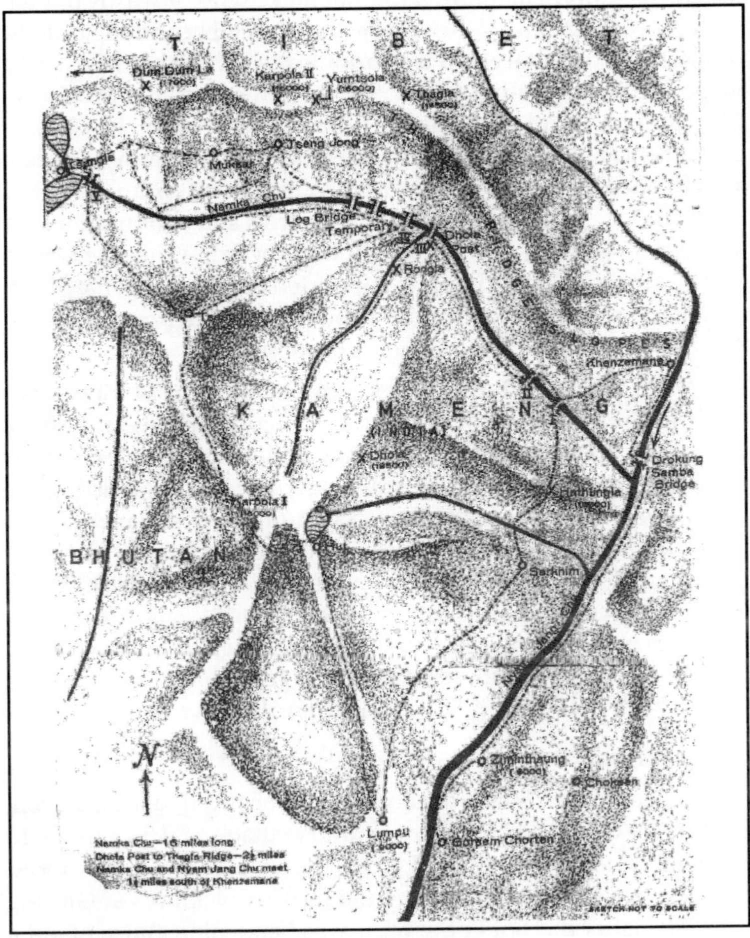

Zhou therefore wrote to Nehru, proposing:

- A negotiated settlement of the boundary;
- That both sides disengage and withdraw twenty kilometers from present lines of actual control;
- A Chinese withdrawal north in NEFA;
- That China and India not cross lines of present control in Aksai Chin.

The Chinese had already advanced 40 to 60 kilometers into Indian Territory. Therefore it did not make sense towards mutual withdrawal by 20 km. Nehru replied on 27 October and suggested a return to the boundary as it was prior to 8th September 1962. Zhou responded by repeating his 1959 offer to return to the McMohan Line in NEFA and MacDonald Line in Aksai Chin. The Indian parliament announced a national emergency and passed a resolution which stated their intent to "drive out the aggressors from the sacred soil of India". The Chinese fought with arms and ammunition and we, like our political masters, fought with rhetoric. While the United States and the United Kingdom supported India's stand, the Soviet Union did not offer the support it had provided in previous years. Once again, Nehru rejected Zhou's proposals.

The fighting in the eastern sector resumed on 14 November (Nehru's birthday). From their strong defensive position of Se La, our troops attacked Chinese positions inflicting heavy casualties. However, the Chinese counter-attacks succeeded in evicting the Indian troops from Se La defences to resume their advance deeper down into Kameng district of NEFA threatening Tezpur in Assam plains, nearly fifty kilometers from the NEFA border (Inner Line). The local government ordered evacuation of civilians in Tezpur to the south of Brahmaputra River. All prisons were also thrown open. In anticipation of a Chinese advance the government officials who stayed behind destroyed Tezpur's currency reserves.

Fighting Resumed

Concurrently Chinese resumed operations in Aksai Chin region. PLA forces launched a heavy infantry attack at 4:35 am on 18 November near Chushul. At 5:45 am the Chinese troops advanced to attack two platoons manning the forward defences at Gurung Hill. The latter did not know what was happening and sent out a strong 'fighting patrol'. As the patrol went out, PLA attacked with greater numbers. Indian artillery could not hold off against superior Chinese forces. By 9:00 am PLA attacked Gurung Hill directly and our troops withdrew from the area. The Chinese had been simultaneously attacking Rezang La which was held by one company of Indian infantry. At 5:05 am, Chinese troops launched their attack audaciously. PLA MMG fire pierced through the Indian tactical defences. At 6:55 am as the sun rose PLA attack on a platoon defended locality began in waves. Indian LMG fire was no match against PLA MMGs. The battle was over in ten minutes, once again highlighting logistical inadequacy of Indian defences. Indian high command believed that their troops were just coming to grips with the mountain combat and finally called for reinforcements. However, the Chinese declared unilateral Cease Fire.

This also signaled end of the fighting in Aksai Chin region where PLA had reached their claim line.

Unilateral Cease Fire

By 19 November 1962 China had reached its claim lines all along the Indo-Tibetan border, therefore it declared a unilateral cease fire that day to come into effect at midnight, November 21. Zhou's Cease Fire declaration stated:

Beginning from 21 November 1962, the Chinese frontier guards will cease fire along the entire Sino-Indian border. Beginning from 1 December 1962, the Chinese frontier guards will withdraw to positions 20 kilometers behind the line of actual control which existed between China and India on 7 November 1959. In the eastern sector, although the Chinese frontier guards have so far been fighting on Chinese territory north of the traditional customary line, they are prepared to withdraw from their present positions to the north of the illegal McMohan Line, and to withdraw twenty kilometers back from that line. In the middle and western sectors, the Chinese frontier guards will withdraw twenty kilometers from the line of actual control.

Here it may be recalled that as early as end September-early October 1962, the Chinese leadership in their directive to PLA had stated that "All Indian troops within China's claimed territories in the eastern sector would be expelled, and the war would be ended with a unilateral Chinese Cease Fire and withdrawal ..." Fantastic forethought and confident military planning! That is real generalship.

The US aircraft carrier USS Enterprise was ordered back after the Cease Fire declaration. Thus, American intervention on India's side in the war came to be avoided. Instead, the US Air Force flew in supplies to India in November 1962. Here, it is noteworthy that neither side had declared war, or used their air force, or fully broke off diplomatic relations throughout the short Border War.

Indian Army suffered much heavier casualties than the Chinese. Indian losses were:

Killed	1383	Missing	1696
Wounded	1047	Captured	3968 (including Brig. J.P. Dalvi, Commander 7 Infantry Brigade)

Chinese losses :

Killed	722
Wounded	1697

Towards the end of the war India had increased her support for Tibetan refugees and revolutionaries, some of them having settled in India, as they were fighting the same common enemy in the region. The Nehru administration ordered the raising of an elite Indian-trained "Tibetan Armed Force" to be later named as "Indo-Tibetan Border Police" composed of Tibetan refugees of Khampa origin, tall handsome well built soldierly personnel. Chakrata, hidden deep in thick jungles of Garhwal Himalayas, was selected as the base, code named "Force Twenty Two", or simply '22'. The CIA had already begun operations in bringing about change in Tibet.

The Chinese military action had been viewed by the United States as part of the PRC's policy of making use of aggressive wars to settle its border disputes and to distract the population at large from its internal issues. Western nations at the time viewed China as an aggressor during the Sino-India border war, and the war was part of a monolithic communist objective for a "World Dictatorship of the Proletariat". This was further triggered by Mao Zedong's views: "The way to world conquest lies through Havana, Accra, and Calcutta". In the past China had been adamant to gain control over regions to which it had a "traditional claim", which triggered the dispute over NEFA and Aksai Chin, and indeed the whole of Tibet too. It would not be far wrong to assume that China might ultimately try to regain control of everything that it considers as "traditionally Chinese" which in its view includes the entirety of South East Asia! The Kennedy Administration was disturbed by what they considered "blatant Chinese communist aggression against India". In a May 1963 National Security Council meeting, contingency planning on the part of the United States in the event of another Chinese attack on India was discussed. Defence Secretary Robert McNamara and General Maxwell Taylor advised the President to use nuclear weapons should the Americans intervene in such a situation. Kennedy insisted that Washington must defend India as it would any ally. The Johnson Administration considered and then rejected giving nuclear weapons technology to India. The non-aligned nations, perhaps unsurprisingly, continued to remain non-aligned, and only the United Arab Republic openly supported India.

As for the causes of the war, Zhou asserted that China did not try and expel Indian troops from south of the McMohan line and that three open warning telegrams were sent to Nehru before the war. However, Indian patrols south of the McMohan line were expelled and suffered casualties in the Chinese attack. Zhou also told Nixon that Chairman Mao ordered the troops to return to show good faith. However, the Indian government maintains that the Chinese military had overstretched far beyond its supply sources and could not advance further south due to logistical problems – a good face saving rationale by our Polity thinking in military terms!

Western nations, in general did not view Chinese actions favourably, but Pakistan, which had a turbulent relationship with India ever since the Indian Partition, took full advantage of Indian discomfort and improved its relations with China. Prior to the war, Pakistan also shared a disputed boundary with China, and had proposed to India that the two countries adopt a common defence against "northern" enemies (i.c. China), which was rejected by India. In the light of subsequent developments it was obviously a Systematic Failure on the part of Indian Polity. Nevertheless, China and Pakistan took steps to peacefully negotiate their shared boundaries. Pakistan also expressed fear that the huge amounts of western military aid directed to India would allow it to threaten Pakistan's security in future conflicts. Mohammed Ali, External Affairs Minister of Pakistan, declared that massive Western aid to India in the Sino-Indian dispute would be considered an unfriendly act towards Pakistan. As a result Pakistan made efforts to improve its relations with China. The following year, China and Pakistan peacefully settled disputes on their shared border, and negotiated the China-Pakistan Border Treaty in 1963, as well as trade, commercial, and barter treaties. On 2 March 1963 Pakistan ceded in favour of China two thousand sq miles of the Northern Territories it had illegally occupied in 1947-48 Indo-Pak War through British connivance. Since the area originally belonged to India, and Pakistan had no legal *locus standii*, the latter had no hesitation in parting with it in favour of China, which benefitted by having a more southerly boundary along the Karakoram Range. The border treaty largely set the border along the MacCartney-Macdonald Line.

Scape-Goat for Nehru

India suffered a humiliating defeat in its war against China, part of which was of its own making. It was a national disaster for India. The aftermath of the war saw sweeping changes in the Indian military to prepare it for similar conflicts in the future, and placed pressure on Indian Prime Minister Jawaharlal Nehru, who was seen as responsible for failing to anticipate the Chinese attack on India. The main lesson India learnt from the war was the need to strengthen its own defence forces and provide them the necessary wherewithal, as well as a drastic change in its foreign policy. Because of India's inability to anticipate Chinese aggression, Nehru faced harsh criticism from the Indian public, the media and also the government officials, for having promoted pacifist relations with China. Nehru's prestige in international affairs suffered a steep downfall. A scape-goat had to be found to save Nehru's skin. The unpreparedness of the Army was blamed on Defence Minister Menon, who was more or less made to resign his Cabinet post to make way for someone who might modernize India's military better. India's policy of weaponization via indigenous sources and self-sufficiency was thus cemented. The fallout from Menon's resignation tempered down Nehru's culpability in this fiasco. General Kaul was also shown the door, and General Thapar too went home soon. Although Menon and the Army brass had been sacrificed to save face for Nehru, the latter knew deep down that ultimately he was responsible for the humiliation the entire nation had suffered. Concurrently, the Indian government commissioned an investigation by Lieutenant Generals Henderson Brooks and P.S. Bhagat, Victoria Cross, to bring out the reasons for India's unpreparedness for war, and to recommend remedial measures. Their Report was highly critical of India's performance in high-altitude combat and led to an overhaul of the Indian Army in terms of doctrine, training, organization and equipment. The report was classified and went a long way in strengthening the Indian Defence Services. India more than doubled her military manpower in the next two years. Military's training and logistic problems were resolved. The Army's capabilities and preparedness were significantly enhanced. Nonetheless the question doing the rounds amongst the middle class India was no longer after Nehru "Who?" the intellectual elite would now ask: After Nehru "What?"

Meanwhile, Mr. Chavan had taken over the Defence portfolio. He had the courage to tell the Parliament:

"This brings me to the next point which is called the Higher Direction of War/Operations. Even the largest and the best equipped armies need to be given proper policy guidance and major directives by the Government, whose instrument it is. An increase in the size or improving the equipment of the Army cost not only money but also needs time."[2]

"Our political philosophies contributed to lackadaisical attitude to defence matters. We did not fear war. We did not seek war to settle any of our problems. We believed that our non-aligned policy and our inflated international prestige would ensure us friends in a crisis. The Indian Government would gladly have disbanded the Army in 1949/50 if the Kashmir problem would have been solvd."[3]

India Request American Arms Aid

The US Ambassador in New Delhi, John Kenneth Galbraith, was called on November 09, 1962 to meet Prime Minister Nehru. A request was made for American arms and military hardware. And the consignments started arriving by late November. This was also virtual end of Nehru's non-alignment policy.

Taking advantage of the tight situation India was in, Pakistan began a policy of provocations against India by border incidents and infiltration into Jammu and Kashmir. Ultimately, a series of such incidents led to triggering the Second Indo-Pak War in 1965. It lasted for thirteen days only but the fighting was indeed intense. However, India had learnt its lesson from 1962 and was prepared to meet Pak aggression head on. The result of the 1965-War was inconclusive and it effectively ended in a stalemate. Two years later, in 1967, there was a short border skirmish known as the Chola Incident between Chinese and Indian troops. In this incident eight Chinese and four Indian soldiers were killed.

Attempts to Find Solution of Kashmir Problem

The humiliating defeat at the hands of Chinese had considerably weakened Prime Minister Nehru, physically and mentally. Yet he had not given up hope of finding a permanent solution of Kashmir imbroglio – It may be recalled that Sheikh Abdullah had been arrested by Government of India in August 1953. No charges were brought against him and he was suddenly released in January 1958. He addressed well attended public meetings all over the State. The one at Hazratbal mosque seems to have unnerved the Bakshi Ghulam Mohammed's Administration. In April he was arrested again on trumped up charges like plotting with Pakistan to break up India, of attempting to facilitate wrongful annexation of the State with Pakistan, create communal disharmony, *et al.* This time he was sent to jail in Jammu. The guilt of putting his old trusted friend behind bars weighed heavily on Nehru. His release was announced by Nehru's confidant Lal Bahadur Shastri with the remarks that Abdullah's detention had been a "matter of pain to the Governmant, and particularly to the Prime Minister." His welcome back to Kashmir was overwhelmingly profuse. In his speeches the Sheikh described his state as a bride cherished by two husbands, India and Pakistan, but neither cared to find out what the bride desired. Since the elections held in Kashmir in 1957 and 1962 were far from being free and fair, the demand for ascertaining afresh the wishes of the people was eminently fair and reasonable.

During his visit to Delhi Sheikh Abdullah stayed with Nehru. Nehru requested Abdullah to discuss the Kashmir issue with an informal committee of advisers consisting of Foreign Secretary Y.D. Geneva, G.Parthasarthy India's High Commissioner to Pakistan and Badruddin Tyabji, Vice Chancellor of Aligarh Muslim University. Various solutions were discussed threadbare. The discussions were thorough and lasted two full days. Abdullah made it clear that he:

- Wanted to promote Indo-Pak friendship;
- Wanted to uphold the secular ideal of Indian Constitution;
- Did not want to weaken the position of minorities in either country.

The foregoing stipulations obviously ruled out a plebiscite. The ground had thus been prepared for Abdullah's forthcoming visit to Pakistan on the invitation of President Ayub Khan whom he met for three hours on May 25 and for four hours on May 26, 1964. After the second meeting Abdullah declared with a broad beaming smile that President Ayub Khan and Prime Minister Nehru would meet in Delhi in mid June 1964, where he (Abdullah) would also be present for any consultations.

Abdullah left for Muzaffarabad in POK where he got the sad news that Prime Minister Jawaharlal Nehru died on the afternoon of that day 27 May 1964. With him also died any hopes of negotiated settlement of Kashmir problem as well as Sino-Indian border dispute.

Notes

1. The Author was working in the Divisional TAC HQ located just to the rear of forward defences in Thag La area. He was responsible for coordinating field-engineering aspects of operations, extremely limited in scope due to paucity of equipment. Only limited mine laying was involved.
2. Quoted by Dalvi J.P. Brig., *Himalayan Blunder*, Natraj Publishers, Dehradun, 1969-1997-2010; p. 397.
3. Dalvi J.P. Brigadier, *op.cit.*, p. 401.

14

SECOND INDO-PAK WAR 1965

Historical Background

On January 17, 1951 General Sir Douglas Garcey relinquished his post as Commander-in-Chief of Pakistan Army. In the absence of any other suitable senior candidate, Lieutenant General Ayub Khan was appointed as the new Army Chief. His rise in the Army hierarchy was indeed meteoric – from major to Army Chief in five short years! Prime Minister Liaqat Ali's assassination in Rawalpindi on October 16, 1951 came as a blessing in disguise to Ayub who was left alone by the politicians scrambling for power to strengthen the Army and sister services thereby creating a well oiled war machine. US military aid to equip and maintain four infantry and one and a half armoured divisions began to flow into the country in 1954. Meanwhile the political turmoil continued. Authority of Central Government had eroded. On October 07, 1958 the President Iskandar Mirza declared Martial Law. But he could not carry the Army with him which was under tight control of Ayub to administer the Martial Law. Therefore, on October 28 he reluctantly handed over power to General Ayub Khan who in turn became the President and Supreme Commander of the Armed Forces. General Mohammed Musa was appointed as Army Chief although he was junior to a few generals, who chose to retire, or were eased out of service. It was obvious that "General Musa had been selected for his dependability rather than merit."[1] His loyalty to Ayub was unquestionable.

India's humiliating defeat in Sino-Indian War 1962 emboldened Pakistan to make another bold attempt to gain the Valley Beautiful, the Muslim majority Kashmir, to accord validity to its 'Two Nations' theory. Pakistan's second full scale attempt to grab Kashmir led to the Second Indo-Pak War 1965 which was a culmination of numerous border incidents instigated by Pakistan that took place between April and September 1965. This conflict came to be known also as the Second Kashmir War fought by India and Pakistan over the disputed region of Kashmir, the first having been fought in 1947-48, a legacy of Jawaharlal Nehru. Pakistan launched its well planned and coordinated "Op Gibraltar"[2] that was designed to infiltrate para-military forces into Jammu and Kashmir, in the garb of Mujahedeen, with the aim of precipitating an insurgency against Indian rule in cooperation with the local separatist elements. The initial success was to be followed by active operations by Pak regular Army.

The Sino-Indian War had acted as a catalyst towards active modernizing of India's defence forces. Y.B. Chavan had taken over November 21, 1962 as India's new Defence Minister. A plan for expansion, reorganization and modernization of equipment was put into effect. Notwithstanding the irritations and pinpricks caused by the non-aligned policies of Nehru Government, seasonal friends like the USA and UK extended a helping hand, quite generously too. The Soviet Union did not lag behind either. Since Nehru had laid strong foundations of long-term friendship with the Soviets, the geopolitics of great power rivalry gave India an added advantage in defence equipment and weapons systems. However, in so far as infantry fire power at fighting sub unit level was concerned, ours was no match for Pakistan because of the qualitative and quantitative tilt in favour of Pakistan in this respect. This in turn instilled in Ayub Khan the confidence to launch his military adventures, first in Rann of Kutch as test drive, and then in Kashmir as a proper military operation to annex the State, or as much of it as was possible. It was the same approach as in 1947-48 – grabbing as much as you can on the battlefield, and then using it as a bargaining chip on the conference table, where Indian diplomacy invariably appeared inept.

On February 23, 1964, after lengthy talks between President Ayub Khan, Mr. Bhutto, and the Chinese Prime Minister Zou-en-Lai, the latter publically declared his country's support for Muslim Liberation Front in Kashmir.[3] However, in this Second War China offered diplomatic and moral support to Pakistan but no direct military support. Much of the war was fought by the countries' land forces in

Kashmir and along the well established and demarcated International Border between the two countries.

Ever since Pakistan came into existence there have been several contentious issues between the two countries. Kashmir was the predominant one. But there were many other irritants too. Accession of the Princely State of Junagarh into India, Pak claims over the Rann of Kutch, were major outstanding issues besides some minor ones too. Junagarh did not have a contiguous border with Pakistan nor a direct land-link; its population was predominantly Hindu but Muslim ruler of the tiny state wanted to join Pakistan. However, it was easily integrated into Indian Union and the ruler with his family took off in a Dakota aircraft for shelter in Pakistan. This caused serious turbulence between the two countries. A similar situation existed in Hyderabad where the ruler, the Nizam, was a Muslim who claimed sovereignty, or accession to Pakistan, but the population was predominantly Hindu.

Rann of Kutch

Soon after American arms started flowing in, General Ayub devised an ingenious plan[4] to administer a phased *coup de grace* to India, which in their opinion was reeling under the effects of famine and language riots, besides of course the crushing defeat at the hands of Chinese in NEFA. The first phase of the Plan was to be of a diversionary nature, a test drive, to draw Indian forces well away from the main theatre of operations, about 1200 km to the south. The second phase was a guerilla infiltration campaign in Kashmir with a view to take over the State. The third phase was deployment of Pak regular forces at an opportune moment of critical significance. Pak Air Force was to assist by way of supply drops.

The die was cast by "Operation Desert Hawk" launched at 3:30 am April 09, 1965 when two battalions of 51 Brigade of Pakistan Army mounted a pre-dawn attack on an Indian police post at Sardar in the Rann of Kutch in Gujarat. Soon it developed into full-fledged campaign that opened with four-pronged attack on April 24 in Kanjarkot-Bier Bet area by Pak Army using M47/48 tanks and infantry in armoured personnel carriers supported by field and medium artillery. India reacted by deploying her forces along the 800-mile West Pakistan border. Lest it develops into full scale war between two Commonwealth countries, the then British Prime

Minister Harold Wilson took the initiative as a result of which President Ayub Khan ordered his forces to cease operations in the Rann on 01 May leading to the two governments signing the Kutch Agreement. Ayub would appear to have equally faithfully copied Mao's political technique. "Having invented a border dispute where none existed, Ayub's next step was to win for the dispute international recognition." Which he did brilliantly! Unfortunately, our Indian diplomatic stand(s) based on idealism mixed with rhetoric have generally led to negative results.

A tribunal was set up under aegis of British Prime Minister to resolve a fictitious dispute. The verdict came later in 1968 which awarded 350 square miles of the Rann to Pakistan as against its original claim of 3500 square miles. Why could we not put up a counter claim for a similar tribunal regarding Gilgit which had been occupied by Pakistan through British complicity and perfidity of British officers? A systematic failure of Indian Polity, to say the least!

On the one hand Ayub ordered cessation of operations in the Rann on 01 May, on the other, at 8:00 pm May 16, 1965 a battalion of Karakoram Scouts surreptitiously attacked one of our posts in Kargil Sector followed by a series of attacks on Indian positions in that Sector so as to cut off our ground L of C to Leh-Ladakh. Ayub's hypocricy and duplicity was thus exposed. India reacted by crossing the Cease Fire Line for the first time on 16/17 May 1965. 4 Rajput evicted the Pakistanis from their two tactically vital features then known as 1360 and Black Rock, which dominated the road axis. In the following incidents sixty Pakistanis were killed, 40 wounded and three captured. On the intervention of General R.H. Nimmo, Chief Military Observer of UNMOGIP, India voluntarily relinquished those posts in June 1965. A major error of judgment, indeed a serious systematic failure, by Indian field commanders; as usual the Indians were taken for a ride! The aggressor had tasted advantage in the high Himalayas, and now in the Rann of Kutch too! Indian politico-military wisdom at its zenith ... CFL violations continued adlib adinfinitum notwithstanding the presence and assurances of UNMOGIP. And these posts were recaptured by Indian troops in the wake of 1965 War and again returned to Pakistan in compliance with Tashkent Declaration. A farcical drama at its best! More about this later in this chapter; nonetheless it was indeed a tragic systematic failure of Indian Polity.

Obsession with Kashmir

Soon after successfully internationalizing the Rann of Kutch issue, Pakistan reverted to its favourite issue of Kashmir. General Ayub Khan believed the Indian Army would be unable to defend itself against a quick military campaign in the disputed territory of Kashmir, more so since the Indian military had been decisively defeated in 1962 in its confrontation with China, and morale of troops was low. Pakistan also believed, albeit erroneously, that the population of Kashmir was generally discontented with Indian rule and that a resistance movement could be ignited by a few infiltrating saboteurs in connivance with some of the known discontented elements in local population. An operation code named "Op Gibraltar" aimed at covert infiltration by Pakistani para-military personnel and discontented elements of the former State Forces as well as deserters from J & K Army was to infiltrate into Kashmir to ignite the resistance movement.

Major General Akhtar Hussain was General Officer Commanding Pakistan's 12 Division for defence of 'Azad Kashmir'. He had 25 infantry battalions to cover a frontage of 400 miles. In early July 1965 his area of responsibility was divided into four sectors, each under a brigadier. He was the spirit behind the concept, planning, and later part execution of the bold and imaginative operation, a reflection of his personality. Op Gibraltar was designed to present a *fait accompli* there before the Indian forces could be alerted ... "There is, however no doubt that there was a miscalculation." The entire operation was conceived on three assumptions:

- Widespread support would be available from local population within POK as well as in the Valley proper;
- India would restrict its operations within the bounds of Azad Kashmir territory only; and
- There was no possibility of India crossing the international border.

As the events unfolded all three assumptions proved wrong. The operation failed because the fundamental difference between commando raids and guerilla operations was never clearly recognized. The selected personnel did not know the area and local language. During the planning stage the Military Operations Directorate had put in a bid for two additional divisions and a corps

HQs. The President had approved the plan of augmentation of forces as demanded. It was also appreciated that infiltrators alone would not be able to wrest Kashmir from India. A complementary operational plan code named "Operation Grand Slam" was already in place, the aim of which was the capture of Akhnur by regular forces of Pakistan using armour and air power. This blitzkreig operation was designed to deliver a disastrous blow to the entire logistic set-up of not only the Indian Army in the Valley but also for the entire State of Jammu and Kashmir.

Pakistan's "Kashmir Cell' was entrusted with the responsibility to train locals for sabotage activities and to train guerillas for induction across the CFL with a view to disrupting conditions in the valley, to arm the locals and help them rise against the Indian Army. The infiltrating force was divided into eight columns given various romantic names like Babar force, Ghaznavi force, etc. Each column had six units of five companies, each of 110 men. The large scale infiltration, particularly in the later half of 1965 caused considerable distress to the Indian civil and millitary establishments. The guerillas were to mix with Kashmiri crowds celebrating the festival of Pir Dastgir on August 08, 1965. The following day a rally to observe the 12th anniversary of Sheikh Adullah's arrest in 1953 was scheduled. Fortunately, these evil designs were discovered by Indian security forces 3-4 days before irreparable damage could be done. On August 09, 1965 the responsibility for dealing with saboteur was entrusted to the Army.

In the words of India's Western Army Commander, Lieutenant General Harbaksh Singh VrC: "The plan was brilliant in conception. The raiders were to infiltrate between 1st and 5th August, concentrate at pre-selected points, and then converge into the Valley from various directions ... the raiders proposed to sneak into the procession fully armed, stage an armed revolt, and in the process capture the radio station, air field and other vital centers. Meanwhile other columns were to cut the roads Srinagar-Jammu and Srinagar-Kargil to isolate Srinagar ... constitute a Revolutionary council, proclaim it as a lawful government, broadcast an appeal to all countries for recognition and assistance ... this was to be signal for Pakistan Army to move in for the kill ..."[5]

"Gibraltar Force"

The Gibraltar Force comprising of about 30,000 all ranks with HQs at Murree under overall command of Major General Akhtar Hussain had assembled for the impending 'war of liberation'. This task force was comprised of men drawn from Pak regular army as well as from the so called Azad Kashmir Militia. In the light of Op Gibraltar the Indian Parliament approved application of Articles 356 and 357 of the Indian Constitution to Jammu And Kashmir State. These provisions allow the President of India to declare President's Rule in the State. Pakistan construed this step as an attempt by India to absorb the "disputed" territory of Kashmir into the Indian Union. There was no doubt that hundreds of infiltrators had entered in Jammu and Kashmir.

India's retaliation to Op Gibraltar was prompt and swift. Indian forces crossed the border on 15 August 1965 and launched an attack on the territory of Kashmir administered by Pakistan (POK). In the rush of initial momentum the Indian Army succeeded in capturing three important mountain positions after a prolonged artillery barrage. However, by the end of August both sides had some success stories. Pakistan had made progress in Tithwal, Uri and Poonch sectors while India had successfully fought the Battle of Bedori, a pre-requisite for success at Haji Pir, leading to capture of the tragically important Haji Pir Pass by 1 Para, eight kilometers into POK followed by Battle of Bisali (4 Rajput), Operation "Faulad" by 93 Infantry Brigade with a view to advance from Poonch to Kahuta, and Battle of Gitian (6 Dogra). Pakistan's reaction to Indian success stories was the move that set the ball rolling for a full scale 1965-War. Op Gibraltar fizzled out as a complete failure setting the stage for the follow-up plan by regular Pak Army.

Pak Army launched a counter attack, code named "Operation Grand Slam" on September 1, 1965: Objective to capture the strategically vital town of Akhnur in Jammu so as to disrupt India's L of C and cut off supply routes. It was a powerful counter attack by Pak Army using technically superior tanks, and infantry in far greater strength. Indian forces were caught unprepared and suffered heavy losses. Pakistan made substantial gains. Failure of Indian Intelligence was writ large. India responded by calling in its air force to blunt the Pakistani attack. The next day, Pakistan Air Force retaliated by attacking Indian ground forces and air bases in both Kashmir and Punjab.

"It is wrong to suggest, as many military historians have done, that Grand Slam was a counter offensive in response to Indian crossing of the CFL in Haji Pir Bulge ... In fact it was a pre-planned operation complementary to Op Gibraltar."

MAP : OPERATION GRAND-SLAM:CHHAMB-JAURIAN SECTOR, SEPTEMBER 1965

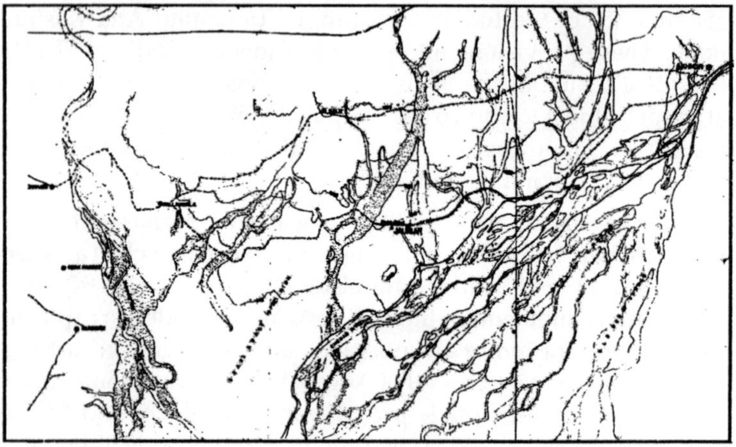

Indian Bold Move Unbalances Pakistan

India found herself in deep waters. In order to release pressure on Akhnurs, India responded by launching a massive surprise attack in the Lahore Sector at 3:30 am, September 06, 1965. As a deception plan it was announced by All India Radio that Pakistan was moving troop formations from Sialkot to Jammu. India decided to open a second front across the International Border in Punjab. That marked the official beginning of Second Indo-Pak War. Pakistan was not prepared for such a totally unexpected bold move by India, but perforce had to relocate troops to defend Punjab. Pakistan was thus forced to thin out in Chhamb-Jaurian Sector. Consequently, Operation Grand Slam also failed. This was perhaps a solitary successful bold story of Indian Polity till it too turned out to be a systematic failure in the end! The same day Pak President declared a state of emergency in his entire country. The responsibility for escalation was therefore solely of Pakistan's own doing, or undoing.

The initial thrust against Lahore by three tank regiments of 2nd Independent Armoured Brigade supported by infantry formations reached the Ichogil Canal (BRB) by 06 September. The Pakistani Army held the bridges over the canal or blew up those it could not hold, effectively stalling any further advance by the Indians on Lahore. However, one unit of the Indian Jat Regiment, 3 Jat, had crossed the Ichogil canal and captured the town of Batapore (Jallo Mur to Pakistan) on the west side of the canal. Indian High Command failed to build up on this unexpected success, yet another instance of systematic failure on the part of Indian military High Command which was not even aware of successful crossing of the Canal by their troops. The same day, a counter offensive by an armoured division and infantry division supported by Sabers of Pakistan Air Force forced the Indian 15th Division to withdraw to its starting point. Although 3 Jat suffered minimal casualties, the bulk of the damage was borne by ammunition and stores vehicles. Strangely enough, the higher commanders had no information of 3 Jat's capture of Batapore! Yet another failure at high command level! Misleading information led the command to withdraw from Batapore and Dograi to Ghosal-Dial. This move brought extreme disappointment to Lt-Col Desmond Hayde, CO of 3 Jat. Dograi was eventually recaptured by 3 Jat on 21 September, for the second time but after a much harder battle. However, Pakistani counter attack took Khem Karan from Indian forces who tried to divert the attention of Pakistanis from Khem Karan by an attack on Bedian and the adjacent villages.

MAP : TANK BATTLES OF KHEMKARAN SECTOR

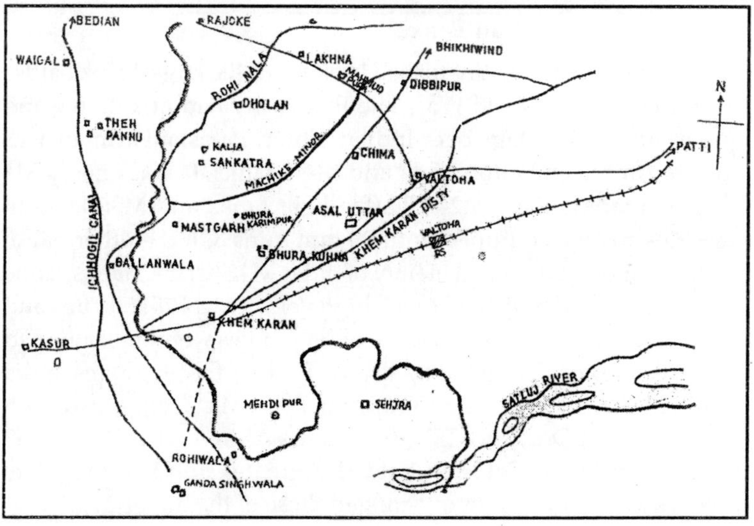

**MAP : BATTLE OF ASSUL UTTAR- KHEMKARAN SECTOR
September 1965**

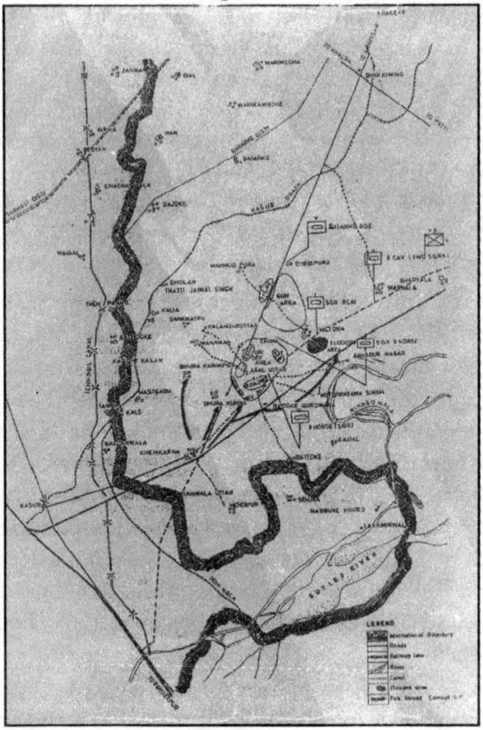

India Battles American Tanks

The 1965 war is distinguished by some of the largest tank battles since the Second World War. The Pak Army had qualitative and quantitative advantage over Indian armor. Pakistani armour was largely American Patton M-47 and M-48 tanks, besides many M4 Sherman tanks, some M24 Chaffee light tanks and M36 Jackson tank destroyers, equipped with 90 mm guns. On the other hand, India's armour comprised mainly of older M4 Sherman tanks; some were up-gunned with the French high velocity CN 75/50 guns and could hold their own, whilst some older models were still equipped with the inferior 75 mm M3 L/40 gun. Besides the Shermans, India also had the British-made Centurion Tank Mk 7, equipped with 105 mm Royal Ordnance L7 gun, and the AMX-13, PT-76, and M3 Stuart light tanks. Pakistan fielded a greater number and more modern artillery; its guns out-ranged those of the Indian artillery.

India's inferiority in numbers and quality of tanks and guns was primarily due to short-sighted policies of Prime Minister Nehru and Defence Minister Krishna Menon who were allergic to America, or their military hardware. They were scared of military coups which were then common amongst newly independent states in South and South-East Asia. Nevertheless it was a serious *systematic failure of Indian Polity*.

At the outbreak of war in 1965, Pakistan had about 15 armoured cavalry regiments, each with about 45 tanks in three squadrons. Besides the Pattons, there were about 200 M4 Shermans re-armed with 76 mm guns, 150 M24 Chaffee light tank and a few independent squadrons of M36B1 tank destroyers. Most of these regiments were allocated to Pakistan's two armoured divisions, the 1st and 6th – the latter was in the process of being raised. As opposed to these, Indian Army possessed 17 cavalry regiments, and in the 1950s had begun modernizing them by the acquisition of 164 AMX-13 light tanks and 188 good old Centurions. The remainder cavalry units were equipped with M4 Shermans and a small number of M3A3 Stuart light tanks. India had only one armoured division, the 1st ('Black Elephant'), which consisted of the 17th Cavalry (Poona Horse), the 4th Hodson's Horse, the 16th 'Black Elephant' Cavalry, the 7th Light Cavalry, the 2nd Royal Lancers, the 18th Cavalry and 62 Cavalry, the two first named being equipped with Centurions. There was also the 2nd Independent Armoured Brigade, one of whose three regiments, the 3rd Cavalry, was also equipped with Centurions.

The Author was commanding an Independent Field Company of Bengal Sappers and was part of the 2nd Independent Armoured Brigade deployed in defensive positions in Khemkaran Sector of Punjab. The Brigade was facing advance of 1st Armoured Division of Pakistan. The assaulting regiments were equipped with latest AMX tanks. In order to channelize/slow down advance of enemy tanks a plan was made to flood certain areas over which assaulting tanks were expected to pass. Since time was at a premium we could not carry out proper engineering survey along the distributory. Of necesiity therefore we resorted to detailed map study of contours along the distributory and, in consultation-coordination with civil canal authorities, canal-distributory passing on the right flank of the Brigade defences was suitably breached by the Bengal Sappers at the selected points to flood the area. The intuitive hunch proved to be a success story of sorts. Part of the forward assaulting regiment of enemy tanks got bogged down in the flooded zone, unable to move forward. The tanks numbering nineteen in all became sitting ducks for our good old Centurions. Since Muslims are afraid of being burnt to death, the crew left their tanks. Next night loud noise emanated from the area of bogged down tanks as if Pak recovery tanks were at the job. The Brigade Commander ordered me to destroy all such enemy tanks *in situ*. Since my unit did not have the resources to destroy such a large number of tanks, and time was at a premium, I decided to disable the tanks so that they could not be put into action in a short time. I deployed my sub units in working groups with orders to blow up the gun breach-block of all the bogged down tanks, as well as the crucial drive sprocket wheel on each track. We managed to disable seventeen tanks that night before returning to our base at first light.

I personally inspected every disabled tank and was astonished to note that some of them had run less than 100 miles! Brand new tanks out of the depot straight into battle action! Obviously, the crew had not trained on their tanks with which they were to go into action. To cut the long story short, Pak 1st Armoured Division assault on Indian defences mainly held by 2 Independent Armoured Brigade did not succeed.

MAP: BATTLE OF CHAWINDA: SEP. 1965[6]

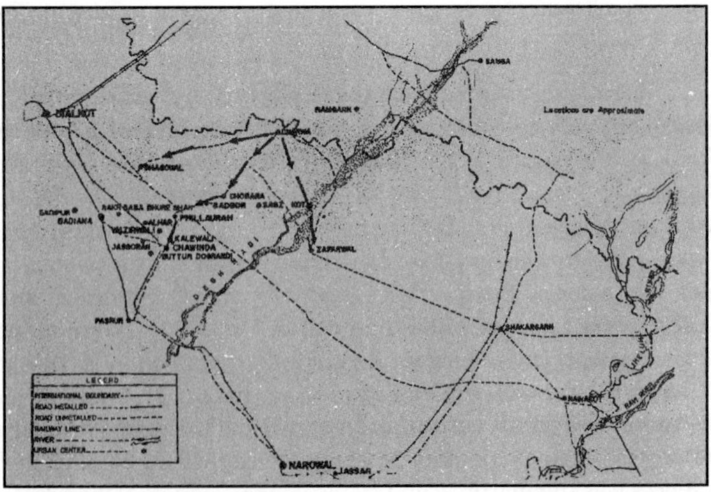

In the same vein India's tank formations experienced similar results. Our attack in the "Battle of Chawinda was the scene of the biggest battle of this short war. It was led by India's elite 1st Armoured Division and supporting units, along with at least three infantry divisions operationg on its flanks. The Pak artillery gave magnificient support to Pak infantry and armour in this 'historic battle' which turned the scales in favour of Pakistan."[7] This major offensive by Indian Army was brought to a grinding halt by newly raised 6th Armoured Division (ex-100 Independent Brigade Group). India lost 12 tanks at Chawinda. One true winner to emerge was our Centurion scene of the battle tank, with its 105 mm gun and heavy armor, which proved superior to the overly complex Pattons and their exaggerated reputation. However, in the Sialkot sector outnumbered Pattons performed exceedingly well in the hands of the 25th Cavalry and other regiments of the Pak 6th Armoured Division, which exacted a disproportionately heavy toll of Centurions from India's Poona Horse and Hodson's Horse. The Indian Army has made much of the fact that some of our Centurions survived repeated hits; yet have failed to point out that the majority of tanks in the Sialkot sector were Shermans whose guns were inadequate even in 1944. Neither the Indian nor Pakistani Army showed any great facility in the use of armoured formations in offensive operations, whether the Pakistani 1st Armoured Division at Asal Uttar or the Indian 1st Armoured Division at Chawinda. In contrast, both proved adept with smaller forces in a defensive role such as the Indian 2nd Armoured Brigade at Asal Uttar and the 25th Cavalry at Chawinda, where they defeated their better equipped but clumsier foes.

Air Operation

The forces of the two countries had previously faced each other in the First Indo-Pak War 1947-48; but that engagement was limited in scale as the two Air Forces (IAF and PAF) were then not involved in combat. However, this war in 1965 witnessed aircraft of the two countries engage in combat for the first time since independence. The IAF was flying large numbers of Hawker Hunter, Indian-manufactured Folland Gnats, de Havilland Vampires, EE Canberra bombers and a squadron of MiG-21s — an assortment of Soviet and European aircraft. The PAF's fighter force was equipped with 102 F-86F Sabres and 12 F-104 Starfighters, along with 24 B-57 Canberra bombers. It has been widely reported and generally believed that the PAF's American aircraft were superior to those of the IAF's, but the experts differ. Nevertheless IAF is believed to have feared the Starfighter but in combat it was not as effective as the IAF's far more agile Gnat fighter. Furthermore, in terms of numerical strength the PAF was out-numbered by around 5:1.

Naval Operations

The navies of India and Pakistan did not play a prominent role in the war of 1965, although Pakistani accounts dispute this. On September 7, a flotilla of the Pakistani Navy carried out a small scale bombardment of the Indian coastal town and radar station of Dwarka, which was 300 km south of the Pakistani port of Karachi. Code-named Operation Dwarka, it did not fulfill its primary objective of disabling the radar station and there was no immediate retaliatory response from India. Later, some of the Indian fleet sailed from Bombay to Dwarka to patrol the area and deter further bombardment. Foreign authors have noted that the "insignificant bombardment" of the town was a "limited engagement, with no strategic value." According to some Pakistani sources their submarine, PNS Ghazi, kept the Indian Navy's aircraft carrier INS Vikrant besieged in Bombay throughout the war. However, INS Vikrant was in dry dock at that time in the process of refitting and therefore the question of PNS Ghazi besieging it does not arise.

Covert Operations

The Pakistan Army launched a number of covert operations to infiltrate and sabotage Indian airbases. On September 7, 1965, the Special Services Group (SSG) commandos were parachuted into Indian Territory. According to Pakistan Army Chief General Musa Khan, about 135 commandos were airdropped at three Indian airfields, Halwara, Pathankot and Adampur. This daring attempt proved to be an "unmitigated disaster". Only 22 commandos returned to Pakistan as planned, 93 were taken prisoner including one of the Commanders, Major Khalid Butt, and 20 were killed in encounters with the army, police or civilians. The reason for the failure of the commando mission is attributed to the failure to provide maps, proper briefings and adequate planning and preparation. The Indian Army diverted 14th Infantry Division to hunt for enemy paratroopers, Pakistan Air Force found the road filled with long columns of transport vehicles, and destroyed many. India responded to the covert activity by announcing rewards for captured Pakistani spies or paratroopers.

Cease Fire

The United States and the Soviet Union joined hands diplomatically to prevent any further escalation of conflict between the two South Asian neighbours. The Soviet Union, led by Premier Alexey Kosygin, hosted Cease Fire negotiations in Tashkent (now in Uzbekistan), where Indian Prime Minister Lal Bahadur Shastri and Pakistani President Ayub Khan signed the Tashkent Agreement, agreeing to withdraw to pre-August lines no later than February 25, 1966.

With declining stockpiles of ammunition and losses in tank-strength, Pakistan feared the war tilting in India's favor. Therefore, they readily accepted the Cease Fire proposals. Despite strong opposition from Indian military leaders, India bowed to growing international diplomatic pressure. However, when the Security Council was pressing for a Ceasefire, Prime Minister Shastri asked his Chief of Army Staff, General Chaudhuri, if India could possibly win the war, were he to delay accepting the ceasefire. The General replied that most of India's frontline ammunition had been used up and the Indian Army had suffered considerable tank losses. Subsequent investigations revealed that only 14% of India's frontline ammunition had been fired and India held twice the number of tanks as Pakistan. By this time, the Pakistan Army had used close to 80% of its ammunition. India was on a winning spree. Prime Minister Shastri was prepared to delay acceptance of premature Ceasefire. But ... It is therefore well on the cards that India would have won a decisive victory against Pakistan but for the shameful ignorant response of India's Army Chief! A serious Failure in the System of military command structure!

On September 22, the United Nations Security Council unanimously passed a resolution that called for an unconditional Cease Fire from both nations. The war ended the following day.

India's Prime Minister, Shastri, suffered a fatal heart attack soon after declaration of the Cease Fire. As a consequence, the public outcry in India against the Cease Fire declaration transformed into a wave of sympathy for the ruling Indian National Congress. The Cease Fire was criticized by many Pakistanis leaders also who, relying on fabricated official reports and the controlled Pakistani media, believed that their leadership had surrendered military gains!

India and Pakistan accused each other of numerous Cease Fire violations. The Cease Fire remained in effect until the start of the Indo-Pakistani War of 1971.

Assessment of Losses

India	Pakistan
3000 men	3800 men
175 tanks	200 tanks
75 Aircrafts	20 aircrafts
1813 sq km	777 sq km

Taking an overall view of military situation of the two antagonists it is beyond doubt that India had an upper hand over Pakistan when Cease Fire was declared.

Air Chief Marshal (retd) P.C. Lal, who was the Vice Chief of Air Staff during the War, points to the lack of coordination between the IAF and the Indian Army. Neither side revealed its battle plans to the other. The battle plans drafted by the Ministry of Defence and Army Chief General Chaudhari did not specify a role for the Indian Air Force in the Order of Battle. This attitude of Gen. Chaudhari was referred to by ACM Lal as the "Supremo Syndrome", a patronizing attitude sometimes held by the Indian Army towards the other branches of the Indian Military. A self-generated superiority complex of an egoistic Chief! Yet another Symbolic Failure at the highest level of command ...

All the foregoing acts of omissions and acts of commission clearly point to repeated Systematic Failures of India's High Command. Indian military intelligence gave no warning of the impending Pakistan invasion. The Indian Army failed to recognize the presence of heavy Pakistani artillery and armaments in Chamb and suffered significant losses as a result.

The Pakistan Army's failures started with the assumption that the generally discontented Kashmiri people, given the opportunity provided by the Pakistani advance, would revolt against their Indian rulers, bringing about a swift and decisive surrender of Kashmir. The people of Kashmiri, however, did not revolt. Instead, the Indian Army was provided with enough information to learn of "Operation

Gibraltar" and the fact that the Army was battling not insurgents, as they had initially assumed, but the enemy was Pakistan Army regulars. Pakistan also failed to recognize that India would attack on the southern sector to open a second theatre of War. Thus, Pakistan had no option but to thin out in Kshamir sector and divert troop reinforcements to southern sector to protect Sialkot and Lahore instead of using them to support penetrations into Kashmir.

Akhnur, a communication center, was primary objective of Pakistan's "Operation Grand Slam" which too was a failure. Many Pakistani commentators criticized the Ayub Khan administration for being indecisive during Operation Grand Slam. Despite progress being made in Akhnur, General Ayub Khan relieved the commanding Major General Akhtar Hussain Malik and replaced him by General Yahya Khan. The change of command at a critical moment led to a 24-hours lull which allowed the Indian Army to regroup thus successfully oppose a lackluster attack headed by General Yahya Khan. "The enemy came to our rescue", asserted the Indian Chief of Staff of Western Command. A serious Systemic Failure on the part of Pakistan at the highest level... The episode closely resembles the First Indo-Pak War 1947-48 when Indian Army was ordered by the top political leader not to pursue the withdrawing Qabailis from Uri to Muzzafarbad! After all, civil and military leaders of both India and Pakistan are sons of the same soil!

Battle of Lahore

Air Marshal Nur Khan, Commander-in-Chief of PAF during the War later said that Pakistan Army, and not India, should be blamed for starting the war. However, propaganda in Pakistan about the war continued; the war was not rationally analyzed in Pakistan, with most of the blame being heaped on the leadership and little importance given to intelligence failures that persisted until the debacle of the 1971-War, when East Pakistan was invaded by India and seceded from West Pakistan, leading to the creation of Bangladesh.

Despite declaration of a Cease Fire, India was perceived as having had the upper hand by virtue of its success in halting Pakistan-backed insurgency in Kashmir. Thus, India was emerging as an Asian power in its own right. In light of the failures of the Sino-Indian War, the outcome of the 1965 War was viewed as a "politico-

MAP : BATTLE OF LAHORE

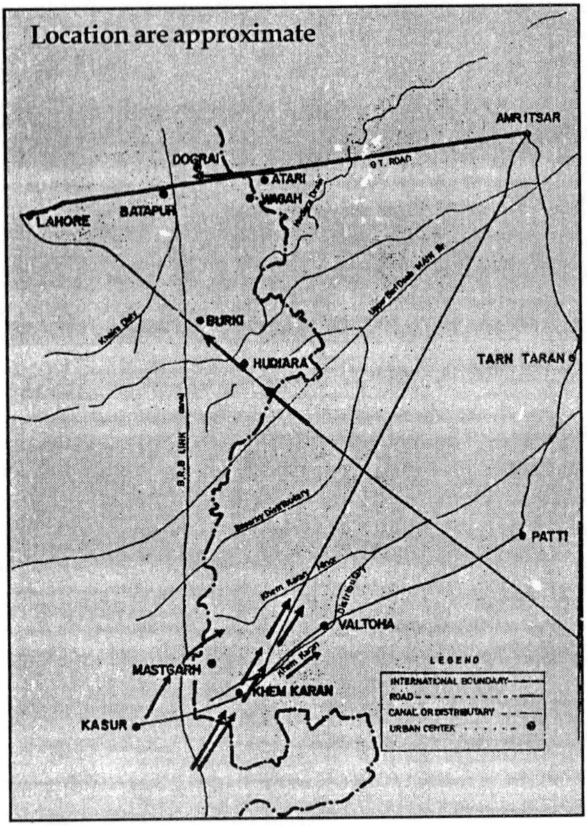

military-strategic" victory in India. The Indian Prime Minister, Lal Bahadur Shastri, was hailed as a national hero. However, Indian military leaders were criticized for their failure to effectively deploy India's superior armed forces so as to achieve a decisive victory over Pakistan. India's Army Chief General Chaudhury was partially responsible for the fiasco of an uncalled for Cease Fire. Though Pakistan "lost heavily" during the 1965 war, India's hasty decision to call for negotiations prevented further considerable damage to Pakistan. Once again a Systematic Failure of Indian Polity! As a consequence, India focused on enhancing communication and coordination within and among the three defence services. Partly as a result of the inefficient information gathering preceding the war,

India established the Research and Analysis Wing for external espionage and intelligence. Major improvements were also made in command and control to address various shortcomings and the positive impact of these changes was clearly visible during the Indo-Pak War of 1971 when India achieved a decisive victory over Pakistan within two weeks.

China's repeated threats to intervene in the conflict in support of Pakistan increased pressure on the government to take an immediate decision to develop nuclear weapons. Despite repeated assurances at the highest level, the United States totally failed to prevent extensive use of American arms by Pakistani forces against India. This considerably irked India. At the same time, the United States and United Kingdom refused to supply India with sophisticated weaponry which further strained the relations between the West and India. These developments led to a significant change in India's foreign policy — India, which had previously championed the cause of non-alignment, distanced itself further from Western powers and developed close relations with the Soviet Union. By the end of 1960's, the Soviet Union emerged as the biggest supplier of military hardware to India. From 1967 to 1977, 81% of India's arms imports were from the Soviet Union. After the 1965 war, the arms race between India and Pakistan became even more asymmetric and India was outdistancing Pakistan by far — a well deserved compliment to India's political and military leadership.

At the conclusion of the war, many Pakistanis considered the performance of their military to be positive. September 6 is celebrated as 'Defence Day' in Pakistan, in commemoration of the successful defence of Lahore against the Indian Army. The performance of PAF, in particular, was commended. However, Pakistan Government was accused by foreign analysts of spreading disinformation among its citizens regarding the actual consequences of the war. After the War the balance of military power had decisively shifted in favour of India. Pakistan had found it difficult to replace the heavy equipment lost during that conflict while India, despite her economic and political problems, had been determinedly building up her strength.

Most observers agree that the myth of a mobile, hard hitting Pakistan Army was badly dented in the war, as critical breakthroughs were not made. Several Pakistani writers criticized the military's ill-founded belief that their "martial race" of soldiers could defeat

"Hindu India" in any war. Rasul Bux Rais, a Pakistani political analyst wrote: The 1965 war with India proved that Pakistan could neither break the formidable Indian defences in a blitzkrieg fashion nor could she sustain an all-out conflict for long.

One of the most far reaching consequences of the war was the wide-scale economic slowdown in Pakistan. Between 1964 and 1966, Pakistan's defence spending rose from 4.82% to 9.86% of GDP, putting tremendous strain on Pakistan's economy. By 1970–71, defence spending comprised a whopping 55.66% of government expenditure. Pakistan was disappointed by lack of support by the United States. After the war, Pakistan increasingly looked towards China as a major source of military hardware and political support.

Another negative consequence of the war for Pakistan was the growing resentment in East Pakistan against the Central Government of Pakistan, particularly for West Pakistan's obsession with Kashmir. The subsequent flare up in East Pakistan had its genesis in as much as all available resources were being squandered in pursuit of Kashmir ambition. Bengali leaders accused the central government of not providing adequate security for East Pakistan during the conflict, even though large sums of money were taken from the east to finance the war for Kashmir. In fact, despite some Pakistan Air Force attacks being launched from bases in East Pakistan during the war, India did not retaliate in that sector, although East Pakistan was defended only by an under strength infantry division (14 Division), sixteen planes and no tanks. Sheikh Mujibur Rahman was critical of the disparity in military resources deployed in East and West Pakistan. Consequently, he demanded greater autonomy for East Pakistan, which ultimately led to the Bangladesh Liberation War, and yet another war between India and Pakistan in 1971.

The Second Kashmir War not only failed to solve the Kashmir problem, it also led to disengagement of United States from the regional entanglements of South Asia. This by itself provided free space for the Soviet Union to expand its influence in the region besides countering the Chinese efforts to play a significant role. Pakistani assessment of Kashmiri sentiment being highly pro-Pakistan proved to be misplaced too. This factor alone made a major contribution towards undermining Operation Gibralar in its early stages itself.

Notes

1. Khan Gal Hassan, Lieutenant General, *Memoirs*, Oxford Karachi, 1993; p. 134.
2. Riza Shaukat, Major General; *The Pakistan Army War 1965*; Natraj Publishers, Dehradun, 1977; p. 18.
3. Bhargava G.S. *Pakistan's Death Wish*, Indian School Supply Depot, Delhi, 1972; p. 13.
4. Harbaksh Singh, Lieut. General; *War Dispatches – Indo Pak Conflict*, 1965;Lancer International, New Delhi, 1991; pp. 26-27 and 74-79. It is rather surprising that the General calls it as "Conflict" rather than War than it was in real sense of the word.
5. As depicted by Brig. A.A.K. Chaudhry, *Pakistan Army*: *op.cit.* p. 74.
6. Chaudhry A.A.K. Brig., *Pakistan Army* : *September 65: Before and After*; Natraj, Dehradun; 1991, p. 74.
7. Soon after the Director od Armoured Corps in British Army visited 2 Armoured Beigade right in our defensive positions. In his opening address he informed that object of his visit to find out how the Indian Army with the British obsolescent managed to take on the modern US tanks equipped with better guns, armour and the necessary ancilliary equipment. He was highly appreciative of the Indian army keeping up the reputation of old British Centurions. (The author was present in that meeting).

15

THIRD INDO-PAK WAR 1971: BANGLADESH

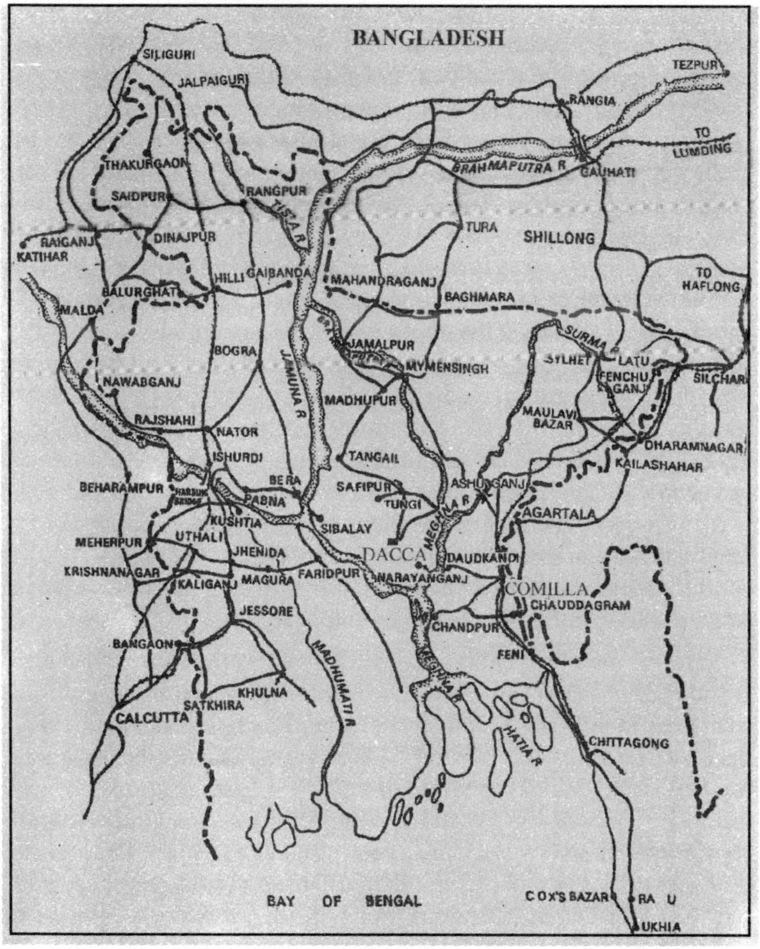

> This was a war in which everything went wrong for the Pakistan Armed Forces. They were not only out-manned but also out-gunned and out-Generaled. Our planning was unrealistic, strategy unsuited, decisions untimely and execution faulty.
>
> ***—Hamoodur Rahman Commission Report***

Yes, it did. But after the fighting was over and Mrs. Indira Gandhi was on Cloud 9, everything went wrong for India.

General Elections in Pakistan

General Yahya Khan succeeded General Ayub Khan as President and Chief Martial Law Administrator of Pakistan. In order to legitamise his position as President he called for general elections based on adult franchise in December 1970, the very first at the national level[1]. The elections were held in early January 1971. General Yahya had hoped that Pakistan Peoples' Party (PPP) led by Zulfiqar Ali Bhutto would win the elections and allow him to continue as President. The entire scheme went topsy-turvy when PPP won 88 seats out of the 144 in West Pakistan while the Awami League led by Sheikh Mujibur Rahman swept the polls in the more populous East Pakistan by winning 167 of the 169 seats. Yahya was shocked. He had hoped that the newly elected assembly would frame a democratic unitary constitution but with the Awami League in power, the constitution would be federal in which the Eastern Wing would have total internal autonomy, perhaps a separate Bangla currency, leaving defence and foreign affairs to the central government. The Sheikh had already thrown hints that the East would manage the foreign exchange generated by exports of its products for the benefit of the Bengali population rather than let the central government fritter away that resource on its adventures in Kashmir and conflicts with India on that score.

Here it may be recalled that the election campaign of PPP was based on the slogan "*roti, kapda aur makaan*" (food, clothing and roof over head) while the Sheikh concentrated on East Pakistan having been victimized by the Western Wing, its anger over suppression of Bengali language, exploitation of its rich natural resources by the military rulers of the Western Wing, besides very poor Bengali representation in Pakistani judiciary, bureaucracy and of course the defence services. In short, the Bengali mind-set severely resented such step-motherly treatment. Furthermore, the West Pakistanis dominated by Punjabi Muslims regarded the Bengalis as effeminate under Hindu influence over ten million of which still lived in their midst. Moreover, many Hindus were doctors, lawyers, professors, and other professionals. The feeling of being discriminated against by an intellectually inferior authority located about a thousand miles away had resulted in piling up of material and psychological grievances over the years.

The West Pakistani elite feared that the constitution framed by Awami League would have a strong Hindu hand in it. In January 1971 Yahya and Bhutto travelled separately to Dacca, the capital city of East Pakistan to hold talks with Sheikh Mujibur Rahman whom they found quite firm on adopting a federal constitution with internal autonomy for the East Wing. The claim of Sheikh Mujib to form the government being the majority party was turned down. Instead Yahya decided to postpone convening of the newly elected assembly. The Awami League thereupon gave a call for indefinite general strike. The protests were quelled by brutal military force which in turn gave birth to the Liberation Movement led by Mukti Bahini. A systematic failure by Pakistani Polity had laid the foundations for disintegration of the country.

Liberation Movement: Rebellion in East Pakistan

Awami League had won a clear majority in the Majlis-e-Shoora, (Lower House of Parliament of Pakistan) and therefore had the right to form the government under its own Prime Minister. Awami League leader Sheikh Mujib presented a 'Six Points' programme to the President of Pakistan and claimed the right to form the government. After the leader of PPP, Zulfiqar Ali Bhutto, refused to yield the primeminster-ship of Pakistan to Sheikh Mujib, President Yahya Khan called the military dominated by West Pakistanis to suppress dissent. Starting with mass arrests of dissidents attempts were made to disarm East Pakistani soldiers and police. After several days of strikes and non-cooperation movements, the Pakistan military cracked down on Dacca on the night of March 25, 1971. The Awami League, the popularly elected majority party, was banned and many of its members fled into exile in India. The police and para-military forces dominated by West Pakistanis (Punjabis) began their offensive with an attack on students of Dacca University who were staunch supporters of Awami League. Many were taken out in darkness of the night, shot and buried in hastily dug mass graves bulldozed over by tanks. The army detachments fanned out to other parts of the city to raid newspaper offices and homes of political leaders. Mujib was arrested at his home on the night of 25–26 March 1971 and taken to a secret location in West Pakistan.

Zia-ur Rahman, a rebellious major in the Pakistani army, broadcast the independence of Bangladesh on behalf of Sheikh Mujib on March 27, 1971. In April, exiled Awami League leaders formed a government-in-exile in Baidyanathtala, popularly known as "Mujib Nagar" in Calcutta. The East Pakistan Rifles, a paramilitary force, defected to the rebellion. A guerrilla troop of civilians, the Mukti Bahini, was formed to help the Bangladesh Army. In the meantime Pak Army fanned out into the countryside seeking to stamp out any signs of rebellion. As the news of Zia-ur Rahman's declaration spread all over the country, East Bengali troops mutinied in several military stations including Chittagong where a major captured a radio station to announce the establishment of the "Independent Republic of Bangladesh". Pak Army countered this slide in the situation by raising squads of local loyalists called 'Razakars' (remember Nizam's Hyderabad?) who put the claims of religion over language, and hence in favour of a united Pakistan.

Genocide in East Pakistan

The Pakistan Army conducted widespread systematic genocide against the Bengali population of East Pakistan, aimed in particular at the minority Hindu population, leading to approximately ten million people fleeing East Pakistan and taking refuge in the neighbouring Indian states. Although most refugees were Hindus, the number of Muslim Bengali refugees was also quite substantial. The Indian Government adopted an "open door" policy right from the beginning. The East Pakistan-India border was opened to allow refugees safe shelter in India. The governments of West Bengal, Bihar, Assam, Meghalaya and Tripura established refugee camps along the border. The resulting flood of impoverished East Pakistani refugees placed an intolerable strain on India's already overburdened economy. "Army officials and soldiers give every indication of believing that they are now embarked on a Jehad against Hindu-corrupted Bengalis."

The Government of India repeatedly appealed to the international community but to no avail. The international silence was deafening and highly disappointing. Prime Minister Indira

Gandhi therefore expressed on March 27, 1971 full support of her government for the independence struggle of the people of East Pakistan. The Indian leadership quickly decided that it was more effective to end the genocide by taking armed action against Pakistan occupation forces in East Pakistan than to simply provide refuge to those who made it across to the Indian side. Exiled East Pakistan Army officers and members of the Indian Intelligence immediately started using these camps for recruitment and training of Mukti Bahini guerrillas.

After the initial swoop Pakistan ordered all foreign correspondents to leave East Pakistan. However, in the summer some were allowed back. They gave harrowing descriptions of damages to towns and villages, destruction of Hindu temples and their homes which were particularly targeted. Evidence of brutal repression was everywhere. During the same period, Indian Army was also running a number of training camps for Mukti Bahini. The trainees were provided arms and ammunition, food, clothing and some sort of housing besides some out-of-pocket expenses. The rank and file of Mukti Bahini included officers and men from the regular army of erstwhile united Pakistan and a number of young volunteers. Every now and then small batches of guerrillas would venture out to East Pakistan, attack army camps and disrupt communications, including demolition of some road-rail bridges[2].

Indo-Russian Treaty

India's hostility towards China dated back to 1950 onwards but that of Russia and China was of recent origin. The armies of the two Communist giants had clashed on River Uri as late as 1969. Both India and Russia shared long borders with China although they did not touch at any point. A treaty of "Peace, Friendship, and Cooperation" between Russia and India was signed in New Delhi on August 09, 1971. The crux of the Treaty was in one sentence in Article IX: "In the event of either Party being subjected to an attack or a threat thereof, the High Contracting Parties shall immediately enter into mutual consultations in order to remove such threat and to take appropriate effective measures to ensure peace and securiries of their countries."

War Clouds in the East

By November 1971 war on the Eastern Front seemed inevitable.

A massive buildup of Indian forces on the border with East Pakistan had begun. Notwithstanding the many attempts at hurrying up the operations, Field Marshal Sam Maneckshaw continued to standby his well considered professional theme: Wait for winter when the drier ground would make for easier operations, and Himalayan passes would be closed by snow, precluding any serious intervention by the Chinese. Yahya Khan declared a state of emergency in all of Pakistan on 23 November and exhorted his people to prepare for war.

At about 5:40 pm on Sunday evening December 03, 1971, the Pakistan Air Force launched a pre-emptive strike on eleven airfields in north-western India, including Agra which was 480 km from the International border.[3] During this attack the Taj Mahal was camouflaged with a forest of twigs and leaves and draped with burlap because its marble glowed like a white beacon in the moon-light.[4] As a result of PAF strike Indian runways were cratered and rendered non-functional for several hours after the attack. Strictly speaking, "Op Chengiz Khan", Pakistan's simultaneous pre-emptive strike on eleven Indian airbases was the spark that ignited the flames of regular war between the two countries. It was Pakistan's 'Chingiz Khan' that started the Bangladesh War, and not India as had been alleged all the time.

MAP : MULTI-PRONGED ATTACKS ON DACCA

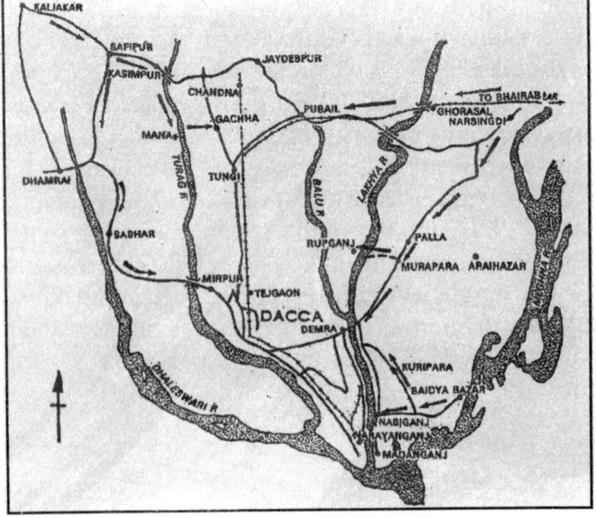

In an address to the nation on radio that same evening, Prime Minister Gandhi held Pak air strikes as a declaration of war against India. The Indian Air Force responded with initial air strikes that very night which were expanded to massive retaliatory strikes the next morning. This marked the official start of the Indo-Pakistani War - 1971, the third since the Partition. Prime Minister Gandhi ordered the immediate mobilization of troops and launched a full-scale offensive against Pakistan. Indian forces responded with a massive coordinated air, sea, and land assault. Indian Air Force started flying sorties against Pakistan from midnight and quickly achieved air superiority. The main Indian objective on the Western front was to prevent Pakistan from entering Indian soil. India had no intention of conducting any major offensive into West Pakistan.

Lasting just 13 days it is considered one of the shortest wars in history producing highly significant results. However, Pakistan considers it to be a part of the overall Bangladesh Liberation War, in which India had been providing direct financial and military support for the Mukti Bahini (Bengali Liberation Forces). Going by the facts on the ground Pakistani version appears to be correct. During the course of the war, Indian and Pakistani forces clashed on the eastern and western fronts. The war effectively came to an end after the Eastern Command of Pakistan Military signed the Instrument of Surrender, following which East Pakistan seceded as the independent state of Bangladesh. Around 97,368 West Pakistanis who were in East Pakistan at the time of its independence, including some 79,700 Pakistan Army soldiers and paramilitary personnel and 12,500 civilians, were taken as prisoners of war by India.

Naval Operations

Pakistan's PNS Ghazi[5], was the only submarine operated by either of the warring nations in 1965. The Ghazi sank off the fairway buoy of Visakhapatnam near the eastern coast of India under mysterious circumstances during the 1971 war, making it the first submarine casualty in the waters around the Indian subcontinent. It is not correct to say that Ghazi was sunk by battle action of Indian Naval Ships; not at all. In the western theatre of the war, the Indian Navy, under the command of Vice Admiral Kohli, achieved commendable success by attacking Karachi's port in "Op Trident" on the night of 4/5 December, which resulted in the sinking of Pakistani destroyer PNS Khyber and a minesweepers PNS Muhafiz while PNS Shahjehan was badly damaged. This resulted in tactical Indian success with Pakistan losing 720 sailors killed and wounded apart from losing reserve fuel and many commercial ships, thus crippling the Pakistan Navy's further involvement in the conflict. 'Op Python' followed 'Op Trident' on night 8/9 December, in which Indian rocket-armed motor torpedo boats attacked Karachi Roads that resulted in further destruction of reserve fuel tanks, as well as sinking of three Pakistani commercial ships in Karachi Harbour.

In the eastern theatre of the war, the Indian Eastern Naval Command, under Vice Admiral Krishnan, completely isolated East Pakistan by establishing a naval blockade in the Bay of Bengal, trapping the Eastern Pakistani Navy as well as eight foreign merchant ships in their ports. From 4 December onwards, the aircraft carrier INS Vikrant was deployed in which its Sea Hawk fighter-bombers attacked many coastal towns in East Pakistan including Chittagong and Cox's Bazaar. One of our IAF bombs in the Chittagong railway yard did not explode. A report was received that the Bomb Disposal Team under a Havildar plans to explode the bomb *in situ,* which would cause major uproar amongst the civil population. I immediately flew over to Chittagong to prevent this tragedy and got the unexploded bomb defused in my presence. However, the Indian Navy suffered its biggest wartime loss on 09 December, when the PNS Hangor sank the frigate INS Khukri in the Arabian Sea resulting in a loss of 18 officers and 176 sailors.

The damage inflicted on the Pakistani Navy stood at seven gunboats, one minesweeper, one submarine, two destroyers, three patrol crafts belonging to the coast guard, 18 cargo, supply and communication vessels, and large scale damage inflicted on the naval base and docks in the coastal city of Karachi. Three merchant navy ships: Anwar Baksh, Pasni and Madhumathi and ten smaller vessels were captured. Pak Navy lost around 1900 personnel while 1413 were captured by Indian forces in Dacca. It is estimated that Pakistan Navy lost a third of its force in this War.

Air Operations

After the initial pre-emptive strike, PAF adopted a defensive stance in response to the Indian retaliation. As the war progressed, the Indian Air Force continued to battle the PAF over conflict zones, but the number of sorties flown by the PAF gradually decreased day-by-day. The IAF flew 4,000 sorties while the PAF offered little in retaliation, partly because of the paucity of non-Bengali technical personnel. This lack of retaliation has also been attributed to the deliberate decision of the PAF High Command to cut its losses as it had already incurred huge losses in the conflict. The PAF also did not intervene during the Indian Navy's raid on Pakistani naval port city of Karachi.

In the east, the small air contingent of PAF, No. 14 Sqn was destroyed, putting Dacca airfield out of commission resulting in complete Indian air superiority in the east.

Ground Operations

Pakistan attacked at several places along India's western border but the Indian Army successfully held their positions The Indian Army quickly responded to PAK Army's movements in the west and made some initial gains, including capturing around 14,000 km^2 of Pakistan territory. However, the land gained by India in POK[6], Pakistani Punjab and Sind sectors was later ceded under Simla Agreement of 1972.

On the Eastern front, the Indian Army joined forces with the Mukti Bahini to form the Mitro Bahini ("Allied Forces"); Unlike the 1965 war which had emphasized set-piece battles and slow advances, this time the strategy adopted was a swift, four-pronged attack by nine infantry divisions with attached armoured units and close air support that rapidly converged on Dacca, the capital of East Pakistan. IAF had already achieved air supremacy while the Indian Naval blockade proved quite effective. Indian ground troops launched fierce attacks on Pak defences. The Indian campaign employed "blitzkrieg" techniques, exploiting weakness in the enemy's positions and bypassing opposition, which resulted in a swift victory. On the night of 13 December 1971 IAF attacked the house of the Governor. The same night Lieutenant General Niazi received a message from General Yahya Khan to surrender since further resistance was not humanly possible. Shortly thereafter all resistance ceased. Faced with insurmountable losses the Pakistani military capitulated in less than a fortnight. On 16 December, the Pakistani forces in East Pakistan officially surrendered to India.

The Instrument of Surrender

The Instrument of Surrender of Pakistani forces stationed in East Pakistan was signed at Ramna Race Course in Dhaka at

16.31 IST on 16 December 1971. Lieutenant General A.A.K. Niazi, Commander of Pakistani forces in Bangladesh signed on behalf of Pakistan while Lieutenant General Jagjit Singh Aurora, General Officer Commanding-in-chief of Indian Eastern Command accepted Niazi's pistol-revolver as a gesture of surrender of Forces under his Command. General Aurora was accompanied by Naval and Air Chiefs of the respective Commands besides his own Chief of Staff, Lieutenant General Jacob. As Aurora accepted the surrender, the surrounding crowds on the race course began shouting anti-Niazi and anti-Pakistan slogans. The same evening Prime Minister Indira Gandhi made an announcement in the Parliament that "Dacca is now a free capital of a free country." Thereafter, she announced on All India Radio a declaration of unilateral Cease Fire on the Western Front by all Indian forces. Twenty-four hours later similar announcements were made by Pakistan.

America Supports Pakistan

The United States supported Pakistan both politically, materially and morally. President Nixon and his Secretary of State Henry Kissinger feared Soviet expansion into South and Southeast Asia. Pakistan was a close ally of the People's Republic of China, with whom Nixon had been negotiating a rapprochement and where he intended to visit in February 1972. Nixon feared that an Indian invasion of West Pakistan would mean total Soviet domination of the region, and that it would seriously undermine the global position of the United States and the regional position of America's new tacit ally, China. In order to demonstrate to China the bona fides of the United States as an ally, and in direct violation of the US, Congress-imposed sanctions on Pakistan, Nixon sent military supplies to Pakistan, routing them through Jordan and Iran, while also encouraging China to increase its arms supplies to Pakistan. The Nixon administration also ignored reports it received of the "genocidal" activities of the Pakistan Army in East Pakistan, most notably the Blood telegram. This prompted widespread criticism and condemnation both by Congress and in the international press. This single episode speaks volumes on the concern for human rights that American Administrations keeps harping on upon from time to time.

When Pakistan's defeat on the Eastern Front seemed certain, Nixon ordered the USS Enterprise into the Bay of Bengal. The

Enterprise arrived on station on 11 December 1971. It has been documented that Nixon even persuaded Iran and Jordan to send their F-86, F-104 and F-5 fighter jets in aid of Pakistan. On 6 December and 13 December, the Soviet Navy dispatched two groups of ships and a submarine, armed with nuclear missiles, from Vladivostok; they trailed U.S. Task Force 74 into the Indian Ocean from 18 December 1971 until 7 January 1972. The Soviets also had a nuclear submarine to help ward off the threat posed by USS Enterprise task force in the Indian Ocean.

The Soviet Union sympathized with Bangladeshis, and supported the Indian Army and Mukti Bahini during the war, recognizing that the independence of Bangladesh would weaken the position of its rivals, the United States and China. Indo-Soviet friendship treaty signed in August 1971 was India's guarantee against Sino-US active participation in the War.

Conclusion

Pakistan lost more than half of its population and had nearly one-third of its army in captivity as a result of the War it had ignited. The end result clearly established India's military dominance of the subcontinent. In spite of the magnitude of Victory, India was surprisingly restrained in its reaction. Most Indian leaders seemed pleased by the relative ease with which Indian forces had accomplished their goals—the establishment of Bangladesh and the prospect of an early return to their homeland of the ten million Bengali refugees who were victims of the War. In announcing the surrender to the Indian Parliament, Prime Minister Indira Gandhi declared:

Dacca is now the free capital of a free country. The people of India hail the people of Bangladesh in their hour of triumph. All nations who value the human spirit will recognize it as a significant milestone in man's quest for liberty.

For Pakistan it was a complete and humiliating defeat, a psychological setback that came from a defeat at the hands of its intense rival, India. Pakistan lost half its territory, significant portion of its economy and its geo-political role in South Asia. Pakistan feared that the two-nation theory was disproved and that the Islamic ideology had proved insufficient to keep Bengalis part of Pakistan. Also, Pakistani military suffered further humiliation by having their 90,000 POWs released by India only after negotiations and signing of the Simla Agreement on July 2, 1972. In signing the agreement Pakistan also, by implication, recognized the former East Pakistan as the now independent and sovereign state of Bangladesh.

The people of Pakistan were not mentally prepared to accept defeat, that too at the hands of "Hindu India". The state controlled media in West Pakistan had been projecting imaginary victories. When the surrender in East Pakistan was finally announced, people could not come to terms with the magnitude of defeat. Spontaneous demonstrations and mass protests erupted on the streets of major cities in West Pakistan. The international community generally recognized emergence of a new nation-state, Bangladesh. The cost of the war for Pakistan in monetary and human resources was very high. General Yahya Khan was demoralized and unable to control the situation. He surrendered power to Zulfiqar Ali Bhutto[7] who was sworn-in on 20 December 1971 as President and as the first civilian Chief Martial Law Administrator.

The loss of East Pakistan had shattered the prestige of Pakistani military. Pakistan lost half its navy, a quarter of its air force and a third of its army. The popular myth that one Muslim had the fighting prowess of five Hindus no longer held any legitimacy. The war also exposed the shortcomings of Pakistan's declared strategic doctrine that the "defence of East Pakistan lay in West Pakistan". Major General Hakeem Arshad Qureshi, a veteran of this conflict noted: "We must accept the fact that, as a people, we had also contributed to the bifurcation of our own country. It was not a Niazi, or a Yahya, even a Mujib, or a Bhutto, or their key assistants, who alone were the cause of our break-up, but a corrupted system and a flawed social order that our own apathy had allowed to remain in place for years. At the most critical moment in our history we failed to check the limitless ambitions of individuals with dubious antecedents and to thwart their selfish and irresponsible behaviour. It was our collective 'conduct' that had provided the enemy an opportunity to dismember us."[8]

Pakistan Government also constituted the Hamdoor Rahman Commission headed by Justice Hamdoor Rahman in 1971 to investigate the political and military causes for defeat and the Bangladesh atrocities during the war. The Commission's report was classified and its publication banned by Bhutto as it put the military in poor light, until some parts of the report surfaced in Indian media in 2000. When it was declassified, it showed many failings from the strategic to the tactical levels. It confirmed the looting, rapes and the killings by the Pakistan Army and their local agents. It laid the blame squarely on Pakistani generals accusing them of war crimes and neglect of duty. Though no actions were ever taken on the Commissions' findings, the Commission had recommended public trial of Pakistan Army's Generals. A further cause for anguish over apathy to genocide is the reaction of the International War Crimes Tribunal which turned a blind eye to numerous acts of commission and omission? A serious failure of International System ...

Bangladesh became an independent nation, the world's third most populous Muslim state. Sheikh Mujibur Rahman was released from a West Pakistani prison, returned to Dhaka on 10 January 1972 to become first President of Bangladesh and later it's Prime Minister.

On the brink of surrender around 14 December, the Pakistan Army, and its local collaborators, systematically killed a large number of Bengali doctors, teachers and intellectuals, part of a pogrom against the Hindu minorities who constituted the majority of urban educated intellectuals. Young men, especially students, who were seen as possible rebels were also targeted. The extent of casualties in East Pakistan is not known. However, Bangladesh Government figures state that Pakistani forces aided by collaborators killed 3 million persons, raped 200,000 women and displaced millions of others. In 2010, Bangladesh government set up a tribunal to prosecute the people involved in alleged war-crimes and those who collaborated with Pakistan. According to the Government, the defendants would be charged with crimes against humanity, genocide, murder, rape and arson.

India emerged as the dominant power in the subcontinent, having washed off its humiliation of 1962. Prestige of Pakistan Army in the eyes of their public suffered a downfall, although they cast the blame on political leadership and tried to find some scapegoat or the other for their battlefield failings. Pakistan's philosophy stood demolished, as was its claim on Kashmir on the basis of commanlity of religion. Moreover, Kashmiri's did not show any interest or anxiety over the fate of West Pakistan in the face of Indian transgression. Pakistan almost turned away from Kashmir.

Now onwards, Soviet Union tilted towards India as a Third World democratic ally of sorts, against US-Chinese nexus. India could also bank on Soviet help if the Chinese misbehaved in future.

Needless to say that Soviet Union came to be India's major supplier of arms, other war equipment and advanced technology for battle readiness. It became a mutually beneficial relationship for both parties.

The Simla Agreement

The Agreement was signed between India and Pakistan on July 02, 1972. It should have been a comprehensive Peace Treaty between the Victor and the Vanquished as it is in international terms. A mere agreement is meaningless in such circumstances, a piece of worthless paper, total failure of Indian diplomacy at the highest political level. The Agreement ensured Pakistan recognized independence of Bangladesh. What good was that to man or beast! Half the world had already recognized Bangladesh as a sovereign independent country. So what if Pakistan did not? Did it matter to Sheikh Mujib, or to India for that matter? And in exchange for that recognition, India, through a sense of misplaced generosity agreed to the return of ninety odd thousand Pakistani Prisoners of War many of whom were guilty of murder, rape, and genocide. What a splendid achievement by the Prime Minister of India!

As a student of military history I cannot cite any such instance in the annals of any international war on record. The agreement not only released more than 90,000 Pakistani POWs in five months; further as a gesture of goodwill, nearly 200 soldiers who were sought for war crimes by Bangaladesh were also pardoned by India — all this unilateral generosity without any *quid pro quo* whatsoever, and that too in the absence of Sheikh Mujib, the President and Prime Minister of the new Nation that had suffered extreme cruelties and atrocities at the hands of the same Pakistanis. What right did we have to play diplomatic games with the assets of that country the President and Prime Minister of which was not even part of the deliberations of the Conference? A Supreme Failure of Himalayan proportions despite repeated sane advice rendered by her trusted advisers.

Having given excellent leadership during the war, the Iron lady had melted like a piece of wax before the sweet-sounding cunning psychophancy of the tall handsome Zulfiqar Bhutto. D.P. Dhar, a close Adviser to Mrs. Gandhi during the War, and Principal Secretary to the Prime Minister and Mr. Haskar, both advised her repeatedly to insist on a comprehensive Peace Treaty, including a final settlement of Kashmir issue and all other outstanding problems, as a pre-condition for repatriation of POWs and return of captured territory, irrespective of pleadings for mercy by Bhutto. But she turned a deaf ear to all sane rational pleadings. She was not open to any advice, not even from a patriotic Kashmiri. Such was the ego of our Iron Lady who, through her leadership, had led the country to a glorious victory. Totally un-statesman-like for deliberately, consciously, obstinately losing an opportunity of a lifetime to resolve All outstanding problems with Pakistan! Indira followed her revered Father's footsteps who committed a similar blunder in 1948 when he ensured survival of Azad Kashmir (POK). His were acts of omission; hers were acts of commission bordering on obdurate irrational obstinacy. The final outcome of Instrumrnt of Surrender was a meaningless good-for-nothing paper agreement, which in international diplomacy had no value at all.

Her genorosity to buy an untrustworthy enemy's goodwill led to yet another Indo-Pak War losing some more precious lives and causing immense grief and distress to the bereaved families of servicemen. Unfortunately, Nehru-Gandhi clan was immune to sufferings of the Defence Services personnel and distress of their families. Mere financial assistance is no compensation for irrational failures.

Indira Gandhi Wrestles with Kashmir Problem

Flush with victory the Iron Lady turned her attention to the Iron Man of Kashmir. She took the initiative to start negotiations with Sheikh Abdullah about the future status of Kashmir. But the Sheikh after almost a decade of house arrest and enforced exile from Kashmir after his release was in no mood to talk to any one about the future status of Kashmir. He had lost faith in Indian political system. However, after much pursuation by one and all the Sheikh finally agreed to send one of his trusted lieutenants, Mirza Afzal Beg to Delhi. Abdullah also made it clear he was interested to know the quality and quantum that India was prepared to concede to Kashmir.

Consequent of Beg-Parthasarthy parleys, Abdullah was allowed to return to Kashmir to resume normal political activity. The Government of India also agreed to examine legislative measures to grant greater degree of autonomy to Kashmir within the Indian Union. This was expected to be harbinger of normalcy and positive relationship between the State and the Central Government. Under such auspicious circumstances Kashmir went to the polls in 1977. By this time Indira Gandhi was out of office and Morarji Desai was the new Prime Minister who made sure that the elections were free and fair in all respects. The Kashmiris came to believe that a gust of fresh air had hit the Valley beautiful to restore it to its past glory and status. The Sheikh died on September 08, 1982. Prior to his death Sheikh Abdullah had successfully groomed his son, Farooq Abdullah, to take his place in the Party and the Government. Meanwhile, Indira Gandhi was back in power. Unfortunately, the concessions on autonomy being granted to Kashmir had a snowballing effect. Punjab, Assam, and other regional groups were vehement in their demands. Indira met them with her usual rhetoric. And she was highly allergic to growth of regional power-centers. She went out of her way to impose her Congress Party where it had no political standing, was out of power and quite unpopular too. Omar was no exception to this tide.

Nehru-Gandhi Politics Derails Positive Swing

Nehru-Gandhi pattern of politics was back in full swing under Rajiv Gandhi. He kept up the Family-traditions. Farooq was persuaded to contest the local elections of 1987 in alliance with the Congess Party. It was a total mismatch. The elections were deeply flawed, openly rigged, as was the past practice with the new avatar of Congress, the Congress (I). The opposition politicians were harassed. Voters were intimidated. Fraud, skullduggery and conceit were the order of the day. The young new generation of Kashmiris were not prepared to acquiesce befor such high level of corruption introduced at the instance of Congress.[9] The protests soon turned violent and took on a secessinonist colour. 1988-89 were the dark period in Kashmir's history after the State joined the Indian Union. The worst was yet to come. Rubiya Sayeed, daughter of Union Home Minister Mufti Mohammed Sayeed, was kidnapped on December 08, 1989 in the heart of Srinagar by Jammu and Kashmir Liberation Front (JKLF) formed in 1976. The Government of India acceded to JKLF demands and released five convicted activists. This one single wrong step emboldened the insurgents so much so that the entire Valley was soon aflame with insurgency. A political blunder of Himalayan proportions!

Ironically, Kashmir's descent into anarchy came at a time when Indo-Pak relations were on a positive swing through untiring efforts of Prime Minister V.P. Singh and his able Forign Minister Inder Kumar Gujral. That positive trend was now derailed; back to square one! After the outbreak of insurgency in Kashmir, Benazir Bhutto openly advocated self-determination for Kashmiris through her familiar inflammatory political rhetoric. Further, troop deployment along sensitive international borders and LOC created deep anxiety in many world capitals so much so that both George W Bush and President Mikhail Gorbachev felt it imperative to issue a joint statement to counsel restraint on Kashmir, both in words and actions.

It is an unfortunate fact of history, may be a coincidence that from 1984 onwards Indian polity went out of its way to resort to deceit, tactlessness and clumsiness in their tackling the internal dimension of Kashmir, thereby further alienating the Kashmiri population. A strange but terrible systematic blunder by Indian Polity!

"The greatest blame, I now realize, lies with Nehru and his daughter, Indira. While his errors were mostly those of omission – supporting Sheikh Abdullah and later abandoning him to the wolves before making a typically gallant but ineffectual attempt at reconciliation – Indira Gandhis sins were those of commission. She, more than any other individual in our history, was the greatest single cause of Kashmir's problems. ... coming a close second to her was Sheikh Abdullah himself, with his foolishly sentimental and idealistic vision to change the course of Kashmir politics outwardly while (perhaps) unwittingly breeding a culture of corruption and dissipation in the Valley's political system, making it one of the worst managed states in the country." India reaped the benefits from the wisdom and leadership of Nehru and his daughter. These were one-time gains, substantial indeed; but those came at an extremely heavy price which has become life long burdens for the country. For how long more? Your guess is as good as mine!

Notes

1. No general election at national level was held in Pakistan during 1947-1970. India's fifth general election was to follow after three months.
2. The Author had personally visited some of the demolished bridges to assess the damage.
3. This pre-emptive air strike came as a blessing in disguise in that Pakistan managed to colour itself as the aggressor, since India's

D-Day was also December 03. The Author can vouch for this since he was present in the operational briefing at the highest level in Fort William when this decision was announced to a few select-members of the Planning Staff.

4. PAF pre-emptive strike code named "Op Chengiz Khan" seems to have been inspired by the success of Israeli 'Operation Focus' in the Arab-Israeli Six Day War. But, unlike the Israeli attack on Arab airbases in 1967 which involved a large number of Israeli planes, Pakistan flew no more than 50 planes to India and failed to inflict the intended damage.

5. PNS Ghazi was originally launched as USS Diablo (SS 479) in December 1944, and commissioned on 31 March 1945 as a long range Tench-class submarine. It was transferred on a four years lease to Pakistan Navy in 1963 and was commissioned into Pak Navy on 01 June 1964 as its first submarine. It sank off the fairway buoy of Vishakhapatnam during Indo-Pak war 1971, perhaps due to a mine explosion while laying mines on the east coast of India.

6. India ceded the reoccupied POK territory primarily because of political immaturity and diplomatic naivette of Indian delegation in the Simla Conference.

6. In 1963 Zulfiqar Ali Bhutto met President J.F. Kennedy in Washington. After a day of talks Kennedy looked at Bhutto and said: " If you were American, you would be in my Cabinet.' Be careful Mr. President, 'Bhutto replied, "If I were American, you would be in my Cabinet." – Wolpert Stanley: *Zulfiqar Bhutto of Pakistan; His Life and Times*, Oxford University Press, New Delhi.

8. Major General Hakeem Arshad Qureshi: *The 1971 Indo-Pak war : A Soldier's Narrative* ; Oxford 1973.

9. I totally agree with all this. However, it may be recalled that for the October 1951 elections for the Kashmir constituent assembly Praja Parishad was also a party. Salient point of their manifesto was : "*Ek Vidhan*", "*Ek Pradhan, Ek Nishan*" (One constitution; one President; one flag". But nomination papers of most of its candidates were declared invalid. The Party therefore boycotted the elections in protest. The result: Sheikh Abdullah's National Conference bagged all the 75 seats, unopposed.

16

INDIA'S POLITICO-MILITARY MISADVENTURE IN SRI LANKA: 1987-1990

MAP : SRI LANKA

The Indian sub-continent underwent a major metamorphosis when Partition of India took place in 1947. But that was all; nothing changed for the multi-ethnic multi-religious Sri Lanka in so far as its integration with the economic-cultural pattern of new India was concerned. It remained as it used to be during the British colonial rule in India. Although there has been some let up in economic relations in as much as capital investment by India's private sector in Sri Lanka was a good omen to begin with, but that has not gone to its logical conclusion in regard to trade, particularly in export trade in tea. That indeed would have been economically more beneficial to Sri Lanka but the political cost outweighed that advantage. Instead of mutual cooperation in economic and security fields, Colombo seems to have been more interested in developing those ties with the ASEAN system.

The "Ceylon Tamil" community in Sri Lanka has been a major festering sore in Delhi-Colombo relations. In the past they have not been involved with Indian political-social system nor have they sought any help or sympathy from the politicians of Tamil Nadu. It is only after the Tamil-Sinhala confrontations that led to violent riots from time to time and the news of atrocities on the Tamils made headlines in world media, that the people and government of Tamil Nadu woke up to the plight of their brethren across the straits. They started pressurizing Delhi to take suitable steps to resolve the problem. This raised Colombo's concerns over perceived threat of Indian intervention, which was further fueled by rhetoric and immature politics of Delhi (more about this later).

The Tamil community has been residing in Sri Lanka for hundreds of years. To label them as migrants defies rationale, to say the least; they are as much citizens of Sri Lanka as the Sinhalas, perhaps more so since Tamils were perhaps the first in that territory, having come across the Palk Straits from mainland Tamil Nadu over a string of islets 35 km long known as Adam's Bridge well before the Sinhalas did. The history of Jaffna-Tamils goes as far back as about 3,500 BC, the period of Indus Valley Civilization (Mohenjodaro and Harappa). On the other hand the "Aryan" Sinhalas came around 600 BC as colonizers from Bengal, Bihar and Orissa region during the period when Buddhism was on a steep decline in India so as to establish Dhamma Shashan in the Dhamma Dwipa[1], while the Tamils followed Saivite Hinduism.

Besides the "Ceylon Tamils" concentrated in the northern and eastern provinces, there is also a community of "Indian Tamils" numbering about one million who had settled in Sri Lanka as migrant labour for tea gardens in the central and southern parts of the country. This community had scrupulously avoided taking sides with insurgent Tamils; nonetheless, being racially connected to the Jaffna Tamils, Colombo sometimes did take harsh measures against them too, but avoided alienating them in the interest of their tea industry which is labour intensive. However, they formed a sizeable chunk of electorate that could influence elections in some constituencies. Therefore, on attaining independence on 08 February 1948 after 450 years of colonial rule, the then ruling party, the United National Party (UNP) redefined the criteria for citizenship which rendered the "Indian Tamils" as stateless. They were deprived of citizenship and denied voting rights by the new Sri Lankan Government. But India refused to accept them back[2]. Some "Indian Tamils" naturally now started looking up to "Ceylon Tamils" and Tamil Nadu for protection and moral support. This constitutional change and other factors like:

- During the colonial era it was the Ceylon Tamils who cornered most of the blue collar jobs. After independence the Sinhala majority naturally wanted this imbalance to be corrected;
- Sinhala was declared the sole official language putting the non-Sinhala minorities at a considerable disadvantage;
- Special constitutional protection was accorded to Buddhism;
- Local autonomy earlier promised to Tamil majority districts was not granted under the new constitutional dispensation;
- Sinhala Police broke into World Tamil Conference held in Jaffna in 1973 causing widespread damage, looting and arson;
- Resettling many Sinhala families in predominantly Tamil areas (perceived by the Tamils as threat at alteration of demographic pattern in the State)

The foregoing factors reignited the fire of ethnic violence.

The rise of Tamil nationalism in TN led to Sinhala distrust of state government. DMK and AIADMK openly proclaimed their support for Tamil homeland in Sri Lanka. The Central Government in Delhi, realizing the depth of emotive nature of this issue, and the necessity of appeasing the sentiments of its own nearly 55 million

Tamil population, Delhi took some diplomatic initiatives during 1980 to cool the temperature. India's policy towards Sri Lanka and the Tamil question underwent a complete metamorphosis. India decided to become the mediator and guarantor of the diplomatic solution of the imbroglio. However, in the SAARC meeting held in August 1983 Sri Lanka reasserted her active support for South-Asian regional system rather than a bilateral system with Delhi. Meanwhile, there was no letup in communal strife in the island State with ever increasing violence and insurgency, nor did Delhi take active steps against well identified training camps for Ceylon Tamil insurgents in South India, active financial, moral and arms support provided by the official and non-official agencies – perhaps with covert support from Delhi. Lest the situation gets out of hand, during late 1985 Indian Prime Minister Rajiv Gandhi started putting strong pressure on Ceylon Tamil insurgent groups to eschew the path of violence and negotiate a political settlement of their grievances. This was attempted in October 1985 when the two parties met at Thimphu, Bhutan, under Delhi's quiet sponsorship. Unfortunately, Colombo's threat perception of Indian intervention on the side of Jaffna Tamils continued as heretofore. The imbroglio continued unabated.

The impression that India's past record of successful military interventions in Junagarh, Hyderabad, Kashmir, Nepal in 1950-51, Goa in 1961, East Pakistan in 1971, Sikkim in 1975, Bangladesh in 1976-77, *et al.*, went a long way to strengthen the threat-perception by Colombo[3], howsoever misplaced that might have been. Be that as it may, the ethnic strife between the Ceylon Tamils and Sinhala majority continued unabated ultimately giving birth to "Liberation Tigers of Tamil Elam" (LTTE)[4] whose primary demand was secession of the Northern Tamil majority areas (Jaffna) to form an independent Sovereign State. It is the world's only guerilla-style force that brought two light aircrafts into action to bomb the country's major airport (Colombo).

Within hours of signing of Indo-Sri Lanka Accord on July 29, 1987 between Indian Prime Minister Rajiv Gandhi and Sri Lankan President J.R. Jayewardene, leading elements of 54 Infantry Division as part of Indian Peace Keeping Force (IPKF) – a totally unprepared ill equipped force – started landing at Palaly Airfield on the east coast of SriLanka. India was neither matured enough, nor its forces trained, prepared or equipped for such a dramatic first overseas foreign venture at such extremely short notice. The Division received no Operational Instructions, issued no Operation Order, and there was no logistical order or movement plan, no formal warning order or NMB (No Move Before) were issued to the Division– all part of basic battle procedures. The grass root leaders did not even have maps[5] of the area they were supposed to operate in, nor compasses and binoculars! LTTE could see us and bring down accurate small arms fire but our infantry's return fire was merely speculative. It was India's first foreign-policy-inspired overseas military venture ("Operation PAWAN" – indeed a whirlwind operation!). Neither the COAS Krishnaswamy Sundarji nor his DGMO Lieutenant General B.C. Joshi ensured even a semblance of logistical planning-deployment for an extremely hurried induction of troops into a foreign land. Perhaps, they could not have done anything in the matter because the entire exercise was controlled by the Ministry of External Affairs and Research & Analysis Wing (RAW) under overall control of Prime Minister Rajiv Gandhi. And he was the Supreme Commander for military, RAW and the bureaucracy!

Involvement of India's armed forces with Sri Lanka may be divided into four phases:

- Phase 1: Induction of IPKF on night July 29, 1987 to ensure implementation of Indo-Sri Lanka Accord signed that very morning at Colombo between Indian Prime Minister and Lankan President J.R. Jayewardene (generally to function as a policing force);
- Phase 2: After breakdown of the Accord on 5 October 1987, capture Jaffna Town and clear Jaffna Peninsula;
- Phase 3: Counter-insurgency operations against LTTE in Northern and Eastern Provinces of Sri Lanka;
- Phase 4: Phased de-induction of the Force ending in March 1990.

In other words, the political task of implementing ISLA by merely "showing the flag" suddenly got transformed into a military task of fighting highly motivated urban guerillas on their home ground. Civilian intelligence agencies and RAW were mainly responsible for this fiasco. They had assured Rajiv Gandhi that LTTE would never attack Indian Army since they were 'our boys' trained and equipped by them!

Lieutenant General Depinder Singh, General-Officer-Commanding in Chief Southern Command was appointed as the Overall Force Commander (OFC) with the following as designated component commanders:

- General Officer Commanding 1 Corps;
- Flag Officer Commanding Eastern Fleet (Navy);
- Chief of Staff of Southern Air Command.

Here it should be noted that since all the three defense services of India functioned as independent entitities in their own right, they were not obliged to follow the instructions of OFC if it did not suit their convenience. In other words, the OFC was to fuction at the goodwill and discretion of Naval and Air Force commanders, and not as a matter of military discipline—a short cut to disruption of chain of command and dislocation of Army's operational plans. To cap it all, you had the coterie of Chiefs of RAW and IB headed by the Prime Minister whose knowledge of military strategy, deployment and tactics could be written on the back of a postage stamp; nonetheless, their word was the last super command in all matters. And there was no Maneckshaw around to stand up to such nonsense. Failure was writ large from Day-One!

A UN panel of experts appointed byUN Secretary General has called for an independent inquiry into "credible" allegations that Sri Lanka committed War Crimes as well as 'crimes against humanity' during its final 2009 offensive against LTTE. Specifically, the Report cited charges of government troops shelling known civilian targets and hospitals in the 'No Fire Zone'. It said that "tens of thousands" of people were killed between January and May 2009 in the final government offensive that resulted in defeat of the separatist LTTE, ending a decade-old ethnic conflict. The Report also cited alleged violations by the rebels for having used the civilians as shields.

The OFC has claimed that contingency planning was taken up by his HQ in April 1987, but no concrete preparations appear to have been made to meet those contingencies. Perhaps, it was more of an academic exercise. And "Operation PAWAN", induction of IPKF, came to be a hurried, haphazard and disorganized affair. This malady was to adversely affect performance of infantry battalions and the formations which came in bits and pieces, more often than not at around 50% of their authorized strength, and that too without much of essential equipment, support elements like mortars, artillery guns and armor, besides absence of organized logistical support. Another major deficiency was lack of preparation, training and psychological preparation at grassroots level for which the units-formations commanders were not given any time. The Politico-Military set up in Delhi was equally, perhaps very much more, responsible for the messy manner of induction of IPKF. It is a lesson for senior military commanders, staff and top political leadership of the future how not to induct troops for an operation, more so overseas in a foreign land. There is no substitute for BATTLE PROCEDURE.

The OFC has gone on record: "The Operational Instruction issued to me was delightfully vague, merely directing me to implement the Accord ... which I interpreted to mean that SLAF and the LTTE were to be separated so that the fighting stopped; we were to accept the surrender of arms and ammunition from the LTTE, ..."[6] Totally unprofessional type of instruction, to say the least!

The island state of Sri Lanka (known as Ceylon during British rule) is 437 km long and 225 km in breadth East-West covering an area of 65,610 km^2. The Northern part comprising about 4/5th of land area is plain while the south-central part is hilly, 900 to 2,000M AMSL. In the present context it is the Northern Areas comprising Jaffna Peninsula, the plains immediately to the south, and coastal belt to the East where the port city of Trincomalee is located, are really relevant. While Sinhalese form about 74% of Sri Lankan population, they constitute only 15% of population of Northern and Eastern Provinces. On the other hand, Tamils form 70% of population in these two provinces, only a little over 50% of Tamils are resident in the two provinces, the remainder being spread over center, west and south of the country. The latter are therefore like vulnerable hostages when hostilities break out between the two major communities. Here it will not be out of place to mention that Jaffna area has a number of lagoons which increase in size during monsoons thereby reducing the usable land area, which in turn leads to wall-to-wall construction of houses, a risky difficult proposition while conducting military operations.

LTTE was banned by Colombo in 1978. But the organization continued to grow in strength and stature. Prabhakaran received massive financial and material assistance from Indian sources, both Governmental and private. Arms and ammunition came in large quantities, so did the instructors from paramilitary forces of India and State Police of Tamil Nadu. LTTE was not the only beneficiary of this largesse; other militant groups like erstwhile Tamil United Liberation Front (TULF), Tamil Elam Liberation Front (TELF), Tamil Elam Liberation Organization (TELO), Elam People's Revolutionary Liberation Front (EPRLF), *et al.*, were also joint beneficiaries on Tamil Nadu soil for which the State Government provided liberal facilities. The cadres were sent back to Sri Lanka after about three months of intensive training and indoctrination. Their material needs and pocket expenses were also taken care of at State expense. During 1983 and 1984 the Intelligence bureau and the Research and Analysis Wing of Central Government were active in coordinating the work of training and allied matters. However, LTTE Supremo seriously resented to what he perceived as an attempt to divide and rule policy of Government of India, perhaps in conjunction with TN authorities. He therefore ordered his cadres to totally eliminate the major rival group TELO. Thus, Jaffna came under exclusive control of LTTE which virtually ran a state within a State. By this time SLAF was confined to their coastal camps only.

Prabhakaran was confident that, whoever else may disassociate from his LTTE, the charismatic Chief Minister of TN (and leader of AIDMK) would continue their moral and material support since that suited political fortunes of TN's ruling political Party's fortunes. Since the Congress Government in Delhi was dependent on his goodwill, and the issue of Lankan Tamils grievances against Colombo commanded massive popular support, his Party's fortunes were on an ascending curve.

The people of India, Tamil Nadu (TN) in particular, were staunch supporters to the cause of Tamil militants. The ethnic connection was indeed strong. The State government of TN actively provided sanctuary, medical aid, financial support, enabled the militants to establish training camps within the state, military training, arms and ammunition, so on and so forth. They enjoyed free access-exit facilities and transport where necessary. In other words, for almost a decade from 1977 till deployment of IKF in July 1987, the State government in concert with the Central Government through its agency, Research and Analysis Wing (RAW), the latter covertly of course, were active patrons of various militant groups fighting the Sinhalese in Sri Lanka. Naturally, Sri Lanka considered these Indian activities as unfriendly acts. Pakistani military dictator, General Zia-ul-Haq offered military assistance to Sri Lanka in its operations against Tamil rebels. Since Pakistani presence in Sri Lanka was inimical to Indian interests, this rang loud bells in the top corridors of power in India. Further, Pakistan had close relations with USA which was interested in obtaining repair and allied facilities in Trincomalee harbour. This was an added complication to an already complex political situation. In order to counter any possibility of Sri Lanka inviting Pakistan or China for assistance, Indian army HQ had earmarked 1 Corps to intervene to pre-empt any such eventuality. Nevertheless, diplomatic moves are initiated towards damage control.

Operation Liberation (by SLAF)

By now it was time for Colombo to act. SLAF reinforced its position in Jaffna Peninsula by inducting additional troops and heavy weapons with a view to launch a major offensive against LTTE. An economic blockade was imposed to cut off entry of men and materials from outside. The operation to wrest control of Jaffna Peninsula was launched by SLAF on May 26, 1987 using heavy artillery bombardment in conjunction with aerial attacks. Point Pedro[7] in the North East of the Peninsula was the center of attention by SLAF. The economic blockade was hurting the civil population the most. There was no electricity, no running water, medicines and supplies in extreme short supply. The Jaffna Tamils were in a deplorable state.

After the slaughter of Jaffna Tamils, Indian Prime Minister was under tremendous pressure from his political partners in Tamil Nadu to put an end to killing of Jaffna Tamils by Sri Lankan Armed Forces. The hardships being faced by the civil population of Jaffna added fuel to the fire. M.G. Ramachandran's loud protestations forced Rajiv's hands. When attempts at mercy mission by sea failed in the face of Lankan Naval resistance, IAF dropped relief supplies from AN-32 cargo aircraft escorted by Mirage 2000 fighters to the beleaguered civil population. Perhaps, this gesture on the part of India partly accelerated attempts at bringing the SLAF offensive to a halt.

Meanwhile LTTE continued to consolidate its position in the heartland of Peninsula besides constantly harassing its opponents in refugee camps in Sri Lanka as well as in TN. Thus, LTTE continued to remain the major, if not the only force fighting for independent homeland for Tamils – *Tamil Elam*. Their discipline was exemplary.

Every single person of military wing of LTTE carried a cyanide capsule on person which added to the cadres' motivation. Above all, LTTE preached the Maoists doctrine: "Power flows from the barrel of the gun"; "Bullet is more powerful than the ballot".

Sri Lankan economy nose-dived in the face of internal strife. Tourism and tea exports – major sources of foreign exchange – had considerably shrunk. The burden of defense continued to rise sharply. External debt kept rising. The cost of fighting the LTTE further drained the scarce resources of the country. The formidable organization and strength, armament and financial and moral support they received from abroad besides TN, their expertise in claymore mines and improvised explosive devices (IED) – were contributory factors in softening the attitude of Sri Lankan Government. Therefore, the Sri Lankan Government became desirous of putting an end to bloodshed and restore normalcy in the State. With that end in view Indo-Sri Lanka Accord (ISLA) was signed between Indian Prime Minister Rajiv Gandhi and President J.R. Jayewardene of Sri Lanka in Colombo on July 29, 1987[8]. The salient points of the Accord:

- Guarantee territorial integrity of Sri Lanka;
- Safeguard India's security interest;
- Restoration and stabilization of economy of Sri Lanka;
- Safeguard interests of all communities in Sri Lanka.

The above objectives were proposed to be achieved through:

- Immediate deployment of Indian Peace Keeping Force (IPKF) in Sri Lanka in order to separate the two warring groups – SLAF and LTTE by enforcing a Ceasefire within **24 hours** of signing of the Accord;
- SLAF to withdraw to its pre-May 1987 positions which were occupied by them prior to launching of Lankan "Operation Liberation";
- Surrender of weapons by LTTE with **96 hours** of signing of the Accord[9];
- Formation of Administrative Council for Northern and Eastern provinces;
- Elections to the Administrative Council to take over from the Interim Council within three months;

- Referendum by end 1988 to decide whether the Eastern provinces would like to merge with the Northern provinces;
- Devolution of more powers to the Administrative Council by Sri Lankan Government.

The above political document formed the basis of IPKF operations in Sri Lanka. It was the genesis of directives for "Operation Pawan" and subsequent operations. The initial force levels and time frame were totally unrealistic and impossible to achieve. The IPKF was doomed to be a politico-military misadventure right from the beginning. It was a classic case of political leadership dictating military terms without an iota of understanding of military implications. Military planning, movements and operations were not taken into consideration. The top military command had no hand in formulation of the Accord, or did not have the courage to render correct military advice to top political leadership (as Manekshaw had done in 1971).

In the opinion of Lieutenant General S.C. Sardeshpande, AVSM, UYSM (Retd.) who served in IPKF first as GOC 54 Infantry Division and later as Deputy OFC:

- The ISLA was a terrible infant - precocious, and complex, with its own chinks ...;
- IPKF was required to disarm militants, confine SLSF to barracks in Tamil Provinces, confront both adversaries if they joined hands - these threefold contradictory implications had not dawned on the politico-military leaders then, but in the end all three eventualities did come about;
- Conspicuous underestimation of SLG in devolving power to the Tamils;
- Tamil militants obduracy to agree to anything short of Elam;
- India lacked the ability to persuade the two antagonists and the will to force it down their throats;

ISLA missed out totally the LTTE's hypnotic hold over Tamils in Sri Lanka as well as India, and their determination to fight even with IPKF, when that became necessary.

Induction of IPKF into Sri Lanka started in the early hours of July 30, 1987. It was more like a fire brigade rushing to douse the flames of a major conflagration. The grass root battalion level units were not given timely 'warning orders' to set the 'battle procedure' in motion to prepare themselves for a foreign assignment. Initially 54 Infantry Division minus its heavy equipment and support elements was the only formation inducted. At that point of time IPKF area of operational responsibility was restricted to part of the Eastern Provinces only. The Division was deployed as under:

• Divisional HQ	Palaly
• 47 Infantry Brigade	Vavunyia
• 76 Infantry Brigade	Trincomalee
• 91 Infantry Brigade	Jaffna

At that point of time tasks allotted to IPKF (54 Infantry Division) were[10]:

- Separate SLAF and LTTE and ensure observance of ceasefire;
- Take over arms and ammunition to be handed over by LTTE and other militant groups;[11]
- Ensure dismantling of all SLAF camps established after May 1987;
- Help local population to return to their homes;
- In general, to maintain law and order.

It was never envisaged that IPKF might be obliged to fight the LTTE trained and armed by the Indians! 54 Infantry Division had made elaborate arrangements to take over all arms and ammunition from LTTE. However, Prabhakaran, the supreme commander of LTTE was not a naive person to part with precious treasure; he refused to hand over a single weapon! Meanwhile SLAF were confined to barracks and commenced to withdraw from positions occupied after May 1987. But their withdrawal and vacating accommodation like schools and hospitals occupied by them in Tamil areas was very slow. LTTE resented these delaying tactics. However, a large number of SLAF personnel continued to be airlifted to Colombo. The ceasefire became virtually effective. The civil population started returning to their homes. This included some Sinhala families too. LTTE questioned the legitimacy of such returnees dubbing it as Colombo's policy of altering the demographic pattern. Mutual mistrust was at the bottom of such allegations, true or otherwise.

With the signing of the Accord, general amnesty was declared to all militants. Sri Lankan security forces had about 1200 Tamils in their custody whose release was demanded by LTTE. In return,

Colombo demanded release of eight policemen held by LTTE. This controversy further delayed the peace process. Yet another negative factor was alienation of Tamil Muslims due to depredations of LTTE against that community while concurrently making efforts to woo them to their side. The overall situation was indeed chaotic.

Formation of **Interim Administrative Council** (IAC) was next item on the agenda to carry forward the political process. The Indian High Commissioner in Colombo was working relentlessly towards that end. He proposed that the Council would comprise of eleven members - six LTTE nominees including one Muslim, two Sinhalas, and two nominees of TULF. LTTE was to give three names for appointment of Chairman out of which the President would choose one. All names for council membership were finally approved by the President. The High Commissioner flew into Palaly on September 28, 1987 where Prabhakaran and his colleagues had already assembled. When the High Commissioner announced the names approved by the President, Prabhakaran objected to the selected Chairman (Sivagnanam) and instead wanted Pathmanathan. This U-turn by Prabhakaran "further lends credence to the theory that the LTTE was apprehensive of fighting an election, and the result was in consequence of the military wing's disagreeing with the assessment of the political wing and prevailing in getting the agreement negated."[12]

Around this time, LTTE propaganda Chief, Thileepan, started his fast unto death on September 15 in the famous Nallur Temple in Jaffna. His demands:

- Stoppage of colonization by Sinhala in Tamil areas;
- Immediate release of all Tamil prisoners held in Sinhala jails;
- Early formation of Interim Council;
- Vacation of school and college buildings by SLAF;
- Holding of elections and referendum as scheduled.

Thileepan died September 26, 1987. The gulf between IPKF and LTTE now became wide and deep. Restoration of political process as envisaged in the Accord appeared hopeless. In fact, it proved that the Accord was an impractical theoretical proposition to resolve an otherwise vexed complicated problem. A hurried politico-military misadventure was not the solution for resolving the ethnic and economic issues involved. India had blundered into the unknown without the top political and military leadership giving a matured thought. Meanwhile the senior bureaucrats in RAW and MEA continued to follow an altogether different agenda – build up other Tamil militant groups, arm and train them as a counter to LTTE intransigence so as to marginalize the LTTE. This double-game being played by India and the High Commissioner Dixit's arrogance put a quick and permanent end to India's fast-eroding-influence with the LTTE."[13]

The proverbial last straw that broke the camel's back was the infamous "Boat Tragedy" incidents in early October 1987:

- A boat carrying 17 LTTE personnel was intercepted by Lankan Navy in its territorial waters on Oct 03, 1987. Since the LTTE had been granted amnesty, and on their insistence, IPKF rescued the prisoners and transferred them to Palaly airbase. Despite OFC and Dixit interceding on behalf of the prisoners on grounds of amnesty, the President did not relent. SLAF decided to take the prisoners to Colombo. When the SLAF started to escort the prisoners to waiting aircraft on October 05, all 17 of them swallowed cyanide capsules. They were immediately rushed to the nearby IPKH hospital, but 12 died including Pulendran[14] and Kumarappa, the Jaffna regional commander;
- In a swift and savage retribution on 5th and 6th October LTTE killed six Indian soldiers, massacred over 200 Sinhalese and rendered over ten thousand homeless. General Sundarji in his usual flamboyant style announced that firm action would be taken against LTTE and Indian Army would finish the LTTE in a week! How naïve ...[15]
- LTTE executed the earlier mentioned eight policemen held as prisoner by them. Their bodies were dropped from a van outside Jaffna Fort in full view of IPKF personnel inside;
- Major General Harkirat Singh, the senior man on the spot, squarely blames the political leadership, diplomats and Army Headquarters for this fiasco.

SLAF garrisons were spread out and had been reduced to barest minimum in accordance with the Accord. IPKF units were therefore milked to provide protection to these garrisons to avoid further complications. It therefore became necessary to augment strength of IPKF. 36 Infantry Division was inducted into Trincomalee and assigned responsibility for the Eastern Province. Indian Army Chief, General Sundarji flew into Palaly on October 06 and was briefed by the OFC. He then took off for Colombo. The same evening Defence Minister K.C. Pant landed at Colombo to meet the President. The next day the Army Chief, while in Colombo, ordered HQ IPKF to use force against LTTE. The order came over the wireless network in clear. Obviously, the political decision to employ force against the one time close ally had already been taken in Delhi where Sundarji and Rajiv Gandhi were hand in glove relationship.

The die had been cast (!), once again, without giving judicious thought to the implications of the decision in favour of hard option. Yes, there were other option(s) but, as usual, the Indian Polity refused to learn lessons from past history, not even from their immediate preceding experiences.

The force level of IPKF at that time was:

- Six infantry brigades of 36 and 54 Infantry Divisions with their field engineer and signal units besides the logistic units;
- One armour regiment;
- One mechanized infantry battalion;
- One artillery regiment;
- One parachute commando battalion;capture of Jaffna.

The area North of Elephant Pass was designated as Jaffna Sector. It was placed under 54 Infantry Division that was already operating in that Peninsula. The remainder area named as Trincomalee Sector was placed under 36 Infantry Division. While Trincomalee Sector had four infantry brigades at that point of time, Jaffna Sector had only two. Since Jaffna symbolized the power of LTTE, capture of Jaffna was accorded the highest priority – to be captured in 4 days!! Totally unrealistic order issued by the high command.The usual failings of Indian polity ...

LTTE strength in and around Jaffna was estimated at 2,500 of which about 75% were armed with AK-47 and G3 automatic rifles which were a definite advantage in favour of LTTE. Moreover, LTTE had at least three tiers of strongly fortified defensive positions which had been well prepared during their fighting against SLAF.

For a start, IPKF carried out some raids on Oct 09 and 10 against some millitant camps as well as Jaffna Town during which 131 militants were captured and 27 weapons, ammunition, explosives etc. were seized. LTTE printing press in Jaffna Town was destroyed and their radio stations, TV transmission facilities were severely damaged. LTTE retaliated by attacking a post of 5 Maratha and ambushed a CRPF convoy killing four Jawans.

MAP: CAPTURE OF JAFFNA

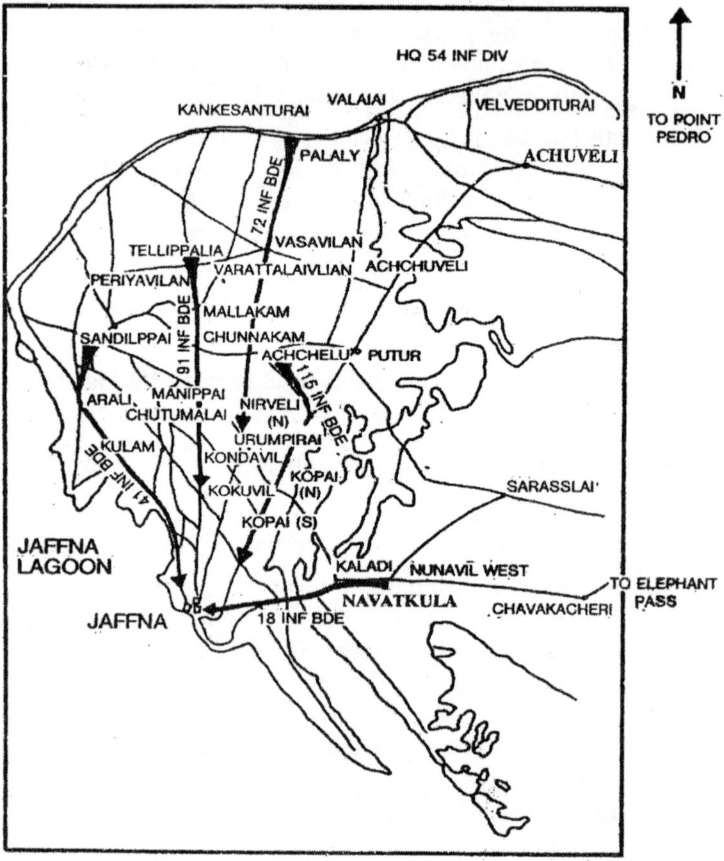

Troops available to 54 Infantry Division for capture of Jaffna Town:

- Three infantry brigades (18, 72 and 91) later to be augmented to five by addition of 41 and 115;
- One armour squadron (between 10-12 October just three T-72 tanks flown in by IL-76 were available) later to be augmented to 65 Armour Regiment less one squadron;

- 831 Light Regiment Artillery less one battery;
- 25 Mechanized Infantry Battalion less two companies;
- 10 Parachute Commando Battalion

The advance by the Division commenced on October 11 on three axes, one from the East and two from the North. It was a slogging march all the way. On arrival in the Sector, 41 Infantry Brigade was deployed in a hook to approach Jaffna from the West along the coastal road since the sea borne assault had been aborted. Since 18 Infantry Brigade was held up in their advance due to fierce resistance put up by LTTE, 115 Infantry Brigade reinforced this axis on 19 October. Both resumed advance to Jaffna. As IPKF neared Jaffna Town, resistance became more and more fierce. As link-up between the various thrusts became imminent escape routes for LTTE had to be blocked. They had assembled numerous boats moored in the Jetty about two km South East of Jaffna. A raid by Para Commandos was mounted through the Lagoon destroying large number of LTTE boats.

Heli-borne Operation on night 11/12 proved to be another fiasco primarily because of lack of coordination between the three services, all for the simple reason there was no one person, a single head acting as the control for all the three services. The Indian High Command had a knack for inter-services rivalry to let down one another—a typical feminine jealousy! Anyway, the plan was to land one company of para-commandos to secure the landing zone (LZ) in the Jaffna University[16] football field, followed by a company of 13 Sikh LI to land in successive waves to take over defence of the LZ. While the Commandos went out on their assigned mission, only one platoon worth of troops of SIKH LI could be landed because of problems with provision of further helicopter sorties. Major Birendra Singh of Sikh LI and his 29 men were left high and dry in the LZ surrounded by LTTE defensive positions. LTTE killed every one of those personnel including the Major except one sepoy who was wounded and captured. Prabhakaran was at the scene and directed his men to spare the man to go and tell the story. Twenty nine Indian soldiers lay dead. Their bodies were put on public display at a temple in typical tribal style, and then burnt after being doused with oil[101] What a shame for Indian Army, to have one of their crack battallions suffer such humiliation for no fault of theirs; their only fault was poor command and control structure.

The use of human shields by LTTE was a major stumbling block for the IPKF. Since IPKF generally operated along roads it made it easier for LTTE to employ this technique. IPKF overcame this unpleasant phenomenon by employing police methods of using tear gas to disperse crowds before they could come close to the advancing troops. Moreover, a number of LTTE men were dressed in lungis as the civilians did; it was therefore difficult to distinguish the unarmed civilians from the armed cadres.

LTTE were urban guerillas. It was a force of middle class educated highly motivated youth armed with most sophisticated weapons, far better than those of IPKF – a formidable combination indeed. While IPKF occupied Jaffna around October 22-23, house by house clearing operations continued to be slow and frustrating battle-experience for Indian soldiers, more so since Indian Army trains for guerilla warfare in jungle-terrain only while urban gurrilla-warfare is practiced as mere academic exercise. Screening of refugees and identification of LTTE elements amongst them posed an insurmountable problem for obvious reasons.

Casualties:[18]

IPKF: Killed – 17 officers, 26 JCOs and 276 OR; Wounded – 53 officers, 67 JCOs and 919 OR.

LTTE: Killed: 1100; Weapons recovered by IPKF: Rifles 167; Sten carbines 17; Rocket Launchers 8; Machine guns 23; Mortars (assorted) 70.

Command of 41 Infantry Brigade was an interesting episode in this misadventure. After their grueling tenure in J & K from 1983 to 1986 the troops were enjoying a well-earned peace station life. Hardly had they settled down in Lucknow, "Exercise Brass Tacks" was inflicted on them during winter 1986-87. 13 SIKH were moved out of Lucknow at 48 hours notice The Battalion moved back to Lucknow in July 1987 to Delhi to provide protection. The Brigade Commander, Brigadier S.S. Mavi (later Major General) had been posted for a long course in USSR. He left end September when the command devolved on his Deputy, Colonel S.K. Singh - a highly respected competent Brigade Commander – pending arrival of new Commander from Ladakh. Meanwhile ISLA was crumbling in Sri Lanka putting Delhi in an awkward position with wide ramifications in TN. Army HQ asked the Brigade on 13 October 1987 to standby for "Aid to Civil Power" in Madras. However, at about 2:00 pm information was received that the task had been changed from "Aid to Civil Power" to induction into IPKF for full fledged battle against LTTE. The Brigade was to be air lifted straight into battle zone in Jaffna Sector! Since the two tasks were of diametrically opposite nature, it naturally caused considerable readjustments in deployment and load tables for move. Instead of rail move it was to be airlifted from Lucknow by Boeing 737 to Delhi, Air bus from there onwards for troops, and AN 32s for "F Echelon vehicles" carrying essential battle loads. This was most unprofessional. On landing at Delhi the Commanding Officer's party was to be met by a Liaison Officer (LO) from Army HQ to guide the troops for onward move. But none came to the Airport! The situation at Madras was no better. A typical nonsense that prevailed in Delhi at that time – civil or military!

The allotment of aircraft for induction of aircraft was grossly inadequate. The battalions were moved into operations in bits and pieces, almost at half their strength. For instance, 13 SIKH was out on "field firing" range and was told that big chunk of the Battalion would rejoin the unit in 3 days. It actually happened in 33 days! Another example of planned fiasco by Delhi! "By then many battles had been fought; many lives lost" with ten soldiers per platoon[19]; three such platoons merely had the potential of a weak one half of a rifle company. Who else except the Indian Army under able leadership of General Sundarji would rush such hotchpotch contingent to a foreign land to fight an invisible urban guerilla enemy, for the simple reason that Mr. Rajiv Gandhi wanted the induction most immediately.

In the meantime distressing news came in that commander of a neighbouring brigade, Brigadier Manit Singh had been side-stepped to take over 41 Infantry Brigade. This Brigadier did not carry a good reputation as a conscientious commander, besides he was under cloud for some unverified things. He was not seen anywhere around during the induction process. In this connection, Major General Harkirat Singh has stated:

> Formation commanders were superimposed without the knowledge of the troops and the staff officers comprising it. Brig. Manjit Singh was Commander of 41 Infantry Brigade during an important stage of the battle. This act virtually broke up cohesiveness of this formation ... Brig. Manjit Singh, an outspoken officer, stated on arrival that that he had walked into the Army Chief's office and sought an opportunity to command a formation in Sri Lanka. Brig.

Manjit Singh terrorized his staff and unit commanders and tension prevailed in this formation."[20]

In the Jaffna operation 41 Infantry Brigade was assigned the task of advancing on the coast road to Jaffna. The Brigade fought its way through opposition losing two BMPs. It made slow but steady progress. On 18 October the Brigade Commander got hold of the third BMP (Infantry Combat Vehicle, or ICV's), took two companies of 5 RAJ RIF and set out for Manipal. The Brigade linked up with the beleaguered company of 8 Mahar and contact with Jaffna Fort garrison was established on 19 October. Brig. Manjit Singh was awarded the Maha Vir Chakra, the second highest award for bravery in the face of enemy. His reputation as self seeker and his performance in commanding the Brigade went back with him to India. He was asked to put in his papers, even though MVC remained his prerogative. While the Brigade Commander was on his jaunt in a BMP, his foot-slogging battalions were looking out for coordination, orders and directions. The troops had been marching for three days without any rest, and practically without any food and replenishment. Logistical support via the Brigade was totally lacking. The Brigade did not have an artillery fire plan either. Finally, the Deputy Brigade Commander took charge of the Battalions as de facto Brigade Commander since Manjit Singh had already achieved what he came to Sri Lanka for.

Jaffna Fort was a solid looking medieval structure, more like an ancient monument but still useful for military purposes. A number of modern style high-rise buildings surrounded the Fort, 'adorning it like a necklace' rather than as after-thought appendages. It was scenic beauty alright, but it was a deadly structure from security angle. The surrounding area was densely populated, like any other growing oriental town. Military operations in such a populated environment where each building could well be a death trap. The fear of the unknown was lurking in the minds of the troops earmarked to clear the low or high-rise buildings, where every room could be a safe haven for the LTTE cadres who were determined to defend Jaffna town to the last. Here there was no front or rear for the assaulting force. Anything could come from any direction. Moreover, LTTE were on their own turf fully conversant with every nook and corner, and it was virtually impossible to distinguish an innocent civilian from an armed guerilla. Improvised Explosives Devices (IEDs) at which LTTE had a special mastery were a serious danger in room to room clearance. Every single room in every house, every floor in every high-rise structure, had to be physically cleared before those in the IPKF could be sure of security in the town.

All this required enormous manpower while the battalions inducted were barely half strength with rifle companies merely having the strength of a platoon, if not still less - thanks to the politico-military masters' ingenuinity to meet the ISLA targets. IPKF could fight the urban guerillas only if they could be pulled out of their hideouts ensconced inside heavily fortified buildings. One of the Sikh JCO's came out with a brilliant idea. "He suggested that we instead of using the road (which we had been doing all along), we should use a rocket launcher to create a hole in the wall of residences and move parallel to the road but through the houses." A brilliant but simple timely solution! This would give protection, save casualties, and would likely draw the LTTE out from their hiding places."[21] The field engineering company was to defuse the IEDs and booby traps.

The action started in the early part of the night as planned. A few rooms of the first building were cleared. It was pitch-dark. The troops had no means of lighting. One could not distinguish friend from foe. No fire support was planned or available and battalions own 81 mm mortars were in peace location; 2 inch mortars were the only fire support! Suddenly there was an earsplitting loud explosion in which thirteen soldiers had fallen, their seriousness yet uncertain; commander of the pseudo-company was the sole survivor. The other company commander persisted in his assigned task of clearing Ashoka Hotel. It was around 3:00 am. 60 Field Company of 3 Engineer Regiment of Madras Sappers rendered valuable support in clearing IEDs, mines and booby traps. The progress was slow but steady. Neutralizing explosive devices was of necessity a time consuming process. By daylight Ashoka Hotel had been cleared, room by room, floor by floor. The Hotel and Cross Roads objectives were in the hands of 13 Sikh, a valiant hazardous operation to say the least.

Constant refrain from the Brigade and Divisional Commanders was to hurry up! Easier said than done, when far removed from the hazards of war ... They appeared to be guided by a new "principle of war" —"COAS General Sundarji had given word to the Prime Minister that Sri Lanka would be cleared of the LTTE in seven days!" ... Advance to and capture of Jaffna town continued to progress, slowly but steadily, and finally successfully too.

Jaffna had a population of ten lakhs besides a refugee population of around 70,000. It was a town without any administration. Relief and rehabilitation of refugees was taken up around October 24. Brigadier R.I.S. Kahlon was inducted as Town Commandant, Jaffna. His immediate priorities were:

- Food supplies: Initially from India by sea, later from Sri Lankan sources by sea and thereafter by rail after rail services between Colombo and Jaffna were resumed;
- Medical: Existing hospitals and dispensaries were initially operated by Army sources from India. Gradually, local medical staff returned to their jobs and relieved the Army personnel;
- Restoration of electric supply, supply of running water, etc were of equal importance. 51 Engineer Regiment played a significant role in this humane endeavour;
- Provision and distribution of petrol, diesel, and kerosene oil;
- Opening of educational institutions;
- Repair-restoration of places of worship;
- Restoration of bus services;
- Return of displaced persons to their homes;
- Restoring policing and judicial services, restoration of radio and TV services, *et al.*

All these administrative measures required large staffs and resources which were augmented and three IAS officers joined the staff of Town Commandant.

Next phase of operations was fighting insurgency—Counter Insurgency (COIN for short). With the capture of Jaffna by IPKF, LTTE made their way out to regroup in nearby jungles and marsh lands. Most fled to the Eastern Provinces. Frequent incidents of ambushes, firefights, and sneak-attacks continued intermittently. LTTE rarely missed an opportunity to keep up pressure on IPKF and quietly disappear thereafter.

LTTE continued to receive moral and financial support from the government and people of TN. They continued to receive consignments of arms and ammunition from abroad through ports on TN coastline. Some explosives and cordite manufactured near Wellington in TN continued to be received by LTTE. LTTE casualties were treated in hospitals in TN at state expense. It is a strange and paradoxical situation that when the country is fighting the enemy, the latter continues to receive material and financial support from a part of the same country. If that is not treason, what is it? Indian Federal democratic system at its worst; just to show the failings, the weakness of India Polity and the dangerous games they play at various levels. It was unfortunate for IPKF that by this time RAW and IB at Delhi had an upper hand in dictating orders to IPKF and COAS could not effectively influence the decision-making process.

A "Battle School" was established in Chennai. Infantry battalions being inducted for COIN were imparted pre-induction counter-insurgency training. During this phase of 'Operation PAWAN' nearly one fifth of India's infantry battalions were deployed in Sri Lanka.

Army HQ issued a fresh directive to IPKF on November 05, 1987 for the next phase of operations. Army HQ also created a new Military Operations Cell for Sri Lanka (MO-SL) which, bypassing all channels of command started issuing direct orders to General Staff at HQ IPKF at Palaly regarding even company and platoon level operations. It was a manifestation, a reincarnation, of the 1962-syndrome of Prime Minister Nehru and Krishna Mennon along with Gen Kaul deploying sections to various points on Indo-Tibetan borders to show flag to the Chinese in civilian style while the Chinese showed their flag in the military manner!

The High Commission in Colombo was of the opinion that LTTE could now be militarily completely neutralized in about 8-10 weeks provided it did not get financial and war-like assistance from TN. But who would bell the cat! It was not probable at all that TN would withhold support from LTTE. This assessment was therefore purely academic and of no value to man or beast. It speaks volumes about ignorance of politico-military matters amongst our political leadership and their bureaucratic executives-cohorts.

The first of such operations was a proposed raid on a hospital overlooking the beach in the northern Vadamarachhari area where Prabhakaran was believed to be hiding according to information given by RAW. A blockade of the area was enforced by Indian Navy. Unfortunately, LSTs required to take 9 Para Commandos deputed for the task did not report till after midnight losing precious hours of darkness. And the operation had to be aborted. Yet another failure of command structure ...

As a result of new directive additional troops were inducted. In January 1988, 4 and 57 Infantry Divisions were brought in besides two more brigades from 23 Mountain Division, making a total of nearly twenty-three infantry brigades with fifty infantry battalions besides a commando brigade worth of Special Forces. Armour element was boosted to almost a brigade worth of tanks, artillery support increased to equal an artillery brigade besides an Engineer Brigade was added to force levels of IPKF. A large number of civil affairs and civil administrative personnel were also inducted. Adequate Naval air support was also catered for, albeit command, control and coordination continued to suffer some deficiencies as heretofore. Hereafter, four separate Divisional HQs controlled the four sectors:

- Jaffna Sector now under control of Major Gen S.C. Sardeshpande. GOC 54 Infantry Division;
- Trincomalee Sector: Maj. Gen. Jameel Mehmood, GOC 36 Infantry Division;
- Batticoloa: 57 Mountain Division commanded by Maj. Gen. T.P. Singh;
- Vavuniya: 4 Infantry Division under Major General Gupta.

Yet another innovation, if one may call it so was: MO Directorate in Army HQ assumed direct control of insurgency operations, without corresponding accountability—a typical phenomenon in uniform of Indian bureaucracy. Lt Gen Depinder Singh merely issued verbal instructions without the usual written confirmatory orders. In other words the Major General, General Staff (MGGS) in HQ Southern Command, Major General A.S. Kalkat (later Lt Gen) could hold formation and unit commanders responsible for any acts of omission, again without any responsibility-accountability on his part, or for that matter on the part of his set-up. Consequently, during November-December 1987 operations to further erode potential of LTTE were accelerated.

By the end of 1988 IPKF had broken LTTE's control in the urban and semi-urban areas of the country. During the elections held in November-December 1988, the peak strength of IPKF deployed came to a staggering 54,802 personnel.

Elections to the Provincial Council were long overdue. Due to strong pressure from Jaffna Tamils IPKF declared a five day cease fire, 15-20 September 1988, to give an opportunity to LTTE to join the political process. In response to strong public pressure the cease fire was extended by another five days. But the LTTE was obdurate. They refused to participate in the polling which was was held on November 19, 1988. The overall polling percentage was 62.71 per cent. EPTLF-ENDLF combine won a clear-cut majority. Varadaraja Perumal was appointed as the Chief Minister of the North Eastern Province. He was sworn in by the Governor General, Lt. Gen. Nalin Saneviratna and the Government assumed office by the end of the month. However, the SLG was reluctant to devolve necessary powers to the Provincial Government and the exercise ended in a natural death.

Deinduction of IPKF

Meanwhile, Sri Lankan Presidential Elections were also due in end 1988. Jayewardene declined to contest. Instead Premdasa was the prime candidate. He adopted a strong anti-India posture. It was a political gimmick to play with Sinhalese chauvinism to win the election. The elections were held simultaneously in both the Northern and Eastern districts on December 19, 1988 along with the rest of Sri Lanka. Premdasa defeated Mrs. Bandaranaike and became the President of Sri Lanka in January 1989. His government made a deal with LTTE which, in turn, made ISLA a defunct entity. This set the stage for de-induction of IPKF.

President Premdasa set the date for withdrawal of IPKF as July 29, 1989. The OFC IPKF, Lt. Gen. Kalkat resorted to the threat of ordering firing on SLAF soldiers if they stepped out of their barracks. Meanwhile TN State Assembly elections in 1989 brought DMK to power and Karunanidhi became the Chief Minister. He had been highly critical of role of IPKF. Moreover, political support base for IPKF was fast eroding both in Sri Lanka and at home in India. By now, it was quite clear that Indian political leadership of the day was totally immature and inexperienced and lacked the ability to launch a well planned coordinated military action in furtherance of its national aim. ISLA was dead, killed more by the beneficiary, Sri Lanka than by the LTTE. There was no political validity for continuance of IPKF. Sri Lanka wanted them out at the earliest. Rajiv

Gandhi, the architect of ISLA, had no option but to order phased withdrawal of IPKF to be completed by March 1990. Unfortunately, the primary task of IPKF of creating a Tamil majority North-Eastern Province with sufficient autonomy remained a utopian dream.

After the Parliamentary elections in India in 1989, the opposition coalition came to power with V.P. Singh as the Prime Minister. His policy: "Leave Sri Lanka to its own Affairs". Gradual phased withdrawal of IPKF contingents continued as heretofore. Violence and turmoil was back in the streets. The killing game continued. In order to ensure peaceful withdrawal of IPKF, the Chief Minister of Tamil Nadu, M. Karunanidhi, sent a personal message to the LTTE Supremo Prabhakaran, through Indian High Commissioner in Colombo, that de-induction process should not be interfered with. He sent a similar message to the Sri Lankan President also, and received positive response.

The IPKF had been in Sri Lanka for 967 days. Casualties: 1155 dead, over 4,500 wounded. Expenditure to the nation: Rs. 300 crores. The withdrawal was more or less peaceful. The IPKF was given a ceremonial send off by SLAF at Trincomalee harbour at 1100 hrs March 24. The last contingent boarded M.V. Akbar and INS MAGAR which was the last ship to leave the shores of Sri Lanka. Tamil Nadu Chief Minister exhibited rather poor taste by pointedly remaining absent from the welcome ceremony to Indian soldiers who had gone through thick and thin in service of the nation on orders of political leaders of Karunanidhi's ilk.

Independent India's first ever overseas military venture in pursuit of its political ambitions was a classic operation, only one of its kind in the annals of modern military history. It was fought by soldiers with at least one hand tied behind their back while the generals were controlled by inexperienced political leadership surrounded by equally incompetent 'yes-men', the bureaucrats with high sounding designations. The flamboyant uniformed top-brass had excellent gift of the gab and ample theoretical military expertise which, for one reason or the other, they totally ignored to put into practice, perhaps under pressure of political compulsions and pressure of circumstances. Rhetoric is no substitute for meticulous planning and preparations. In a nutshell: India was still an immature country unaware of politico-military implications of military intervention in neighbouring countries, particularly across a sea obstacle.

In the first place, India decided to provide material and military aid to Tamil minority of Northern Sri Lanka to face Sinhala onslaught. Training camps were established, arms, ammunition and pocket expenses provided. Their ethnic 'brethren' in Tamil Nadu went all out to give moral and financial support, besides safe sanctuaries, medical and transit facilities. After three months of intensive military training the trained cadres, "our boys", were inducted back into their homeland to fight their tormentors. So far so good!

The home country found itself unable to face the surge of well trained highly motivated guerilla style combatants, armed with sophisticated weapons and expertise. So they decided to take recourse to conference table where a young cub faced a cunning fox. Outcome: Indo-Sri Lanka Accord (ISLA). Its time frame was totally unrealistic and its terms were completely one-sided, trapping India to fight Sri Lanka's battles, while their own soldiers were safely ensconced in their barracks. Tables were turned against India by its own politico-military naïveté. Eventually, India was out to fight its "own boys"! This document (ISLA) should have been consigned to a trash-can (where it finally reached) but it did only after Indian Armed Forces had suffered humiliating reversals and were literally pushed out by the host country. Nonetheless, ISLA did form the very basis of a military "Operation Instruction" for three years of grueling campaign, innumerable hardships for the battle-worn-soldiers and their families back home, besides numerous casualties, dead and wounded, widows and orphaned children back home.

Bahût bay âbroo hô kâ târâ kûche sâ hum niklâ!

Notes

1. Extracted from LTTE web site – The Sinhalas do not accept this version of ancient history and insist that the Tamils came in the wake of invasion by the Chola King of Tamil Nadu around 100 CE.
2. An agreement was signed between India and Sri Lanka in 1964 under which India agreed to repatriation of over 500,000 disenfranchised Tamil labourers and grant them Indian citizenship. After signing the pact, Sri Lankan authorities came to the grim realization that their tea industry would suffer irrepairable damage if this vast work force left. UNP turned a blind eye to the agreement which died a natural death. None of the Indian Tamils were repatriated.

3. Rose E. Leo: *India's Regional Policy: Nonmilitary Dimensions* in *The Security of South Asia*, edited by Stephen Philip Cohen, Vistar Publications, New Delhi, 1988; p. 21.
4. LTTE was formed by Velupillai Prabhakaran in Jaffna in 1972.
5. Since Army Headquarters could not provide maps of areas of operations, Lt. Gen. Depinder Singh approached the College of Military Engineering, Kirkee, Poona, which promptly got sufficient copies of relevant maps printed and sent them to HQ OFC.
6. Depinder Singh, Lieutenant General: *Indian Peacekeeping Force in Sri Lanka*; Natraj Publishers, Dehradun, 2001.
7. Velupillai Prabhakaran, Chief of LTTE, hailed from Point Pedro.
8. In the first place the proposed time-frame gives an impression that Mr. Rajiv Gandhi and the President were playing a game of chess rather than dealing with movements and deployment of military formations!

   The sense of euphoria generated by the Accord was marred by the ugly incident during departure ceremonies when a naval member of Guard of Honour being reviewed by Indian Prime Minister attacked him.
9. In actual practice, LTTE surrendered only a handful of weapons and that too of old vintage. They continued to retain bulk of their sophisticated weapons till de-induction of IPKF in 1990.
10. Depinder Singh, *op. cit.*, p. 38.
11. LTTE was reluctant to hand over arms. Some arms were of course surrendered and the ceremonial surrender came to an end on 21 August. In his book "*Tigers of Jaffna*" narrates: "Jaffna's population was receptive to IPKF despite LTTE's growing restiveness. On 12 August, two IPKF members including Jaffna-born Major Dilip Singh died when they stepped on a land mine: When Jaffna Traders Association tried to collect money for dead soldiers' families, LTTE intervened and quietly but firmly asked them to drop the idea." (Quoted in *Sri Lanka Misadventure* by Gautam Das and M.K. Gupta-Ray; p. 55) "Born in Jaffna and died in Jaffna. IPKF's first casualty, Major Herbert Dalipsingh, was a Tamilian; Commissioned into Corps of Engineers, was in 8 Engineer Regiment of Madras Sappers and Miners.
12. *Ibid., op. cit.*, p. 70.
13. Gautam Das and M.K. Gupta-Ray, *op. cit.*, p. 60. These two authors had served in Indian Army. The first was an infantry officer of 11 G.R., commanded troops in counter-insurgency ops, was a qualified instructor in counter-insurgency and jungle warfare and holds an

MA in Defence studies of Madras University. The second was an officer in Sikh LI and took part in Indo-Pak War 1971. He commanded 16 Sikh in IPKF in Jaffna sector.

14. Pulenderan had been involved in bus massacre in April 1987 when LTTE cadres had stopped a bus, ordered all passengers to disembark, separated the Sinhalese and murdered them in cold blood. Incidentally, Kumarappa had been married for just thirty days.
15. The Author had personally known Sundarji while in Calcutta during planning stage of 1971 Bangladesh War. The General certainly had a great gift of the gab, and had a convincing manner of speech in whatever he believed.
16. Jaffna University was the place where the seed of this war of attrition had been sown. The Sinhala Government imposed their arbitrary rule to restrict admission of Tamil students in the University scoring marks higher than the Sinhalese students, thereby depriving the Tamils of their rightful place in their own domain. This proved the turning point and educated youth took to militancy.
17. Gautam Das &, *op. cit.,* p. 94.
18. Depinder Singh, *op. cit.,* p. 102.
19. A platoon is the very basic subunit of an infantry battalion. Its standard strength is one platoon commander and thirty five soldiers. If the strength goes below twenty two, then the platoon is considered unfit to take part in any active operations.
20. Quoted in *Sri Lanka Misadventure;* p. 143.
21. As narrated by Lieut. Col M.K. Gupta, CO 16 Sikh; *Sri Lanka Misadventure;* p. 199 (parenthesis mine).

17

KASHMIR AND INDO-PAK RELATIONS 1971-1999

Soviet Arms Package

India had century's' old economic-cultural ties with Afghanistan. Notwithstanding Soviet support for India in 1971 and the treaty for friendship, India's reaction to Soviet attack and occupation of Afghanistan in December 1979 was adverse and highly critical. However, Soviets were particularly keen on maintaining their friendly ties with India. With that end in view as well as the prevailing international situation, in May 1980 they offered an exceptionally generous arms package to India in the face of US large scale armaments-aid to Pakistan. The Soviet arms package included T-72 tanks and MIG-25 'Foxbat' aircraft costing about $1.63 billion repayable over an extended period of 10-15 years[1]. Nothing comes free in the free world! In return, Soviets asked for silence during the debate on Afghanistan in the UN General Assembly. Of course India kept its part of the bargain.

India's stand in the UN on the Afghanistan issue did not at all go down well with the United States. By this time Rajiv Gandhi was the Prime Minister. He visited the US in June 1985 to put at rest American misgivings regarding India's relationship with the Soviets, but to no avail. The strain continued. It was further accentuated when the Americans decided to 'sell' Hawkeys EC-2 AWACS aircraft (Advanced Warning and Control Systems) to Pakistan. Naturally, these aircrafts would confer significant battlefield advantages to Pakistan, thereby further increasing India's security concerns.

Chill-Wind from Siachen Glacier

While Aksai Chin was the bone of contention between India and China, Siachen Glacier in the Eastern Karakoram Range took its place in the ever worsening Indo-Pak relations. The Glacier is 70 km long, varies in width from 2-8 km. Its depth is more than 300 metres and is the second longest glacier in the world covering in all an area of about 10,000 sq km. It falls from 18,875 ft at its head to 11,875 ft at its terminus. The crest of the Saltoro Ridge varies between 25,330 ft to 17,880 ft AMSL. Average annual snowfall is 35 ft and the surface temperature on the glacier can drop to as low as -50 degrees C in winter with winds upto 150 knots. Perhaps, that is why Raspal Khosa calls it the 'Third Pole'![2]

Actual Ground Position Line (AGPL)

The genesis of the dispute lies in inadequate demarcation-delineation of the Cease Fire Line (CFL) at the end of First Indo-Pak War 1948-49, and under the agreement arrived at in 1949. Because of the terrain and extreme climatic conditions, the CFL terminus was left in the air at map grid point NJ 9842. "Beyond Point NJ 9842 on the Ladakh Range is the 110 km long AGPL along the Saltro Range going up to the Indira Col."[3] This terrain is one of the bleakest and one of the most hostile terrains found anywhere on Planet Earth. However, the terrain of the LoC before that is marginally better.

SKETCH : ACTUAL GROUND POSITION LINE (AGPL)

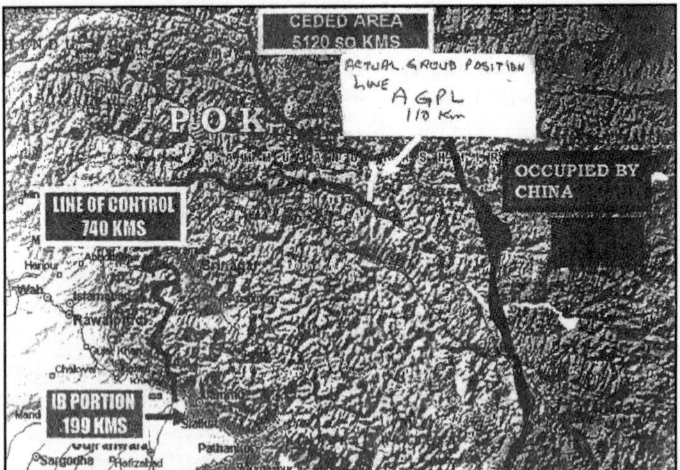

ROUTES OF INTRUSIONS FROM POK

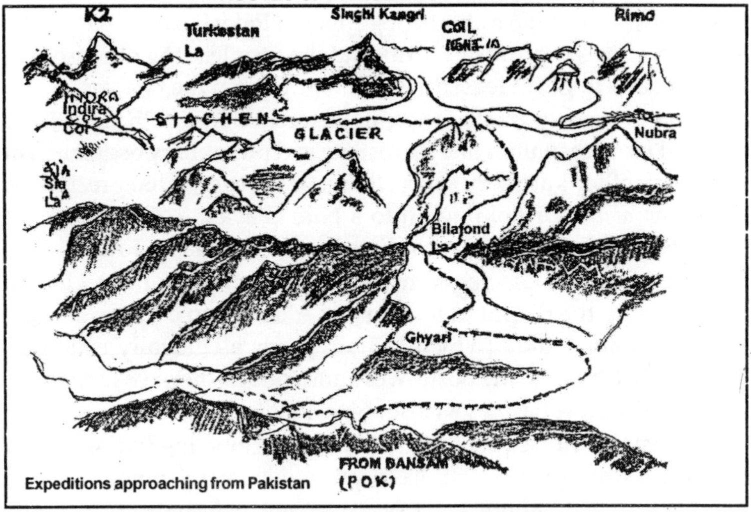

Intrusion by several expeditions to glacier from POK

Routes of Ingress from POK (Siachin Glacier)

The Nubra River flowing down from the Siachen Glacier joins the Shyok River. Thereafter it flows down into Pakistan across the LoC near Turtuk. This strategic stretch of land was wrested from Pakistan during the 1971 War. A motorable road from Leh to Turtuk along the River passing over Khardung La is the highest road in the world. It is the only communication link between the two high altitude places. The added importance of this road lies in the feeder road that takes off from it to the base of Siachen Glacier. Another feeder road following the Shyok River upstream provides line of maintenance from Pakistan's military base at Skardu to the LoC to support operations in Siachen.

Sometime during early 1984, intelligence reports poured in HQ Northern Command that Pakistan was planning to occupy the Glacier claiming it for Pakistan. The Army Commander of India's Northern Command, Lieutenant General M.L. Chibber took pre-emptive action to launch military operation code named "Meghdoot" ("Cloud Messenger") and Indian troops occupied the Glacier because of its strategic location, despite the extremely inhospitable conditions. An excellent example of Systematic Success of Indian Military High Command, both by the Army Commander and his Chief! (Did the General(s) have the approval of MOD? May be, may be not .) Pakistan retaliated by immediately launching its own operation code named

'Abadeel' ("Swallow") in April 1984, but did not succeed in evicting our troops. One of the military objectives of Pakistan in initiating the Kargil War was capture of Turtuk and the spur leading therefrom to the Glacier – to get at least an initial foothold on the Glacier.

Due to the extremely inhospitable conditions, both sides have suffered more casualties due to frostbite and pulmonary oedema than from each other's artillery shells. If that be the case, what precisely is the *raison d'être* for holding on to a bare Glacier — Obviously, its strategic location is the answer. In the words of Raspal Khosa:[4]

"The Siachen Glacier complex which abuts the Indo-Tibetan border along the disputed territory of Aksai Chin on the one side, the Shaksgam Valley (which India regards as illegally ceded by Pakistan to China) to the north-west, and the Northern 9842 triangle, is a wedge that separates a closer Sino-Pak territorial nexus ..."

Pakistan's subsequent many attempts at evicting Indian troops from the strategic Glacier have proved in vain. Since the two combatants just cannot trust one another, negotiations towards demilitarization of the Glacier in order to save human suffering and high maintenance costs have not been successful either.

Here it may be recalled that, of late, Pakistan was losing ground in Kashmir. In order to regenerate the issue and to internationalize the same to gain maximum advantage in subsequent negotiations, it had become imperative for Pakistan to do something out of the ordinary. They were also suffering from psychological trauma for having repeatedly failed to capture Siachen Glacier, if not the whole, then at least to gain a foothold on that highly strategic real estate, and thereby the respect of their public. The revenge for Siachen defeats was in their blood. That background is indeed the raison-de-etre for the Fourth Indo-Pak War in KARGIL. Pakistan's expertise in proxy wars via intrusions-infiltrations in the guise of so called Mujahideens who hardly had any significant presence.

Notes

1. Duncan Peter, J.S., *The Soviet Union and India;* Council on Foreign Relations, New York, 1989; p. 47.
2. Malik V.P. General, *Kargil: From Surprise to Victory;* Harper Collins, New Delhi 2010; p. 66.
3. Khosa S. Raspal, *Siachin Glacier Dispute: Imbroglio on the Roof of the World;* Contemporary South Asia, Vol. 8, No. 2 ,1999; p. 199.
4. Kind Courtesy General V.K. Malik, *Kargil : From Surprise to Victory;* Harper Collins, New Delhi, 2010.

18

KARGIL
The Fourth Indo Pak War 1999

The story of Pakistan is the story of ambitious and adventurist Generals denying the people their rights.

— Former Air Chief, Mohammed Asghar Khan, 1983

Historical Background

Kargil used to be part of Baltistan district of Ladakh, which was an integral part of the Princely State of Jammu and Kashmir. After India gained Independence from the British Empire in 1947 J&K acceded to the Indian Union thus it became part of independent India. The First Indo-Pak War (1947–48) concluded with the Line of Control bisecting the Baltistan district, with the town and district of Kargil lying on the Indian side in Ladakh subdivision of the Indian state of Jammu and Kashmir. Under the Simla Agreement signed after Indo-Pak War of 1971, both nations agreed not to attempt to alter the resultant boundary by force. In other words, LOC remained a *de facto* boundary instead of being converted into a *de jure* boundary which should have been the normal outcome of 1971-War. So it remained a matter of mutual trust between the two antagonistic states. And can you ever trust Pakistan, its generals and politicians! But for Pandit Jawaharlal Nehru and his illustrious daughter Indira Gandhi, this war, the Kargil War 1999, could never have come about.

Geographical Background

The town of Kargil is 205 km from Srinagar via a typical mountain road. It is strategically located opposite the Northern Areas across the LOC and is merely 173 km from POK controlled military base of Skardu which is potentially capable of providing logistical and artillery support for any operations in the Kargil region. The climate is temperate with cool summers and frigid nights, while winters are long and chilly with temperatures often dropping to 48°C on hill-tops. Indian national highway (NH 1D) connecting Srinagar to Leh passes through Kargil proper. This road is overlooked by high ridges. The heights on the side of POK dominate this only road link between Srinagar and Leh. The area that witnessed the infiltrations and fighting is about 160 km long stretch of ridges overlooking this road link. From the military stand point, the road is most vulnerable by enemy action from the dominating ridge-line. The military outposts on the ridges above the highway were generally around 16,000 ft high, with some as high as 18,000 ft. and had clear visibility all along the road. Thus, Pakistan could cut off this supply route at will besides causing casualties to men and vehicles.

With the best of will and resources in the world, you cannot possibly man every single hill feature in higly mountainous terrain. Of necessity therefore some features have to be left physically unoccupied, although some of them may be covered by fire. It is the existence of such unoccupied features that tempted Pakistan military to selct Kargill as the target area to avenge their humiliating defeat of 1971. In any case they had to revive the Kashmir issue and this long stretch of strategically located ridge line provided the best option for surreptitious infiltration and occupation of defences, more so since the Kargil region is sparsely populated with diverse ethnic, linguistic and religious groups living in isolated valleys separated from one another by some of the world's highest mountain ranges with toughest steep slopes. Surreptitious infiltration therefore may not easily come to notice of Indian defenders. Apart from the district capital, Kargil, the populated areas near the front line included the Mushko Valley and the town of Drass, southwest of Kargil, as well as the Batalik sector and other areas, northeast of Kargil.

Kargil region had the added advantage for Pakistan in that the surrounding terrain lent itself pre-emptive seizure of unoccupied military positions. With tactically vital features and well-prepared defensive posts Pakistanis atop the peaks would enjoy advantages akin to a fortress.

Pakistani Infiltrations/Intrusions

The withdrawal of Soviets from Afghanistan in 1989 left

thousands of victorious foreign Mujahideen looking out for a new cause. The notorious ISI drafted them for *jihad* in Kashmir. Suicide terrorists attacked Indian Parliament House on December 13, 2001 killing fourteen people. The perpertrators of this terror attack were traced to a Kashmiri militant group, Lakshkar-e-Toiaba (The Army of the Pure) based in Pakistan.

As in the past, Pakistan used its expertise at covert operations via infiltration-intrusions to start its wars by proxy, and jump into the fray as and when appropriate, or otherwise. The Kargil War of 1999 was no exception to their well established *modus operandi*. The Kargil Conflict took place between May 08 and July 14, 1999 in the Kargil district of Kashmir and elsewhere along the LoC: The cause

INFILTRATION OPERATIONS IN J & K (Kargil)[1]

of this was infiltration of Pakistani soldiers (some in civil dress as Mujahideens) and Kashmiri militants, mostly into positions on the Indian side of the LoC, which served as the *de facto* border between the two states. During the initial stages of the war, Pakistan blamed the fighting entirely on independent Kashmiri insurgents, but documents left behind by casualties and later statements by Pakistan's Prime Minister and Army Chief clearly established involvement of Pakistan's paramilitary forces and regulars led by General Ashraf Rashid. The intrusions were a complete surprise for the Indian military and intelligence officials and that too not for the first time either. As usual, the top civil intelligence agencie(s) let down the army in the lurch.

This War is one of the most recent examples of high altitude warfare in mountainous terrain, which posed significant logistical constraints for the combating sides. This was only the second direct ground war between any two countries after they had developed nuclear weapons; it is also the most recent[2].

Since Indo-Pakistan War of 1971 there had been a long period with relatively few direct armed conflicts involving the military forces of the two neighbours - notwithstanding the efforts of both nations to control the Siachen Glacier by establishing military outposts on the surrounding mountain-ridges and the resulting military skirmishes in the 1980s. During the 1990s, however, escalating tensions and conflict due to separatist activities in Kashmir, some of which were supported by Pakistan, as well as the conducting of nuclear tests by both countries in 1998, led to an increasingly belligerent atmosphere. In an attempt to defuse the situation, Indian Prime Minister Atal Behari Vajpayee inaugurated a bus service in February 1999 with much fanfare between border cities of Amritsar and Lahore. At the end of his trip the two Prime Ministers signed the Lahore Declaration, promising to provide a peaceful and bilateral solution to the Kashmir conflict. This conference was believed to have de-escalated the tensions that had existed since May 1998. However, the subsequent developments proved that the Conference and its deliberations were merely a ruse to deceive India. The major motive behind the operation was to help in internationalizing the Kashmir issue for which global attention had been flagging for some time. The intrusion-plan was the brainchild of Pakistan's Army, Gen Pervez Musharraf and Lt Gen Mohammed Aziz, Chief of General

Staff. They are reported to have obtained only an 'in principle' concurrence, without any specifics, from Prime Minister Nawaz Sharif.

Infiltration by Regular Army Troops

During the winter of 1998-1999, some elements of the military of Pakistan were covertly training and sending Pakistani troops and paramilitary forces, some allegedly in the guise of Mujahideen, into territory on the Indian side of the LOC. The infiltration was code named "Operation Badr"; its aim was to sever the link between Kashmir and Ladakh, and cause Indian forces to withdraw from the Siachen Glacier, thus forcing India to negotiate a settlement of the broader Kashmir dispute. Pakistan also believed that any tension in the region would internationalize the Kashmir issue, helping it to secure a speedy resolution.

According to India's then Army Chief Ved Prakash Malik much of the background planning, including construction of logistical supply routes, had been undertaken much earlier. On several occasions during the 1980s and 1990s, the army had given Pakistani leaders, Zia ul Haq and Benazir Bhutto, similar proposals for infiltration into the Kargil region, but the plans had been shelved for fear of drawing the nations into all-out war. However, it is believed that blueprint of attack was reactivated soon after Pervez Musharraf was appointed chief of army staff in October 1998. After the war, Prime Minister Nawaz Sharif claimed that he was unaware of the plans, and that he first learnt about the situation when he received an urgent phone call from Atal Behari Vajpayee, his counterpart in India. Sharif attributed the plan to Musharraf and "just two or three of his cronies". Musharraf, however, asserted that Sharif had been briefed on the Kargil operation 15 days ahead of Vajpayee's journey to Lahore on February 20. Can you ever trust Pak politicians? Or generals for that matter!

There were three major phases to the Kargil War:

- Infiltration of Pak forces into Kashmir and occupation of strategic positions enabling it to bring NH 1D within range of its artillery fire;
- India discovers infiltrations, mobilizes forces and plans to deal with the threat;
- Recapture of every single Pak strongly defended positions by

Indian forces, one by one, inflicting heavy casualties till ultimate capitulation and total withdrawal of all Pak infiltrators leading to restoration of *status quo ante*.

Infiltration/Intrusions Discovered

121 Infantry Brigade sent out a routine reconnaissance patrol on May 05, 1999 to Kaksar area along the LOC to ascertain snow conditions in the region. The patrol was never heard of again. Perhaps all its members were killed. During the winter season, due to extreme cold in the snow-capped mountainous areas of Kashmir, it was a common practice, a sort of gentlemen's agreement, to abandon some forward posts on their respective sides of the LOC and to reduce patrolling in the areas. As and when weather conditions became less severe forward posts would be reoccupied and patrolling resumed. During February 1999, the Pakistan Army began to re-occupy the posts it had abandoned on its side of the LOC in the Kargil region, but also sent forces to occupy some posts on the Indian side of the LOC too. Untrustworthy as usual! Troops from the elite Special Services Group as well as four to seven battalions of the Northern Light Infantry (NLI: a paramilitary regiment) set up bases on vantage points in the Indian-controlled region. These Pakistani forces were backed by Kashmiri guerrillas and Afghan mercenaries.

Pakistani intrusions took place in the heights of the lower Mushkoh Valley, along the Marpo La ridgeline in Drass, in Kaksar near Kargil, in the Batalik sector east of the Indus River, on the heights above the Chorbat La sector where the LOC turns North, and in the Turtok sector south of the Siachen area. The only Himalayan mountain pass connecting Kargil area to the Kashmir Valley, Zoji La, normally opens by the end of May or beginning of June. Thus, moving of reinforcements by surface means from Srinagar would not have been possible till then. Pakistan Army calculated that even if the intrusions were discovered in early May, as they were, the Indian Army's reaction would be slow and limited, thereby allowing them to consolidate the intrusions more effectively. In the event, however, mother-nature opened Zoji La in early May itself. Thus, the basic assumption of the Pak plan became off balance. However, the Pak plan was top secret and all possible measures had been taken, besides deception measures to ensure Indian suscpicions were not aroused.

There had existed a sort of "gentlemen's agreement" between India and Pakistan that the armies of either side will not occupy posts from 15 September to 15th April of each year. This had been the practice since 1977. When even written-signed agreements were not being honoured, how come our field commanders trusted Pakistani's unwritten so called gentlemen's agreements ! Shall we ever learn the methodology and deceitful practices of Pak military? Anyway, but in 1999 this agreement was unilaterally cast aside by Pakistan Army in hopes of trying to gain the upper hand in Kashmir and plunging the Indian subcontinent in a brief limited war besides raising the specter of nuclear war.

The Kargil Mountains are a formidable constituent of the Greater Himalayas. Unlike other similar high altitude areas, the Kargil Mountains lose snow cover rapidly as the summer progresses. Below the peaks and the ridgelines are loose rocks, which make climbing extremely difficult for the assaulting troops. If it is not the snow cover, then it is the rocks that hinder movement causing extreme hardships on the attacking troops.

The Pak finalized plan was put into action towards the end of April. The main groups were broken into a number of smaller sub-groups of 30 to 40 each for carrying out multiple intrusions along the ridgelines and occupy dominating heights.

By the second week of May an Indian patrol team led by Capt Saurabh Kalia was ambushed. A tip-off by a local shepherd in the Batalik sector led to the exposure of the infiltration. Initially, with little knowledge of the nature or extent of the infiltration, the Indian field commanders assumed that infiltrators were Mujahedeens who could be evicted within a few days. Subsequent discovery of infiltration elsewhere along the LoC established that hostiles had occupied as many as seventy positions along and across the LoC. Obviously enemy plans were on a much grander scale. The total area seized by the ingress is generally estimated as between 130-200 km^2. However, Musharraf stated that 500 square miles (1,300 km^2) of Indian Territory was occupied.

Indian Mobilization

Over the next six weeks India had moved five infantry divisions, five independent brigades and 44 battalions of paramilitary troops to Kashmir. The total Indian troop strength in the region had reached 730,000. The build-up included the deployment of around 60 frontline aircrafts, besides of course heavy artillery and mortars. Since Zoji La opened early on account of the unseasonal melting of snows, Indian Army's reaction was far swifter and more vigorous than Pakistan had anticipated. Indian Army Patrols detected intruders atop Kargil ridges during the period 8-15 May. Indian army launched operations which succeeded in cutting off the infiltrators in Drass sector while those in Batalik sector were pushed back. A colossal effort and concentration of such large forces with their heavy armament was a commendable achievement.

Thus, by 30 June 1999 Indian forces were prepared for a major high-altitude offensive.

The Intruders on the heights were an amalgam of professional soldiers and mercenaries. They included the 3rd, 4th, 5th, 6th and 12th battalions of the Pakistan Army's Northern Light Infantry (NLI). Among them were many Mujahideen and members of Pakistan's Special Services Group (SSG). It was estimated that the strength of intruders was around 5,000 stretching over a length of about 160 km. A complex logistical network was in place from bases in POK. The intruders were well equipped and armed with AK 47 and 56, mortars, artillery, anti-aircraft guns, and Stinger missiles.

Op Vijay

From May 15-25 military counter-operations were planned, troops moved to their attack locations, artillery and other equipment were moved in and the deficiencies made good. Indian Army's offensive named "Operation Vijay" was launched on May 26. Indian troops moved towards Pak occupied positions under IAF air cover.

Artillery Firepower

Operation Vijay was a joint Infantry-Artillery endeavour to evict regular Pakistani soldiers of NLI who had surreptitiously occupied vacated-high-altitude ridgelines-peaks on our side of LOC. It soon became apparent that before the infantryman could assault and evict the the enemy, massive and sustained firepower was required to destroy the *sangars* (fortification). The enemy's will to fight had to be broken through a process of attrition. A unique saga in the history of employment of Artillery Firepower in mountain warfare, with the gallant infantry man leading the assault on well entrenched enemy fortified positions was in the making. That was the crux of Indian success story — a totally new concept of artillery in direct firing role in support of infantryman.

Tololing in the Drass subsector was the first victim of the new concept of employment of artillery fire power. It was captured on June 13 after several weeks of bitter fighting. Infantry assaults were preceded by sustained fire from over one hundred Artillery guns, mortars and rocket launchers firing in concert. Thousands of shells, bombs and rocket-warheads wrecked havoc and prevented the enemy from interfering with the infantry assault. The 155 mm Bofors medium guns/howitzers and 105 mm Indian field guns in direct firing role pulverized all visible *sangars*, which forced the enemy to abandon several positions. The arcs of fire trailing behind the Bofors high explosive shells and the Grad rockets provided an awesome sight.

Tiger Hill

The capture of the Tololing complex involved liquidation of a series of fortified positions in depth, one after another. It was a time and ammunition consuming process, a stepping stone for launching successive assaults on the formidable Tiger Hill complex. A multi-directional attack was called for. Over 1,200 rounds of high explosive rained down on Tiger Hill causing large-scale deaths and devastation. Once again, the Gunners of the Indian Artillery fired

SKETCH : CAPTURE OF TIGER HILL

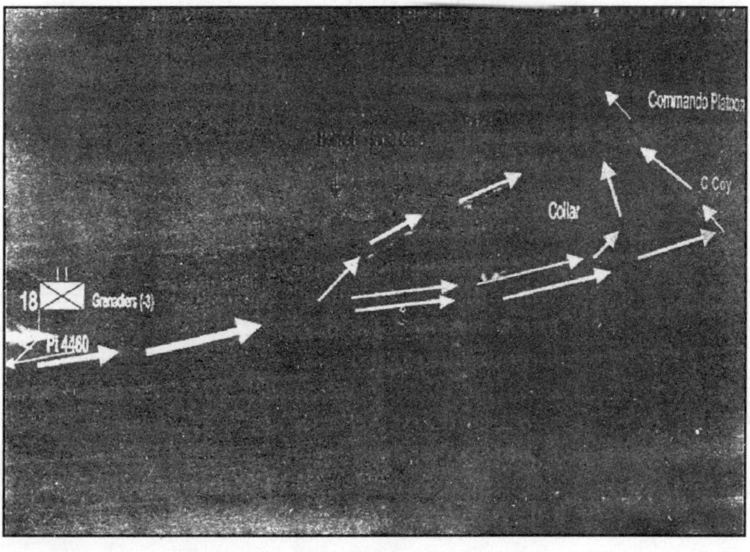

their guns audaciously in the direct firing role, under the very nose of Pakistani artillery observation posts (OPs), without regard for personal safety. Even 122 mm Grad multi-barrel rocket launchers (MBRLs) were employed in the direct firing role! Hundreds of shells and rocket warheads impacted on the pinnacle of Tiger Hill in full view of TV cameras. I and my family enjoyed the spectacle of a live battle with heavy weapons firing in unison. It was once in a lifetime opportunity to watch the might of Regiment of Artillery, the cousin brother of the Sappers. Tiger Hill was re-captured on July 5 and Point 4875, another dominating feature to the west of Tiger Hill and jutting into Mashkoh Valley, was re-captured on July 7. Point 4875 was later re-named "Gun Hill" in honour of the stupendous performance of the Gunners in Drass and Mashkoh sub-sectors.

The terrain in the Batalik sector was much tougher and enemy was far more strongly entrenched. The containment battle itself took almost a month. Artillery OPs were established on dominating heights and sustained heavy Artillery fire was brought down continuously by day and night allowing the enemy no rest. Our casualties were heavy. However, steady progress was maintained. Point 5203 was re-captured on June 21 and Khalubar on July 06. Within the next few days further attacks were pressed home against the remaining Pakistani posts in the Batalik sub-sector and these fell quickly after being pulverized by Artillery fire. Once again, Artillery firepower played a vital role in softening the defences and destroying enemy headquarters and logistics infrastructure.

The Indian Artillery fired over 2,50,000 shells, bombs and rockets during the Kargil War. Approximately, 5,000 Artillery shells, mortar bombs and rockets were fired daily from 300 guns, mortars and MBRLs. Such high rates of fire sustained over long periods had not been witnessed anywhere in the world since the Second World War.

This systematic success story by Indian military High command washed off many sins and blemishes of previously catalogued systemic failures of both civil and military Polity.

The battle casualties: 524 Indian soldiers killed in action and 1,363 wounded; 696 Pakistani soldiers and approximately 40 civilians killed.

The 1971 War was "Sappers' War". Kargil was 'Gunners War'! But every war is Infantryman's war!!

Air Operations

During the period May 11 to 25, ground troops supported by the Air Force tried to contain the threat, assessed the enemy dispositions and carried out various preparatory actions. "Entry of the Air Force into combat action on May 26 represented a paradigm shift in the nature and prognosis of the conflict." It was indeed a bold decision on the part of the Vajpayee Governement. In operation "Safed Sagar" the IAF carried out nearly 5,000 sorties of all types over 50-odd days of operations. Of these, 550 sorties were flown in Kargil, though just about 80 were on or close to the target. Undoubtedly, the shoulder-fired missile threat was omnipresent. An IAF Canberra reconnaissance aircraft was damaged by a Pak Stinger fired possibly from across the LOC. On the second and third day, the IAF lost one MiG-21 fighter and one Mi-17 Helicopter to shoulder-fired missiles. In addition, one MiG-27 was lost on the second day due to engine failure just after the pilot had carried out successful attacks on one of the enemy's main supply dumps. These events only went to reinforce the tactics of the IAF in carrying out attacks from outside the Stinger-SAM envelope and avoiding the use of helicopters for attack purposes. The fact that the enemy fired more than 100 shoulder-fired SAMs against IAF aircraft indicates the great potential and intensity of enemy air defences in difficult mountainous terrain. However, the success of IAF tactics, especially after the first three days of the war when not a single aircraft received even a scratch, also shows how quickly our Air Force devised suitable tactics to counter enemy threat.

In high altitude warfare the aircrafts have to fly at about 20,000 feet where air density is 30% less than at sea level. This causes reduction in pay-load, reduces manoeuvrability, increases radius of turning, deteriorates engine performance, and adversely affects trajectory of weapons.

The Indian airfields nearest to Kargil were Srinagar, Avantipur and Adampur and IAF operated from these three bases. The planes used for ground attack were MiG-21s, MiG- 23s, MiG-27s, Jaguars and the Mirage- 2000. The MiG-21 is capable of operating in restricted spaces which was of importance in the Kargil terrain. Mirage-2000s were used for electronic warfare, reconnaissance and ground attack. It caused considerable devastation to Pakistani bunkers on Tiger Hill and Muntho Dhalo. In the Mirage attack on Muntho Dhalo Pakistani troops suffered 180 casualties. The load-carrying Mi-17 was modified to carry 4 rocket pods with air-to-ground rockets and proved effective in engaging Pakistani bunkers.

Naval Operations

Strike elements from the Eastern Fleet were sailed from Visakhapatnam on the East Coast to take part in a major naval exercise called 'Summerex' in the North Arabian Sea. This was envisaged as the largest ever amassing of naval ships in the region. The message had been driven home. Pakistan Navy, in a defensive mode, directed all its units to keep clear of Indian naval ships. As the exercise shifted closer to the Makaran Coast, Pakistan moved all its major combatants out of Karachi. The naval focus now shifted to the Gulf of Oman. Rapid reaction missile carrying units and ships from the fleet were deployed in the North Arabian Sea for carrying out missile firing, anti-submarine and electronic warfare exercises. In the absence of the only aircraft carrier, Sea Harrier operations from merchant ships were resorted to.

The Indian army launched its final attacks in the last week of July. Soon after Drass subsector had been cleared of Pakistani forces, the fighting ceased on July 26. Pakistan capitulated, again. The day has since been marked as "Kargil Vijay Diwas" (Kargil Victory Day) in India. By the end of the war, India had resumed control of all territory south and east of the Line of Control, as was established in July 1972 as per the Simla Agreement. Later, Prime Minister of Pakistan, Nawaz Sharif disclosed that Pakistan was left with just six days of fuel to sustain itself if a full-fledged war had broken out.

Comments

The LoC had been clearly delineated by the two sides in 1972 but Pakistan claimed that the LoC separating the two sides was not clearly defined. Pakistan also tried to use Kargil to project the Kashmir issue as a potential nuclear showdown so as to encourage international intervention. India also demonstrated that the Mujahideen were a mere façade in the Kargil conflict. Indian restraint to restrict operations to Kashmir alone ensured that conflict did not spiral out of control and result in nuclear war. Thus, Pakistan's attempts at "nuclear blackmail" totally failed. By early July it was apparent that Pakistan was on the verge of being pushed back out of positions they had surreptiously occupied on the Indian side of the LOC in flagrant violation of the long standing practice and gentlemen's agreement on the subject. The ultimate triumph of diplomacy occurred as Pakistani Prime Minister Nawaz Sharif travelled to Washington D.C. in early July to seek a face saving device, perhaps a negotiated settlement of the conflict. At this time, defeat of the Pakistani occupying forces seemed assured as Indian armed forces had taken back almost all of the peaks in their respective sectors. The only remaining occupied peaks were the ones closest to the Line of Control, where Pakistani artillery fire could provide cover to the invaders. Under the circumstances Pakistan had no option but to withdraw its troops from the remaining locations in a set time frame.[3]

Lessons for India

- Do not trust Pakistan — A cunning enemy: Poltical or military;
- Defence Services need constant funding to maintain a state of readiness;
- Up date weapons and equipment of the three services:
- Organize and improve intelligence setup and ensure information reaches the user without loss of time;
- Introduce system of accountability, particularly in the fields of intelligence gathering-dissemination, and in generalship;
- Close cooperation and coordination of three services via Chief of Defence Staff. (Don't be afraid of a coup. *Diversity of Indian Defence Services in their culture, language and ethnicity is more than sufficient insurance against any possibility of a coup-d'etat!)*
- Don't be scared of nuclear retaliation by Pakistan.[4]

Conclusions

Soon after the War came to a close, *Deccan News Service* reported that Indian Army Chief had hinted that in a new military mis-adventure by Pakistan India might as well cross the LOC first. Concurrently *Hindu* went a step further by suggesting that the Defence Minister, George Fernandez, had hinted at emergence of a new "Doctrine of Limited War" while retaining sufficient capability for a conventional war. Of course both of them had made these remarks with reference to Pakistan and its attempt to blackmail India and the world at large with its nuclear option.

While a proposed Indian strategy to counter the next mis-adventure by Pakistan involving occupying short and shallow chunks of Pakistan territory all along the international border may be risky, nevértheless, "limited, calibrated incursions across the LOC" are certainly within the realm of possibility, notwithstanding nuclear capabilities of both antagonists. No doubt statesmanship on both sides would preclude an all out war lest it escalates into a nulear conflagration.

Ever since its creation Pakistan has made four, possibly five specific attempts to wrest Kashmir by military force. But for some marginal success it has failed, and lost, every time. The institutional interests of Pakistani Armed Forces lie in maintaining continuous state of conflict so as to retain their top position in country's hierarchy. Kashmir is the obvious target which, it has been from Day-one of birth of Pakistan.

Nehru-Gandhi Dynasty has twice failed the nation in resolving the Kashmir imbroglio once and for all — changing the *de facto* border into *de jure* border. Even today, Division of Kashmir on those lines remains the crux of a permanent solution together with significant changes in Kashmir's federal relationship with India in letter and spirit

Notes

1. Ganguly Sumit: *India-Pakistan Tensions Since 1947*; Columbia University Press, New York, 2001; p. 114.
2. During this War when Pakistan found itself in a tight corner, it did not retaliate with nuclear option; instead its Prime Minister went to Washington to seek US intervention. Nuclear option is not such a simple matter easy way out — CNN-IBN News Channel interview with General Bakshi, May 08, 2011.
3. *Times of India,* April 23 and May 01, 2011.
4. *Ibid.,* dated May 09, 2011.

EPILOGUE

The ripe fruit of Kashmir Valley Beautiful did not fall in the lap of Jinnah, much to his disappointment. But it was bestowed on India much to the disillusionment of Pakistan, which could not reconcile to a Muslim majority state going to 'Hindu majority' India. And what did India do with the precious prize of 'Switzerland of the East'? India just did not have the capacity to digest the Sweet Fruit! When all the top cards were in Indian hands, our esteemed polity frittered away the golden opportunity through neglect, mismanagement and uncalled for excessive use of force to control the docile, peace loving, spiritually inclined people of the Valley Beautiful. Our Army came to be equated with the army of occupation through Indian polity's acts of omission and commission over a period of time, without sitting back to give a cool thought to the problem at hand. The consequences of such ill conceived approach are loudly painted on the world screen.

Notwithstanding its irrational claim based on its shattered ideology, Pakistan cannot possibly renounce its claim on Kashmir. And that holds good for India too because of its proven sound ideology of secularism without any discrimination on religious grounds. The 'stands' of both contenders are mutually exclusive and irreconcilable. Result? The people of Kashmir are at the receiving end of violent reactions from both antagonists. Such a situation must not be allowed to drift, to remain in place *ad infinitum*. A via media has to be found, a solution to the imbroglio has to be worked out, to restore peace and harmony in the region in the interest of the people at large in both countries. Indeed, they are the ones who are suffering.

Crux of Solution of Kashmir Imbroglio

India and Pakistan must refrain from interfering in the internal affairs of Kashmir. Division of Kashmir along the LOC has come to be taken for granted as *de facto de jure fait accompali*. This must be internationally recognized and guaranteed. Jammu and Ladakh are to be detached from the Valley Administration. Constitution of India is to be amended to make it truly 'federal' in letter and spirit, providing full and unfettered internal autonomy to the Valley. However, India shall retain control of defence, foreign affairs, external communications and currency, to be managed by India with honest consultations and concurrence of the Valley Administration; all other subjects being left at the entire discretion of the local government.

Incorporation of the highly controversial Article 370 in the Constitution providing for special treatment for Kashmir turned out to be a catastrophic provision for the unity and security of the country. It forbids Indian nationals from settling down in Kashmir, or to buy/own property in that State. By implication, it meant that Indians were foreigners in Kashmir while Kashmiris were at full liberty to live and own property in the rest of India. The Congress had overwhelming majority in the Constituent Assembly and must be held culpable for this major error of judgment. It was yet another serious failure of Indian National Congress. However, the present prevailing situation in Kashmir does not warrant abrogation of Article 370; that would only make matters worse. What is required at present is an amendment of constitutional provisions so that Kashmiri women who marry a non-Kashmiri man and Indian citizens are free to buy/own landed property in Kashmir, and are also free to settle down therein. Every Indian shall have as much right to live in Kashmir, and own real estate there as any Kashmiri has in India. The internal autonomy aspect should not be tinkered with, not for the present at least.

Financial assistance to Kashmir shall be at par with the other states of the Indian Union. No special favours shall be shown to Kashmir in this, or any other regard.

Both antagonists must cut down their military forces in the region to absolute minimum level, just so much as to ensure that the LOC cannot be violated by any of the antagonists, and that its security is ensured and guaranteed internationally. The Indian and Pakistani troops are restricted to operate in a pre-defined, pre-determined strip of land agreed between Indian and local Governments. Any dispute(s) between the two governments shall be subject to judicial review by the full bench of Supreme Court of India whose decision with 2/3rd majority shall be final and binding. The Chief Justice of

Kashmir High Court shall be deemed to be a judge of the Supreme Court for this purpose.

Travel across the LOC by local populations shall be permitted liberally, being controlled by a simple permit system for which Srinagar shall frame necessary rules and procedures. Srinagar shall be free to interact with Muzaffarabad.

Pakistan's concurrence to, and adoption of, the foregoing self-imposed Indian constraints would obviously be *sine qua non* for successful implementation of the proposed permanent solution of the Kashmir problem.

After the aforesaid measures have been implemented, the Central Government shall finalize the *modus operandi* of resettling all the Kashmiri Pandits who were turned out of their own homes, to which the secular popularly elected Kashmir Administration and the Delhi Governement were mute spectators. Further, the semi-autonomous government of Kashmir must undertake and fulfill its obligations towards safety and security of Pandits and other minorities.

India's Defense Strategy

Indian defense strategy against Pakistan must be drastically revised in as much as idealism and rhetoric are no substitute for sound military strategy. Proactive defence is to replace against existing passive defence.

Indian political leadership must shed the fear of a military *coup d'etat*. India's unity in diversity is a strong insurance against such an eventualitiy. India is much too diverse etnically, linguistically, religiously and regionally to fall a prey to military dictatorship. In any case, such a form of governance militates against the very ethos of Indian political psychology. These factors are our positive assets against army rule in the country. Remember Nehru-Menon apprehensions?

Therefore it is high time now that the Government must go ahead with the system of CODS to ensure coordinated integrated response to threats to India's security, which can come from more than one quarter.

Kashmir is just one facet of our national problem, amongst many others, with international ramifications. The internal insurgency, Naxalite and Maoism whose basic ideology is based on mindless violence, killings ad lib, irrespective who is killed, or how many, and how the dead are involved in this vicious imbroglio – all this is none of their business. The grievances of the have-not vs the 'haves' are understandable. Unfortunately, the bureaucracy treated these symptoms as mere law and order problem and the political leadership failed to provide the right guidelines to the bureaucracy in as much as the insurgency and accompanying violence were in real terms reflection of socio-economic morass to which the landless and rural poor had been subjected to by the tyranny of the rich and powerful elite. The symbolism of the upsurge was completely lost.

Use of force, more often than not, brutal and cruel led to further accentuation of the grievances. This in turn gave rise to further violence from both sides. The vicious circle continued *ad lib ad infinitum* with the result that more than two third of the countryside is engulfed in Naxal-Mao ideological battle. Our political leadership is not prepared to face the reality. Instead, they play games with various factions, castes and communal elements, stoop down to deals for power sharing, *et al.*, and the chaos continues.

Mizoram is one outstanding example of sensible handling of a very difficult situation, thanks to Narsimharao. Punjab is not far behind. The Naga insurgency is on the decline, but for how long? Your guess is as good as mine. A powerful faction still has a government in exile craving for soverign independent 'Nagalim', all Nagas under one administrative control right from Arunachal Pradesh down to Manipur and Burma, all inclusive. Orissa was in the news in a big way. When the Naxal-Mao sruggle is on the negative slide, kidnapping is the effective technique. The insurgency in Andhra and parts of Kerala is on an upward swing. So where do we go!

It is pointless to enunciate the various symptoms. The malady is chronic and deep rooted. It requires major radical surgery to sort out the mess our worthy leaders have got the country into. The process of recovery is going to be long and painful. But who will bell the cat, and how?

A fairly large Commission representing all walks of life should be appointed by a Chief Justice of Supreme Court of India with impeccable credentials. No politician or bureaucrat will be appointed on this Commission. It would be composed entirely of persons from public life of high personal integrity and morality, representing all professional classes and religious communities. The farce of elections to this body will not be resorted to. The Commission should be divided into various committees, each dealing with a specific aspect of our socio-economic system – form and content of our present so called democracy, judicial system.

The Commission will aim at total overhaul of the system that we inherited from the Colonial masters who had their own axe to grind while formulating the administrative system in the subcontinent.

The high-powered Commission will publish its Report-Recommendations within one year. All recommendations of the "Commission for Overhaul of Socio-Political-Judicial System" of India will be binding. The fate meted out to Sarkaria Commission will not be repeated. The Governmnt, military, police – the list of necessity will have to be long of the day will have to resign and the Commission will take necessary measures to implement its recommendations to put the new setup in place.

A very tall order indeed, utopian in character! Otherwise, a dictatorship appears to be the only alternative, unless the country is prepared to continue to suffer under the existing thoroughly corrupt, inefficient and ineffective administrative setup run by self seekers.

Lest I be accused of negative approach and brushing one and all with the same colour, I do wish to state that the country has survived many vicissitudes of the past because of the microscopic minority of honest sincere and devoted bureaucrats, and an odd politician.

GLOSSARY

Bagh: Garden.

Baluchistan: A western province of Pakistan in which an agitation- movement for autonomy has been in progress for quite some time.

Chauri Chaura: A town in Gorakhpur district of Uttar Pradesh state of India. During the Non-Cooperation Movement launched by Gandhiji the finale came in Chauri Chaura on February 5, 1922 when a Congress and Khilafat procession got out of control in the face of police behaviour. A section of the crowd attacked the police who fired in return. This provoked the entire huge procession. They attacked the police force. The police took shelter in the Police Station. The crowd retaliated by setting the building on fire. Those who tried to escape the fire were caught, hacked to death and their bodies thrown into the fire. In this gruesome incident twenty-two policemen were brutally killed. On hearing of this extremely unfortunate incident Gandhiji decided to withdraw the Movement. He realized that his attempt to foster secularism had not made an auspicious start.

Chowkidars (village guards): In order to boost village-level police force these guards were appointed by the Administration. Their wages were to be paid out of funds specifically created for the purpose through chowkidara tax levied on the villages.

Dar-ul-Harb: "Abode of War", a land ruled by infidels that might, through war, become the "Abode of Islam".

DPs: 'Displaced Persons': The Partition of India in August 1947 led to massive transmigration of populations. There were brutal killings, rapes and murders, forcible conversions, untold atrocities, etc., leading to most Muslims of border areas migrating to Pakistan while all Hindus and Sikhs of West Pakistan migrated to the safety of India. However, about 50% of Sindhi Hindus stayed on in Sind albeit a trickle continues even now.

Ezhavas and Pulayas: Low caste Hindus of Kerala state of India could not come within 16 and 72 feet respectively of the higher caste Hindus.

Fatwa: A Muslim religious edict imposing some obligatory social prohibitions/restrictions.

Ganapati: A Hindu god, son of Parwati and Shiv, born with a human body and the face of an elephant; He is the most revered god in the Hindu pantheon.

Hartal: General shut down of business ativity.

Hindi-Chini Bhai Bhai : A relationship of mutual brotherhood between Indians and Chinese cultivated as a result of the Bandung Conference.

Jagirs: Estates bestowed on nobles in the court of a Raja or king.

Jatha: A band of people, armed but very lightly if at all, for a specific cause. Usually Sikhs.

Khalistanis: Extremist Sikhs.

Khilafat: It is the Caliphate that used to establish the authority of Allah on earth, and the Khalifa strived to uphold that authority within the community of followers. The Khilafat Movement was active in India in the early 1920's. The Caliphate came to an end with Turkey becoming a Republic.

Khudai Khidmatgars (Servants of God): Khan Abdul Gaffar Khan, a Congress leader from NWFP popularly known as "Frontier Gandhi", had set up a formidable, well-disciplined, non-violent revolutionary organization popularly known as "Red Shirts". They were destined to play an extremely active role in the Civil Disobedience Movement and in the struggle for freedom. They were opposed to Partition of India.

Kisan Sabha: An informal organization of farmers.

La: In Tibetan, means a 'mountain pass'.

Lashkar: The Pathan unit of fighters comprised of one thousand tribesmen.

Lathis: A long bamboo/wooden stick usually used by the Indian police to beat up/break up a crowd. Also used by ordinary citizens in self defence.

Maulvis: Muslim religious teachers.

Mazdoor Sabha: An informal organization or meeting of labourers.

MERA BHARAT MAHAN!: My country, INDIA, is great.

Mohajirs: Indian Muslims who migrated to Pakistan of their own free will in quest of better jobs and salaries.

MQM (Mohajirs Quami Movement): Mohajir National Movement.

Mullahs: Muslim priests.

Muslim Madrasas: Muslim religious schools curriculum of which is generally restricted to Islam only; Undergoing a change, of late

Prabhat pheris: Group of people on morning walk singing patriotic/religious songs.

Praja Mandals: Organized public groups in the erstwhile Indian Princely States.

Pukhtunistan: Land of Pukhtoons people (belonging to NWFP and Afghanistan).

Qabaili invaders: Tribal raiders (into Kashmir) from clans of NWFP.

Sarf khas: Reserved land. It constituted ten per cent of the total area of the pre-1947 State of Hyderabad. Its income went directly to the Nizam to meet his personal royal expenses.

Sati: Act of a widow throwing herself on the funeral pyre of her departed husband thereby killing herself.

Satyagraha: Agitation for truth.

Shahenshah: King of Kings; the Great Emperor.

Swadeshi: Made in, or manufactured in, one's own country. Swadeshi Movement was formally proclaimed in a meeting held in Calcutta Town Hall on 7th August 1905 when the famous Boycott Resolution was passed urging the country to boycott of Manchester cloth and Liverpool salt.

Swaraj : Freedom; complete independence.

Toshakhana: Strongroom for cash and valuables in a Sikh Gurdwara: Sikh Temple.

Vethi: South Indian Telgu language word, meaning exactions and forced labour.

Wahabi: A sect of Muslims.

Zamindars: Landlord.

APPENDIX

UPDATES: April 30, 2011

Ref. ULFA 11-2: In order to restore peace in Assam and to bring ULFA into political process, the State Government has released a number of top leaders of the banned outfit. The last one to be released on bail is the ULFA chairman Rajkhowa.The violence perpetrated by ULFA during the past more than three decades has been phenomenal. The level of violence reached a peak during 1982 and 2001 when ULFA is reported to have killed 642 civilians and 269 security personnel. The extent of violence abated during 2003 to 2007 when the outfit unleashed a reign of terror in Upper Assam when the militants mowed down 66 Hindi speaking people, mainly Biharis working in brick kilns. Their most brutal act was massacre of 13 schoolchildren in a blast at the Dhemaji Parade Ground during Independence Day celebrations in 2004. On the eve of initiating unconditional peace talks with the Center, their 'foreign secretary', Sasadhar Choudhary virtually apologized for all the killings by ULFA. While announcing the unconditional peace talks, the outfit admitted all the killings it had carried out during its armed struggle for 'Sovereign Assam', particularly "The Killing of 13 school children in a bomb blast was a mistake. In fact, all the killings that we had carried out were a mistake."The foregoing statement and initiation of unconditional peace talks led to a vertical split within the outlawed ULFA when their elusive so called 'C-in-C', Paresh Baruah, rejected the February 2011 proposed talks between New Delhi and all the eight top rebel leaders now out on bail. The ULFA publicity secretary said: "The decision taken by the general council cannot be considered legal as the General Council itself was unconstitutional." However, the leadership announced that the General Council meeting chaired by the ULFA Chairman Arabinda Rajkhowa decided to open unconditional peace talks with the Government and that all the resolutions adopted by the council were conveyed to Paresh Baruah.

That meeting was also attended by vice chairman Pradeep Gogoi, deputy 'C-in-C' Raju Baruah, 'finance secretary', 'cultural secretary' and of course the 'foreign secretary' too. Nevertheless, Historic talks between the insurgents and the Government proved to be 'ice breaker' with the Government Committing for "an honourable and just" settlement. (*TOI*, Dated 7 and 9 February 2011) The Prime Minister Dr. Manmohan Singh during his election tour of Assam, while downplaying the threats to the Congress Party issued by the Paresh Baruah faction ahead of the Assembly polls, went on record saying that talks with ULFA hold a "good future". He went on to say that "both the Government and the insurgents are committed to take the peace process forward and the process is on to bring other underground outfits of the North East to the negotiating table." Both sides agreed to set up a seven members committee comprising of three ULFA members and two members each from the State and Central Governments. Since then, the armed wing of ULFA in Assam has been reorganized by dismantling all battalions and brought all armed cadres under one 'mobile military headquarters'. Consequently, posts of battalion commanders have been abolished. However, Assam Chief Minister Tarun Gogoi stated that the Center has agreed to pay a certain amount of money to pro-peace faction towards maintenance of their cadres till they can settle down to peaceful means of earning a livelihood. It is indeed heartening to note that a citizen's group under chairmanship of scholar Hiren Gohai of Sanmilita Jatiya Abhibartan (SJA), assigned by ULFA to prepare a charter of demands, has proposed a J&K-like status for Assam, and has dropped demand for sovereignty.

BIBLIOGRAPHY

Abdullah Sheikh Mohammad: *Autobiography of, Flame of Chinar,* Viking, New Delhi.

Akbar Khan Maj. Gen. *Pakistan Army : Raiders in Kashmir,* Pakistan Publishers, Karachi; 1970.

Akbar M.J.: *Kashmir Behind the Vale,* Viking, London, 1991.

Asghar Khan Mohemmad, Air Marshal *Pakistan Air Force: The First Round – Indo-Pak War 1965,* Vikas Publishing House, Delhi, 1979.

Atal Hira Lal: Major General: *Nehru's Emissary to Kashmir,* Army Education Stores, New Delhi, 1972.

Ayub Khan, Field Marshal Pakistan Army: *Friends Not Masters,* Oxford University Press, London, 1967.

Bamzai Prithvi Nath Kaul: *History of Jammu and Kashmir: Political-Social- Cultural from Earliest Times to the Present Day,* Metropolitan Book Company, New Delhi, 1962.

Bazaz Prem Nath: *Kashmir in Crucible,* Pamposh Publications, New Delhi, 1967.

Bhagat P.S., VC, Lieut. General: *The Shield and the Sword;* Vikas Publishing House, Delhi.

Bhattacharjea Ajit: *Kashmir: The Wounded Valley,* UBS Publishers, New Delhi, 1994.

Bipin Chandra: *India's Struggle for Independence;* Penguin Books, 1988/1998.

Birdwood Lord: *Two Nations and Kashmir,* Robert Hale London, 1956.

Brines Russel: *The Indo-Pak Conflict;* Pall Mall. London, 1968.

Brunel Francis: *Kashmir,* Rupa and Co., New Delhi.

Candeth K.P., Lieutenant General: *The Western Front, Indo-Pak War 1971,* EBD, Dehradun, 1997.

Chaudhry A.A.K. Brig.: *Pakistan Army: September '65: Before & After*; Natraj, Dehradun, 1991.

Chhibber M.L. Lieutenant General: *Pakistan's Criminal Folly in Kashmir*, Manas Publications, New Delhi, 1998.

Doughty Marion: *Afoot Through the Kashmir Valley*, Reprint by Sagar Publications, New Delhi, 1971.

Duncan Peter: J.S.: *The Soviet Union and India*; Council on Foreign Relations, New York, 1989.

Evans Humphry: *Thimaya of India – A Soldier's Life*, Harcourt Brace, New York, 1960.

Ganguly Sumit: *India-Pakistan Tensions Since 1947*; Columbia University Press, New York, 2001.

Gazetteer of Kashmir and Ladakh, Intelligence Branch, Manas, New Delhi, New Delhi, 1992.

Gopal S: *British Policy in India, 1885-1905*, Cambridge, 1965.

Grigg John: *Myths about the Indian Independence*; Austin University of Texas Press, 1998.

Grover Verinder: *The Story of Kashmir: Yesterday and Today*, Vol. I-III, Deep and Deep Publications, New Delhi, 1995.

Guha Ramachandra: *India After Gandhi*, Harper Collins, 2007

Gulati M.N.: *Military Plight of Pakistan*, Manas, New Delhi, 2001.

Gupta Sisir: *Kashmir – A Study in Indo-Pak Relations*, Asia Publishing House, New Delhi, 1966.

Harbaksh Singh, Lieut. General: *War Despatches – Indo Pak Conflict, 1965*; Lancer International, New Delhi, 1991.

Hasnain F.M.: *Gilgit, the Northern Gate of India*, Sterling Gate of India, Sterling Publishers, New Delhi, 1978.

Jacob J.F.R.: Lieutenant General: *Surrender at Dacca: Birth of a Nation*, Manohar, New Delhi, 1997.

Jinnah M.A.: *Speeches and Writings*; edited by Jamil-ul-Din, Vol. I, Lahore, 1960.

Jones Owen Bennet: *Pakistan, Eye of the Storm*; Yale University Press, USA, 2002.

Kalkat O.S. Major General: *The Far Flung Frontiers*, Allied Publishers, New Delhi, 1993.

Kapaia Harsh: *The Battle of Roses Kautilya's Arthashastra.*

Karan Singh, Dr.: *Heir Apparent: An Autobiography*, OUP, New Delhi, 1982/1984.

Karim Afsir, Major General, *Kashmir: The Troubled Frontiers*, Lancer Publishers, New Delhi; 1994.

Kashmir in Crossfire & Joshi Manoj: The Lost Rebellion – Kashmir in the Ninetees; Penguin; Excerpts from a Review by Ashok Banker.

Khan Gul Hassan, Lieutenant General: *Pakistan Army; Memoirs*, Oxford University Press, Karachi, 1993.

Khosa S. Raspal: *Siachin Glacier Dispute: Imbroglio on the Roof of the World;* Contemporary South Asia, Vol. 8, No. 2 ,1999, p. 199.

Knight E.F. *Where Three Empires Meet*, Longman Green and Co.; London, 1919.

Korbel Josef: *Danger in Kashmir*, Princeton University Press, Princeton, 1954.

Krishna Rao, General: *Prepare or Perish: A Study of National Security*, Lancer Publishers, New Delhi; 1991.

Lachman Singh, Vr C. Maj. Gen.: *Missed Opportunities: Indo-Pak War 1965;* Natraj, 1997.

Lamb Alastair: *Kashmir: A Disputed Legacy;* Oxford Books, UK, 1991.

Madan Vijay, Lieutenant General: Jammu & Kashmir Operations, 1947-48: The Other Version; *USI Journal*, July-Sep, 1992.

Manekar D.R.: *Twenty Two Fateful Days;* Manaktalas, Bombay, 1966

Mansergh Nocholas: ed. in chief, *Constitutional Relations between Great Britain and India – Transfer of Power*, Vol. 9.

Menezes S.L. Lieutenant General (Retd.): *The Indian Army*, Viking, Delhi.

Menon V.P.: *Integration of Indian States*, Orient Longman, New Delhi, 1956.

Musa Mohammad, General: *Pakistan Army: My Version: India Pakistan War 1965;* Lahore, 1983.

Nanda K.K., Lieut. General: *Conquering Kashmir: A Pakistani Obsession*, Lancer Books, New Delhi, 1994.

Niazi A.A.K., Lieutenant General: *The Betrayal of East Pakistan;* Manohar, New Delhi, 1998.

Palit D.K., Vr C., Major General: *The Lightening Campaign: Indo-Pak War 1971*; Lancer, New Delhi, 1972.

Panikar K.M.: *The Founding of the Kashmir State*; George Allen & Unwin, London, 1953.

Puri Balraj: *Jammu & Kashmir-Triumph and Tragedy of Indian Federalism*; New Delhi, 1981.

Qureshi Hakeem Arshad, Major General *Pakistan Army: 1971 Indo-Pak War: A Soldier's Narrative.*

Rahman Tariq: *Language and Politics in Pakistan*, Oxford University Press, Karachi, 1996.

Rajinder Nath, Major General: *Military Leadership in India from Vedic Times to Indo-Pak Wars;* Lancer Books, New Delhi, 1990.

Read Anthony & David Fisher: *The Proudest Day*: W.W. Norton & Co, New York, 1997.

Riza Shaukat, Major General: *The Pakistan Army War 1965*; Natraj Publishers, Dehradun, 1977.

Rizvi Janet: Ladakh: *Cross Roads of High Asia*; Oxford, New Delhi, 1983/86.

Schofield Victoria: *Kashmir in Conflict; India, Pakistan and the Unfinished Conflict*, I.B. Taurus, London, 2000.

Sharma B.L.: *The Kashmir Story*; Asia Publishing, Bombay, 1967. Kashmir Awakes Vikas, New Delhi, 1977.

Sinha S.K.: Lieutenant General: *Operation Rescue: Military Operations in Jammu & Kashmir*, 1947-49; Vision Books New Delhi, 1977/1997.

Sitaramayya Pattabhi: *Report of the Liguistic Province Commission: 1948*; p.942.

Sufi G.M.D.: *Kashmir* (two Vols); Light & Life Publishers, 1974.

Tendulkar D.G.: *Mahatma, Life of Mohandas Karamchand Gandhi*, 8 volumes, New Delhi, 1969, reprint Vol. 2.

The History of the Struggle for Freedom in Kashmir, Cultural and Political, from the earliest Times to the Presenr Day, Pamposh Publications, 1967.

Thomas Raju G.C.: *Perspective on Kashmir: The Roots of Conflict in South Asia;* Westview, USA, 1992.

Trivedi Vijya R.: *Facts About Kashmir;* New Delhi, 1990.

Verghese B.G.: *India Answers Pakistan*; Konark, New Delhi.

Wakhla Khem Lata & Wakhlu O.N.: *Kashmir Behind the White Curtain;* Konark, Delhi, 1992.

Wolpert Stanley: *Zulfiqar Bhutto of Pakistan; His Life and Times*, Oxford University Press, New York, 1993.

Yasin Mohammad: *History of the Freedom Struggle in Jammu & Kashmir*; New Delhi, 1980.

Young husband Sir Francis: *Kashmir*; Adam & Charles Black, London, 1909.

Zutshi G., Zutshi G.: *Khan Abdul Ghaffar Khan: Frontier Gandhi;* National, Delhi, 1970.

INDEX

G

P

T